I0828287

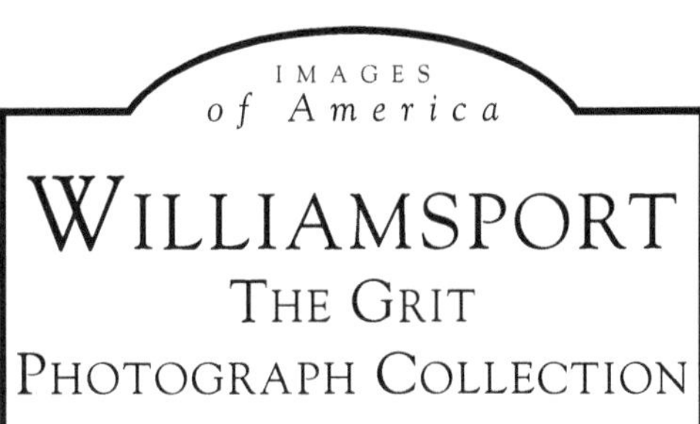
IMAGES
of America
WILLIAMSPORT
THE GRIT
PHOTOGRAPH COLLECTION

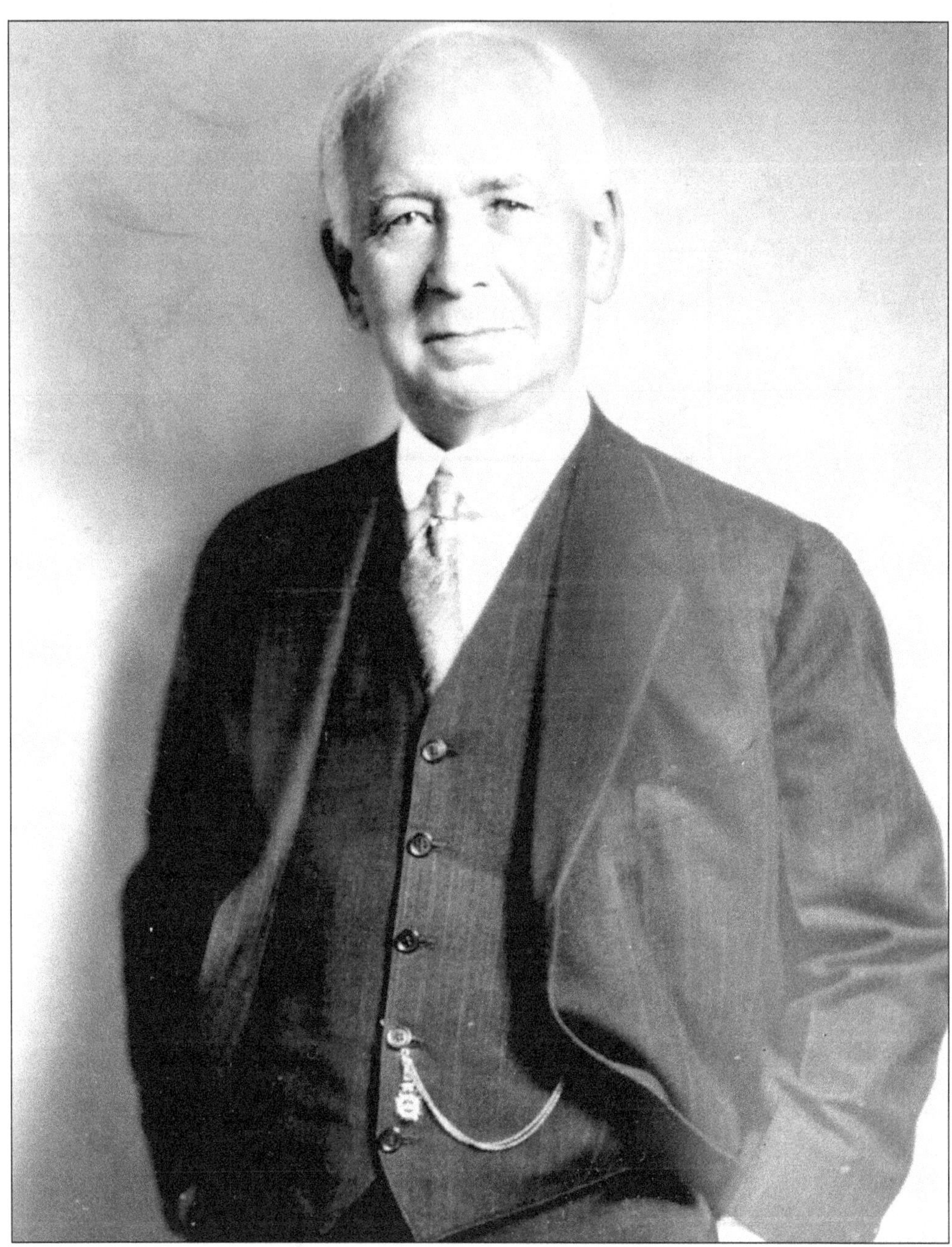

Many in small-town America remember the *Grit* Sunday newspaper with warmth, made possible by Dietrick Lamade, a German immigrant and self-made man. Lamade was born on February 6, 1859, in Goelshausen, Germany, one of nine children of Johannes Dietrick and Caroline Stuepfle Lamade. The *Grit* was one of the first newspapers in America to feature color and fictional supplements. By 1900, it had a national audience, and by the late 1970s, its circulation was more than 1.2 million.

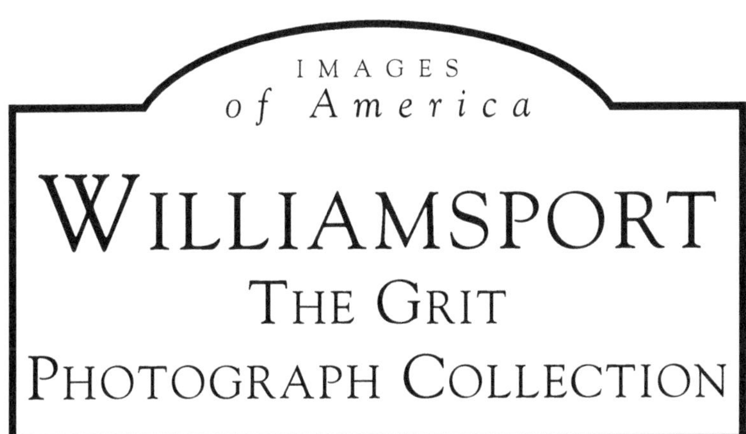

Robin Van Auken and Louis Hunsinger Jr.

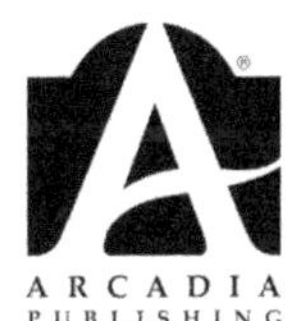

ISBN 978-1-5316-2029-5

Published by Arcadia Publishing
Charleston, South Carolina

Library of Congress Catalog Card Number: 2003114951

For all general information contact Arcadia Publishing at:
Telephone 843-853-2070
Fax 843-853-0044
E-mail sales@arcadiapublishing.com
For customer service and orders:
Toll-Free 1-888-313-2665

Visit us on the Internet at www.arcadiapublishing.com

For the faithful architects and constant readers of the Grit, *then and now.*

Contents

ACKNOWLEDGMENTS

The unity of thought, purpose, and effort that existed between *Grit* and its employees is found in very few industries. From the first day that Dietrick Lamade acquired *Grit*, he never lost touch, and he never overestimated himself. He gathered about him the best men and women, calling them his *Grit* family. Growing from three employees (himself included) to more than 250 in the Williamsport office, plus hundreds of correspondents and contributors nationwide, Lamade's newspaper never reduced wages and never missed a payday for any of its employees (even during its infancy and the Great Depression).

"Sometimes we had to borrow the money back again from the men to operate the business," Dietrick once said, "but we never really missed a pay day."

"*Grit*," he added, "did not simply grow of its own accord. No one works for *Grit*. We all work with *Grit*."

We would like to acknowledge the millions of small-town Americans who have shared the joy of *Grit*. We are most grateful to John Yahner, publisher, and Dave Troisi, editor, of the *Williamsport Sun-Gazette* for their continued support in our quest to document the region's history, and Ogden Publications, the parent company of *Grit* and the *Sun-Gazette*.

We also would like to thank the James V. Brown Library for the use of its extensive microfilm collection and the continued support of its gracious librarians, including Director Janice Trapp, Helen Yoas, Wanda Bower, Nancy Shipley, Tricia Haas, Rosemary Heffner, Beth Albertini, Linda Aston, and Mary Buchanan.

We are grateful to Sandra Rife from the Lycoming County Historical Society for her careful protection of the county's historical assets and to the society for the continued generosity it and its staff offers when its patrons seek knowledge.

Above all, we would like to recognize that this book would not have been possible without the photographic excellence of *Grit* photographers, including D. Vincent Smith, Putsee Vannucci, and Ray Wentzel.

Finally, we need to recognize Lance Van Auken for his invaluable editorial advice.

Introduction

Each weekend in the 1950s, 30,000 boys knocked at the doors of more than 700,000 American small-town homes and were welcomed with a smile and a dime as they delivered the weekly edition of *Grit*.

For more than 100 years, *Grit* delivered news, features, fiction, coupons, and comics to families across the nation. More than a million children have sold *Grit*, some for a few weeks, some for several years. It was an experience many look back on with pride.

This book honors the photojournalistic tradition of the *Grit* newspaper as it recorded local timely events and celebrated family and community through good times and bad. Many of the photographs are endearing and touching portraits that chronicled Williamsport's progress and misfortune.

Grit was founded in 1882 as a Saturday edition of the *Daily Sun and Banner* in Williamsport, Pennsylvania. It was a short-lived venture, however, and in less than two years, it was sold to Dietrick Lamade. His story is typically American—the story of a young man who sought and found opportunity, and who, in 50 years, created one of the miracles of modern publishing.

Lamade was a German immigrant whose family moved to Williamsport in 1867. On January 1, 1869, Johannes Lamade died from typhoid fever. The day after his funeral, his ninth child was born. At the age of 10, Dietrick Lamade, along with his older brothers and sister, quit school and helped support the family. He worked as an errand boy for various stores until, at 13, he began working in the office of a local German-language weekly, *Beobachter*. His weekly salary was $3.

At 18, Lamade got his first experience as a publisher. During the holiday season of 1877, he devoted his spare time to producing several issues of the *Merchants' Free Press*, a free, four-page advertising pamphlet. Later he published a theater program, and in the summer of 1880, he published a small paper called the *Camp News*, while the Pennsylvania National Guard bivouacked in Williamsport.

In 1882, Lamade was made advertising compositor and assistant composing room foreman at the plant of the *Daily Sun and Banner*. He typeset the first head for *Grit* and created all of its forms that first year.

By 1884, he left the *Sun and Banner* to help revive a weekly publication called the *Times* that was scheduled to become a daily. The ill health and lack of finances of its owner caused it to fold, just as *Grit* began to crumble. For the first time in his life, he was without a job. The 25-year-old, who had married in 1881 and now had a wife and two children to support, envisioned opportunity for the first time. He would become a publisher.

Lamade gambled and, with two partners and a combined investment, bought the *Grit* name and good will from the *Sun and Banner* to use for his new publication and the equipment of the *Times*.

The first year of the *Grit* was one of adversity and uncertainty, as it owed more than it was worth and went through seven business partners. But Lamade did not lose faith. The circulation was about 4,000, and many more subscribers would be needed if the paper were to survive.

Lamade decided to interest new subscribers with drawings. Coupons in the paper provided chances for readers to win various prizes, including a piano, a gold watch, a marble-top bedroom set, a rifle, and a silk dress. His partners thought his new idea was impractical and costly, and one threw up his hands in horror at the idea of more debts and announced that he was through with the enterprise. That did not deter Lamade, whose favorite saying was, "difficulties show what men are." He enlisted his younger brother as a new partner, and the *Grit* was on its way.

Five days a week, from May until November 1885, Lamade traveled all over north-central Pennsylvania, using his lottery to stimulate statewide circulation of the *Grit*. His efforts would save his newspaper and transform it into a national institution.

He carried two large suitcases of *Grit* advertising materials and convinced many small stores and newsagents to carry the publication. He tacked flyers to buildings, fences, and trees, and hired boys to put circulars in all the houses. After his week on the road, he returned to the paper's office and slept on a folding cot on Friday and Saturday nights to ensure that the paper was shipped to the out-of-town agents on Saturday mornings and that the Williamsport edition was ready for Sunday mornings.

On Thanksgiving Day 1885, the grand prize drawing was held at Williamsport's Academy of Music. Five prizes were given out, three to out-of-towners and two to local residents. Lamade's tireless efforts more than doubled circulation and helped to stabilize the *Grit*'s finances.

In 1886, *Grit* showed a weekly circulation of 14,000, and its books showed all bills paid with a cash balance of $400. Lamade and his partners shook hands, patted themselves on their backs, and gave themselves raises from $12 to $15 a week. They bought equipment and moved to a first-floor location. By 1887, circulation had reached 20,000, and the partners ordered their first newspaper perfecting press at a price of $8,000.

In 1891, *Grit* and its 40 employees moved into its new home at the corner of William and West Third Streets. Circulation averaged 53,000 copies weekly in most states east of the Mississippi. Lamade expanded circulation even more by using direct mail and hiring newsboys in locations throughout the country to sell the paper. By the 20th century, circulation reached 100,000, and then tripled by 1916. The *Grit* was one of the first newspapers in America to feature color and fictional supplements. By the late 1970s, its circulation was more than 1.2 million. Competing with metropolitan dailies and national magazines was never Lamade's goal. He wanted only to serve small towns and villages removed from the influences of big cities, places that had no daily newspaper of their own. Although Lamade's 5¢ price tag eventually increased to 25¢ because of higher taxes, wages, and materials, the *Grit* never changed its 80:20 percent ratio of editorial matter to advertising content. "If I have succeeded," Lamade once said, "it is because I have concentrated on one thing."

Lamade read his newspaper each week with a critical eye and always encouraged optimism. "Make every issue of *Grit* ring the joy bells of life," was his sage advice. Lamade died on October 9, 1938, at the age of 79, a beloved figure mourned by many. His descendants remain prominent today in Williamsport.

One

Williamsport: Backdrop for a Newspaper

Famous in the 19th century for its lumber products, Williamsport, Pennsylvania, once boasted more millionaires per capita than any American city. It began as a budding pioneer village on the West Branch of the Susquehanna River with easy access to virgin forests of the finest hemlock and white pine. It is a city blessed by a diverse cultural heritage, noble mountains, grand valleys, and fertile farmland.

Michael Ross founded the city of Williamsport. Ross was born on July 12, 1759, of Scottish origin. He and his mother became indentured servants to land speculator Samuel Wallis, who had an estate near Muncy.

Ross became a surveyor's assistant, and at the conclusion of his servitude in 1779, Wallis gave him a favorable recommendation and 109 acres of land. To his holdings, he later added 285 acres of land, which he bought from William Winter. Ross became a successful surveyor and farmed on a large scale. He acquired various tracts of land and added to his acquisitions until he owned plots on both sides of the West Branch of the Susquehanna River.

Williamsport, the lumber capital of the continent, provided more than one and a half million logs annually, which were transported by rafts, canal boats, and the railroad.

Eventually, Williamsport declined as the lumber barons denuded the mountainsides. Zealous timbering, forest fires, and disastrous floods toppled the lumbering companies. Its heyday over, Williamsport turned to agriculture.

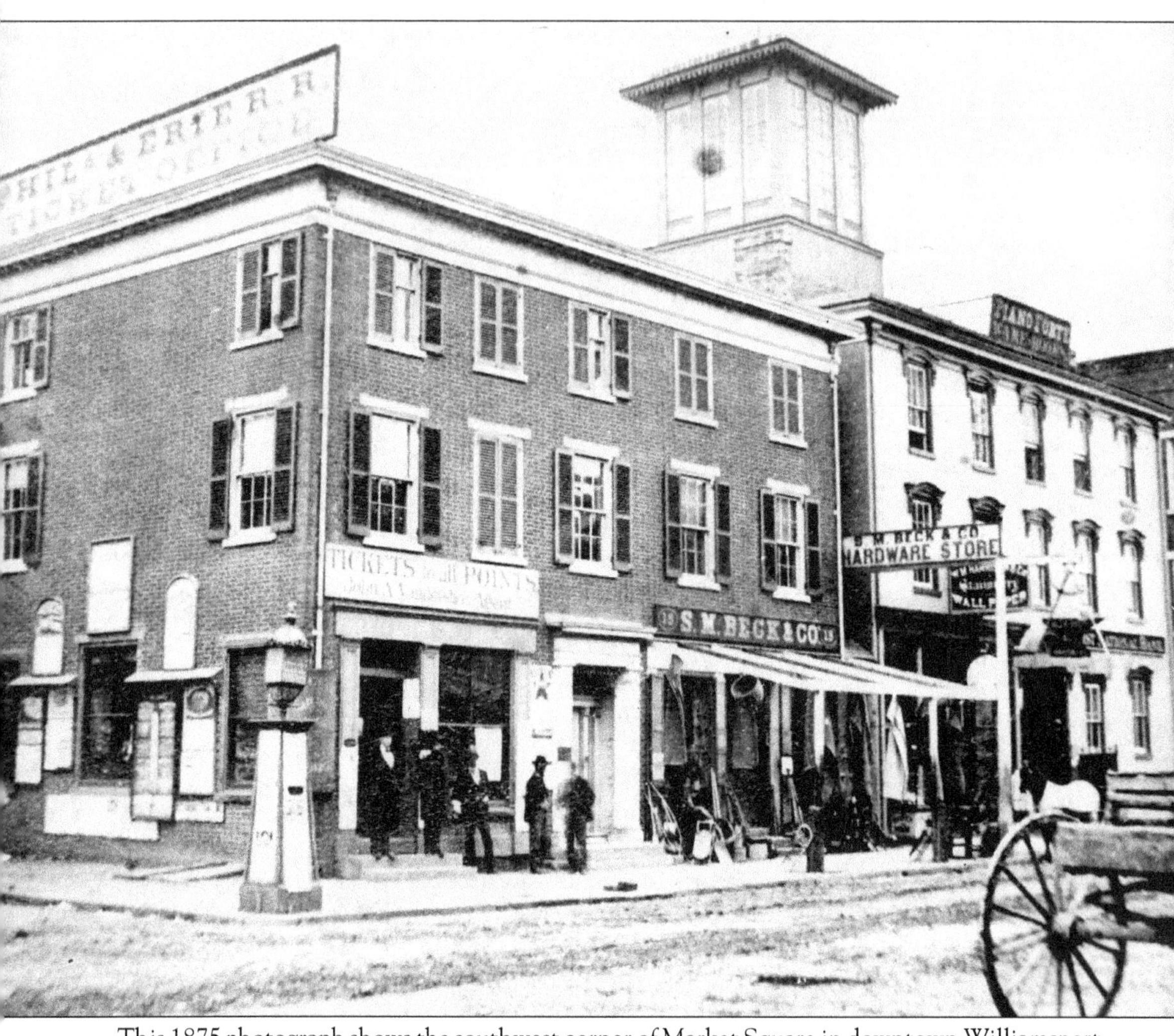

This 1875 photograph shows the southwest corner of Market Square in downtown Williamsport. Bustling with downtown traffic despite the muddy thoroughfares, Williamsport's booming lumber trade summoned entrepreneurs eager to capitalize on the region's wealth and new construction. The block featured a ticket office for the Philadelphia and Erie Railroad Company, a hardware store, and a pianoforte maker. Michael Ross, an indentured servant of Scottish origin, founded the city. In 1793, Ross bought 285 acres of land from William Winter. The original plot of land was a rectangular figure containing 111 acres and divided into 302 lots with streets and alleys crossing each other at right angles. He sold the first lots in what would become Williamsport on July 4, 1796.

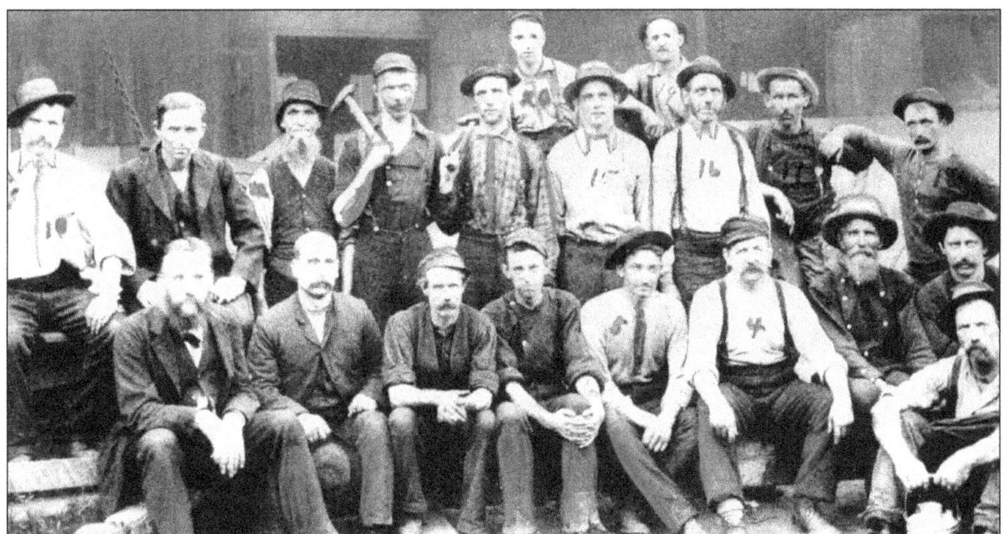

Employees of the E. Keeler Company pose for an 1887 photograph. From left to right are the following: (first row) Isaac Barton, William Hammond, William Kay, Thomas Costello, Samuel Zelman, Isaac Mallinson, George Sands, Joseph Wein, and Harry Hall; (second row) Morris Gahan, James Kelley, John Hauntz, James Costello, James Dolan, George Eoute, Pat Carney, Edwin Quay, and William Williams; (third row) Simon Sands and William Sands.

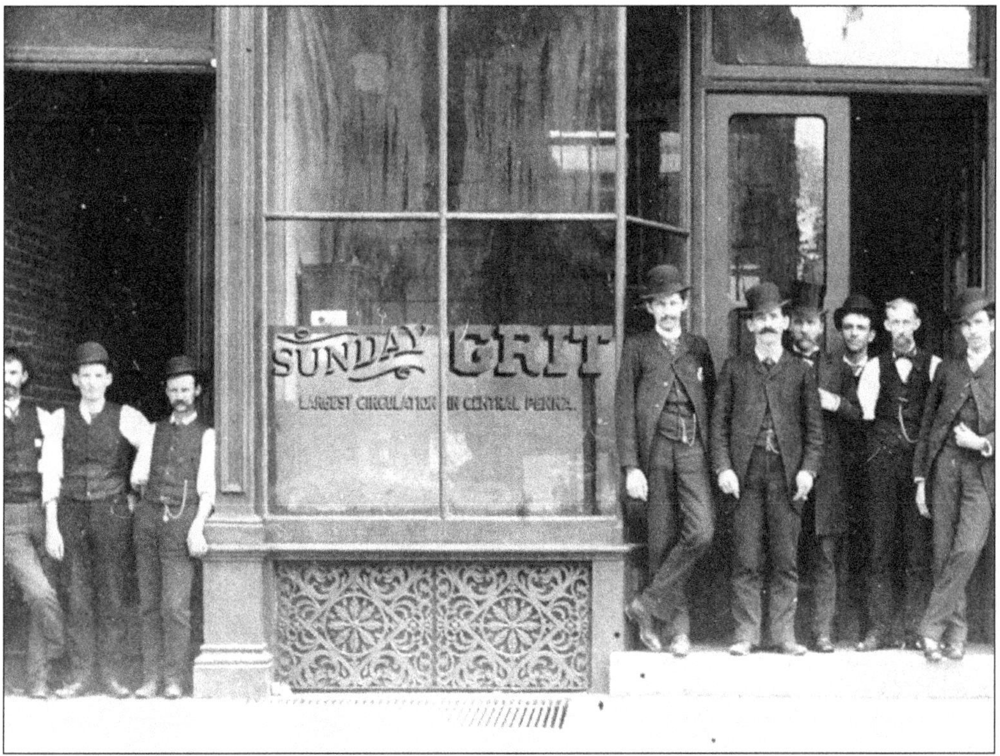

The *Grit* newspaper moved from its one-room, third-floor location in 1886, to new quarters, boasting a first-room floor and basement. Dietrick Lamade and his partners contracted for a $2,700 second-hand newspaper press, a job press costing $400, an engine, and a boiler.

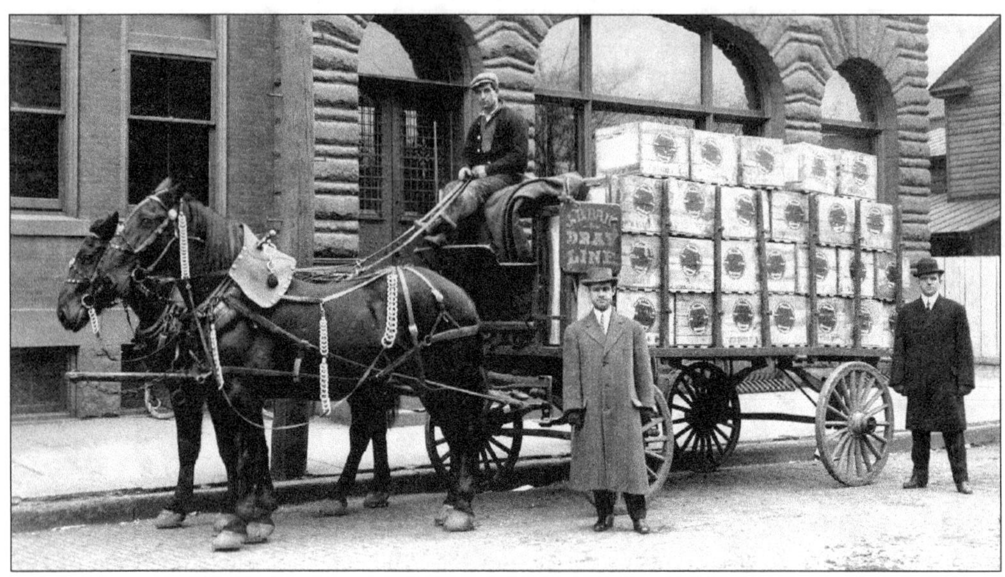

A shipment of Remington typewriters arrives at the *Grit* on the J. B. Bair Dray Line in 1892. The Sholes & Glidden Type Writer was produced by gun makers E. Remington and Sons in Ilion, New York, from 1874 to 1878. It was not a great success (not more than 5,000 were sold), but it founded a worldwide industry, and it brought mechanization to dreary, time-consuming office work. Among the first users was Mark Twain, who fiddled around with it before putting it aside.

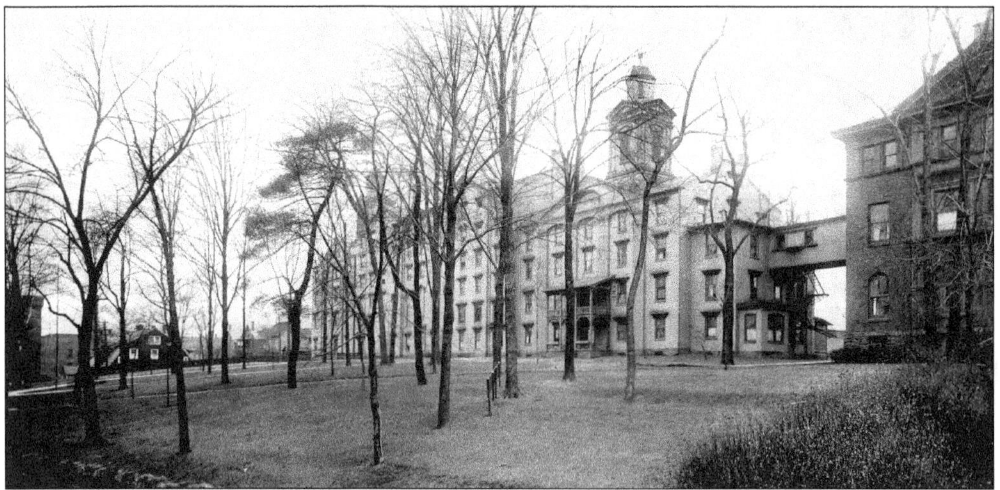

Pictured here is a venerable old landmark on the campus of Dickinson Seminary, now Lycoming College. It was Old Main, and unfortunately it fell to the wrecker's ball in the late 1960s, under the guise of progress. In the spring of 1847, the Reverend Benjamin H. Crever heard that the Williamsport Academy, which was established in 1812, was for sale. He walked to Williamsport to make an offer and purchased it on behalf of the Methodist Church, whose officials then offered Crever a job as principal. He turned them down and suggested Dr. Thomas Bowman. Crever became the school's financial agent and a teacher of experimental sciences. His wife, Susan Caroline Follansbee, became the preceptress, or dean, of the school. The school was called Dickinson Seminary because of the preparatory relationship it had with Dickinson College in Carlisle. It had 212 students in its first year.

Two

A NEW CENTURY

During the turn of the century, many families turned to agriculture. A great deal more, however, were obliged to move from the area to seek employment. Business and industry were at a standstill. Plucky Williamsporters sought to avert financial and industrial collapse by forming a trade association to attract new industries to the county and revitalize the region. During the 20-year period from 1894 to 1914, virtually every aspect of life in Lycoming County communities was affected by sweeping changes. The disastrous floods of 1889 and 1894 were catalysts of change. Other changes were propelled by developments in communication and transportation. Extensive unemployment and lower living standards accompanied business panics in 1893 and 1907. Throughout it all, D. Vincent Smith was a familiar sight, lugging his box camera on the back of his heavy-duty bicycle. He left behind a priceless photographic heritage for *Grit*.

From the 1890s through the first two decades of the new century, streetcars dominated travel in Williamsport. Trolley parties were popular during the summer, and parents often would charter a trolley for children's outings. The streetcars also prospered ferrying residents to favorite recreation spots. For example, the Vallamont loop served a nine-hole golf course located west of Woodmont Avenue, as well as Vallamont Park. For 10¢ residents could ride round trip to the park, which included free admission to a matinee performance in the pavilion. The loop also served Athletic Park, home of the Williamsport Millionaires of the Tri-State Baseball League.

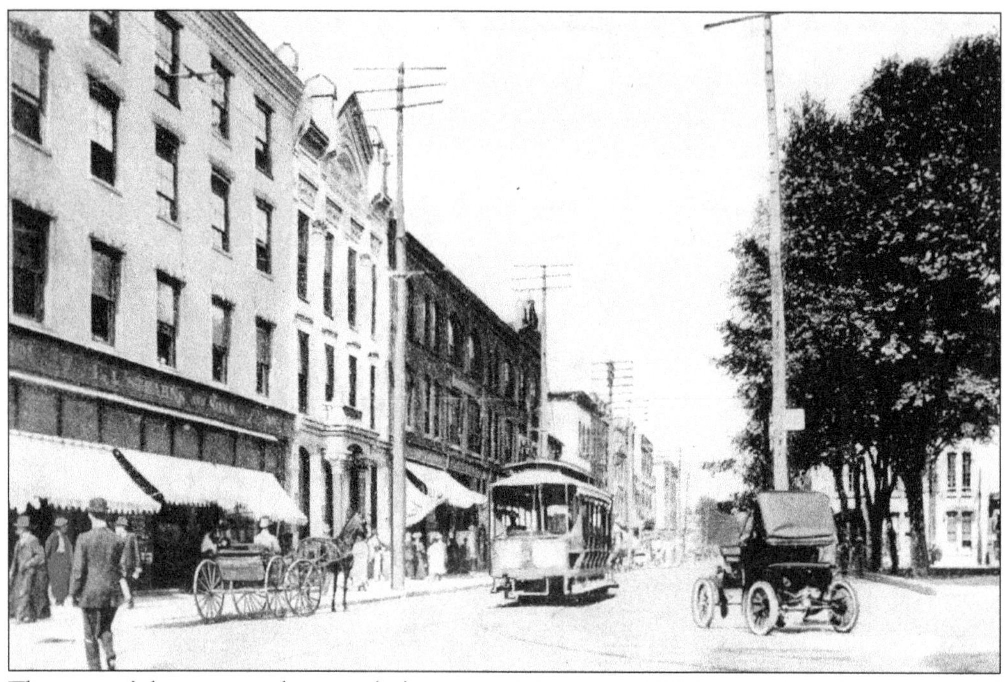

This turn-of-the-century photograph shows one of downtown Williamsport's busiest commercial crossroads, the intersection of West Third and Pine Streets. On the left is the L. L. Stearns business and on the right are the lawn and trees of the courthouse. Also significant are three modes of transportation—the horse-drawn buggy, the streetcar, and the newfangled automobile. And, of course, the familiar pedestrian shoppers also are on the scene.

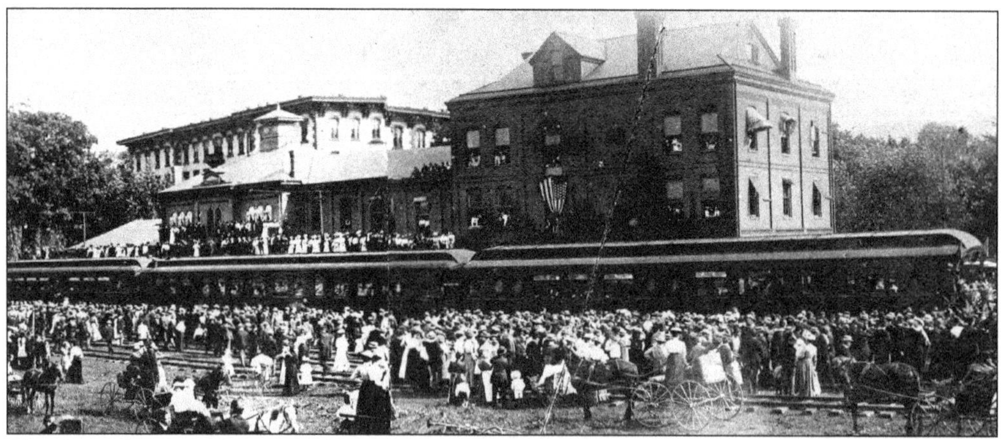

The funeral train of Pres. William McKinley passed through Williamsport's Park Hotel rail station on September 16, 1901. Hundreds of people came out to mourn their fallen president, who was assassinated at the Pan American Exposition in Buffalo, New York, on September 6, 1901, by anarchist Leon Czolgosz.

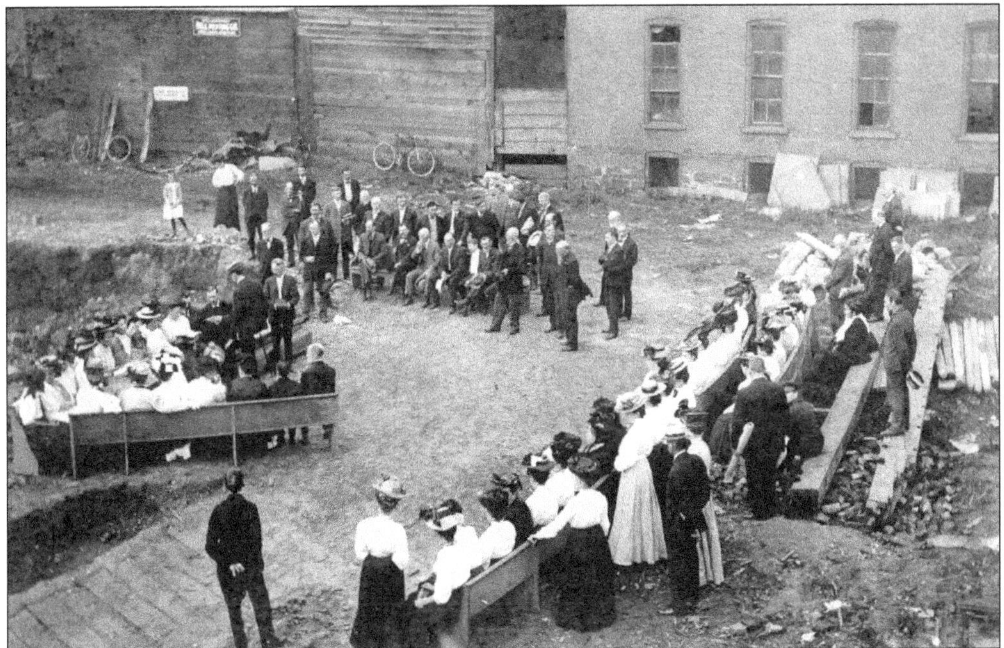

A service of consecration was held on July 8, 1907, as preparations were made to break ground for the new Pine Street Methodist Episcopal Church. The facilities were dedicated in 1910 and seated 2,500 persons. The church has pioneer beginnings. In 1769, John Wesley appointed two missionaries to America. In 1770, an Englishman named Amariah Sutton built a cabin near Lycoming Creek. Richard Parriot, a Methodist circuit rider, organized the area's first Methodist class in the home of Amariah Sutton in 1790.

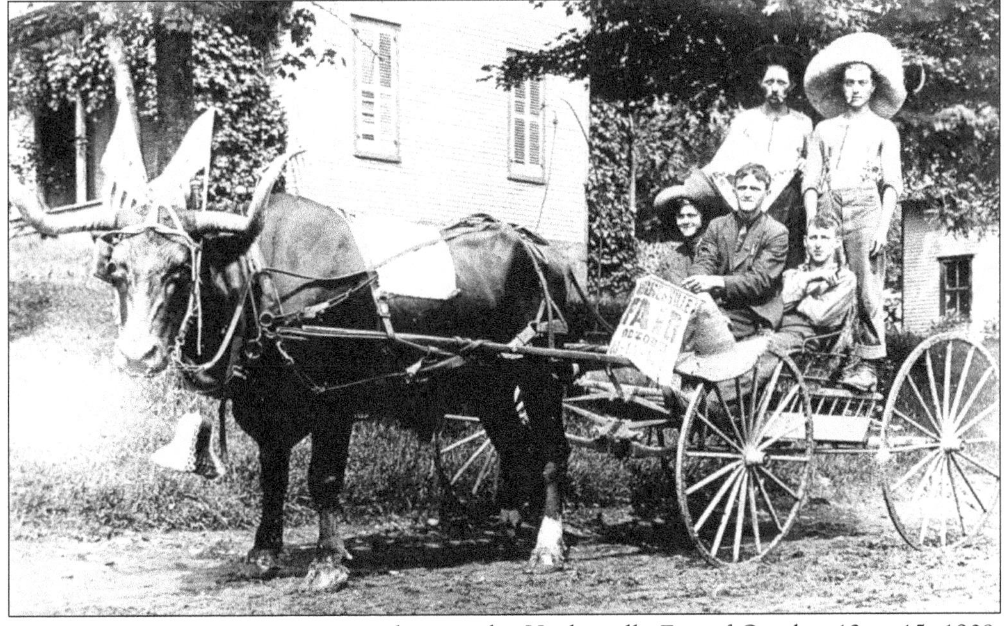

This family is seen setting out to advertise the Hughesville Fair of October 13 to 15, 1908. Even the ox was festooned with advertising posters as well as Old Glory. During its history, the Lycoming County Fair has been at several locations, including the fairgrounds in Hughesville.

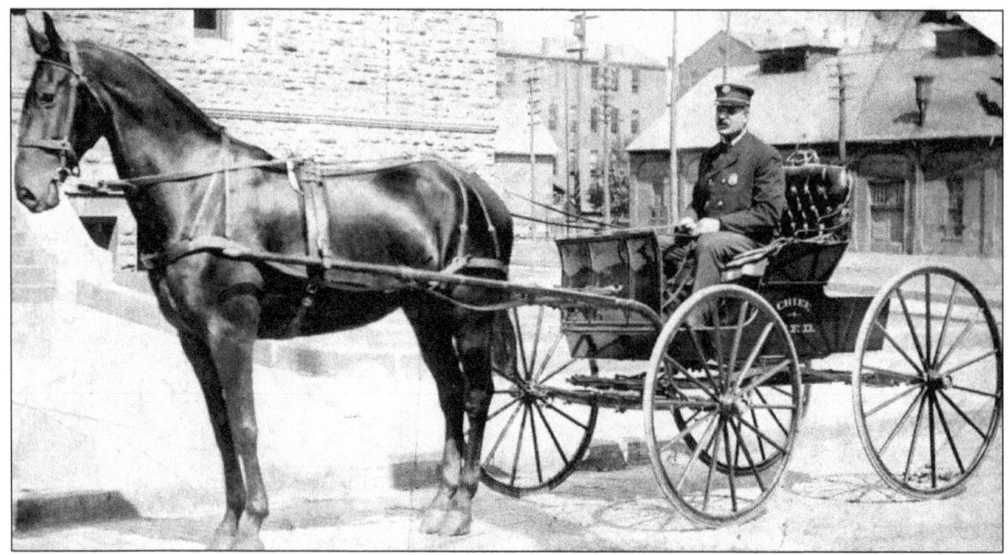

Pictured here is Fire Chief Frank F. Stryker in a 1912 photograph. He was one of the most popular and efficient fire chiefs Williamsport ever had. When Stryker was chief he made his rounds in a rubber-tired buggy driven by John, a horse that had many admirers.

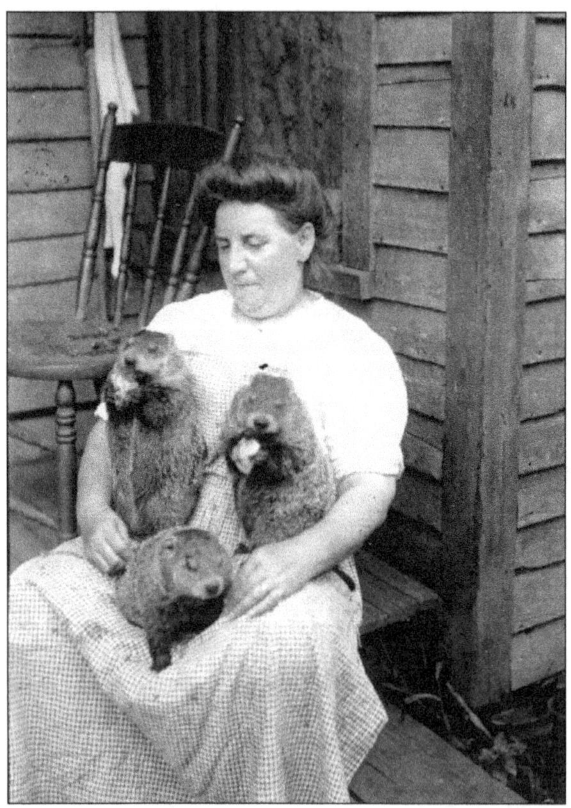

Catharine Hipple poses with her three pet groundhogs for this September 8, 1912, portrait in Williamsport. Also known as woodchucks and considered vermin, these animals suffer many of the maladies of humans and die from liver cancer, heart attacks, and strokes resulting from hardening of the arteries. Few wild chucks ever reach it, but their potential life span is estimated at eight years.

Flags and bunting decorate the West Branch National Bank building that later became a part of the L. L. Stearns store on Pine Street. This photograph was taken during a large Knights Templar convention that was held in Williamsport in September 1912. Allen P. Perley, a longtime director of the West Branch National Bank of Williamsport, was chosen president of that institution, the largest and strongest financial concern in the city at the time.

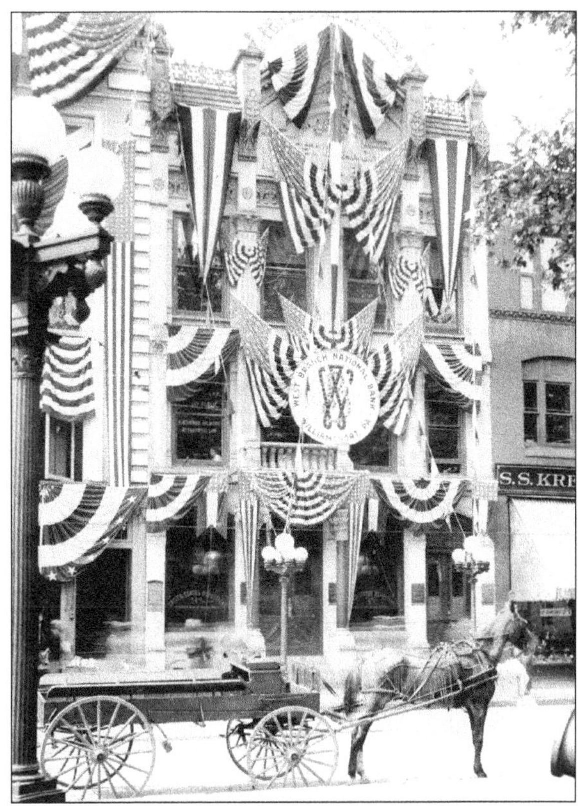

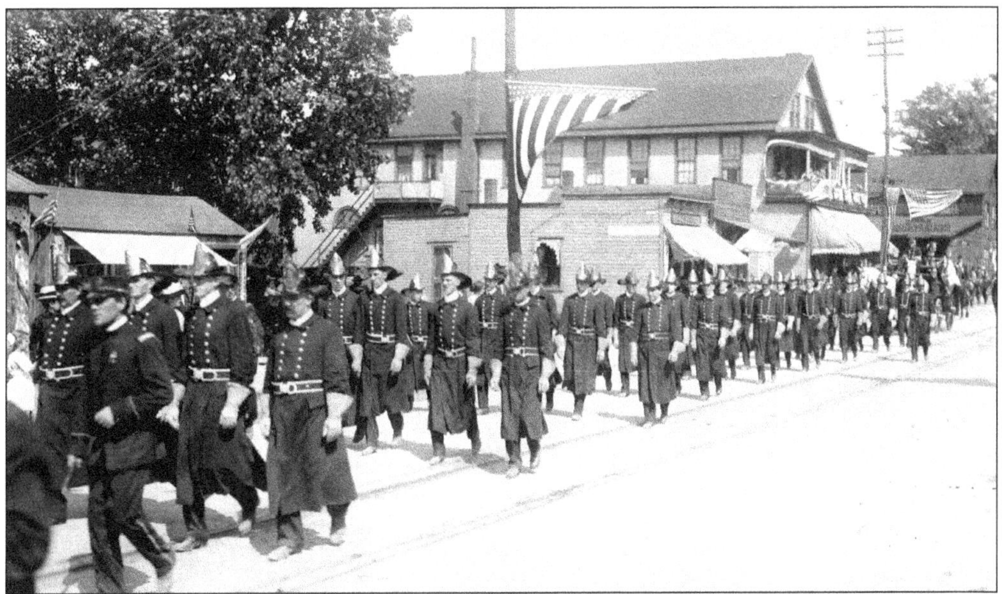

Here is a portion of the mammoth firemen's parade held in nearby Jersey Shore on August 24, 1913. Firemen from a city fire company are shown here marching smartly in their pressed formal uniforms. A parade of this magnitude and featuring Williamsport fire companies was a major event in a small town like Jersey Shore.

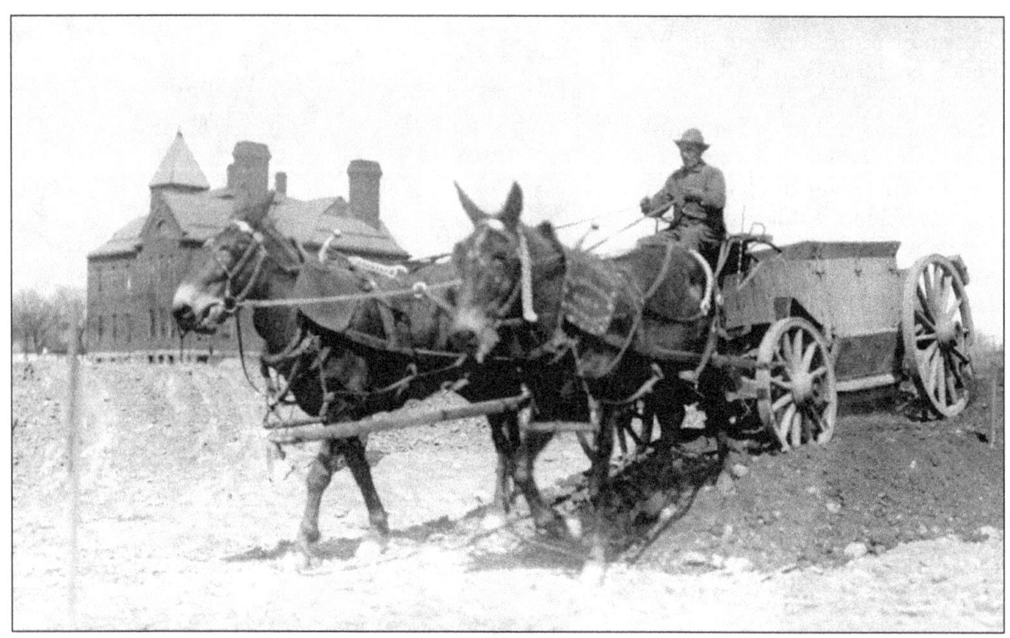

A man grades the Williamsport High School athletic field on West Third Street in April 1913. The wagon, pulled by a team of mules, is seen dumping earth on the low spots of the field. The field was used as the athletic and football field for Williamsport High School until 1972.

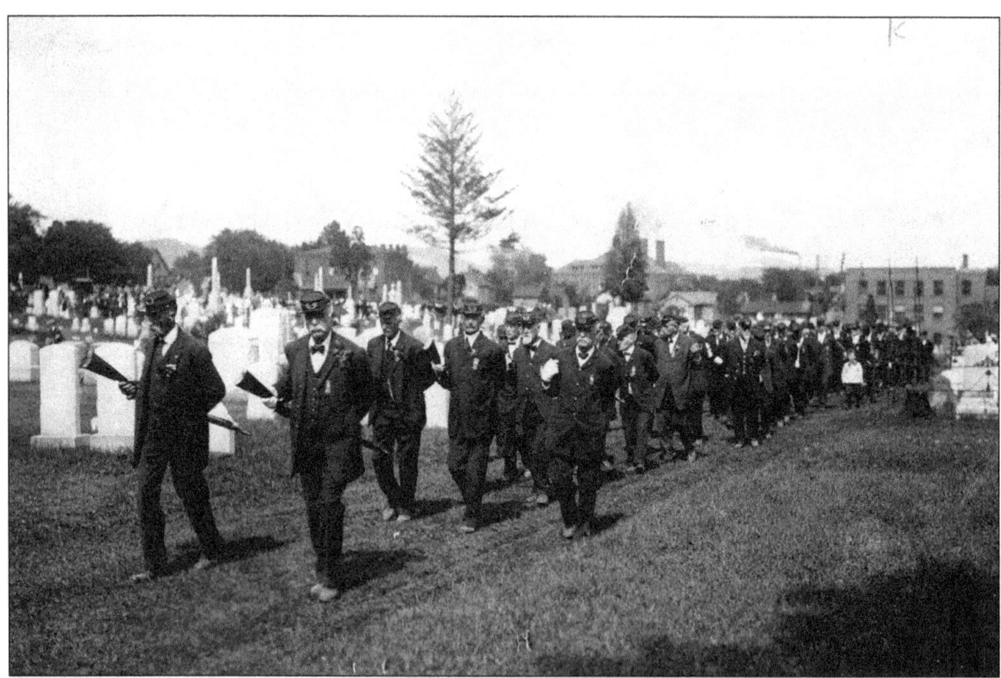

Civil War veterans march in Wildwood Cemetery as they pay homage to their departed comrades on Memorial Day 1913. In his *History of Lycoming County*, John Meginness wrote, "When war came the enthusiasm of the people broke forth in flame. Monster meetings were held and the citizens demonstrated in the most unmistakable manner they were solid for the Union."

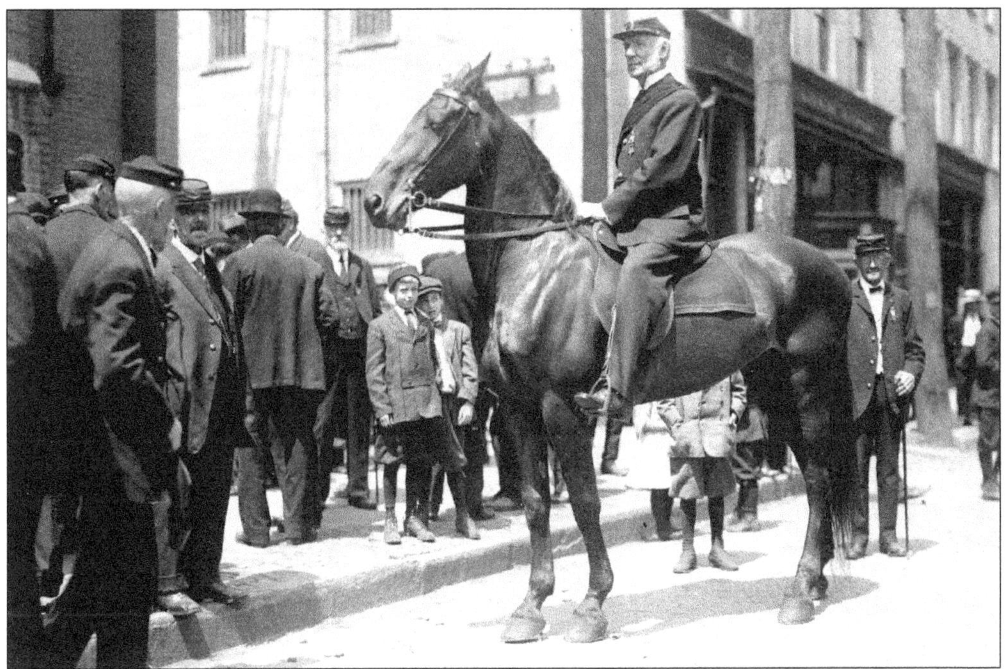

A regal looking Hyman Slate, an aged Civil War veteran, is admired by young boys as he sits proudly atop his horse as an aid to the chief marshal of the Memorial Day commemoration held by Grand Army of the Republic Reno Post 64 in 1913.

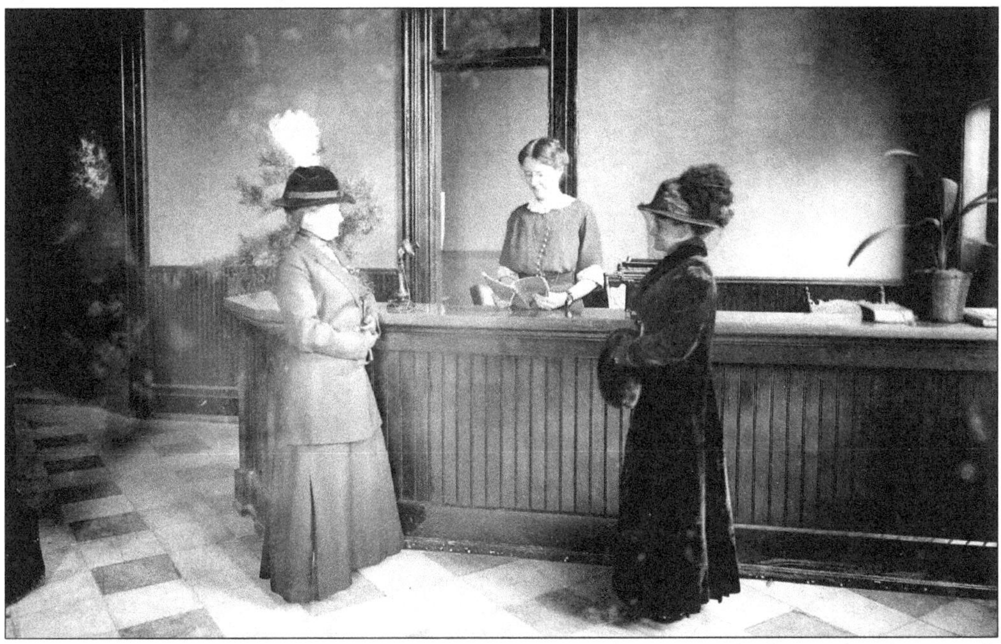

Miss Williams works the main desk of the YWCA as two other women look on. This photograph was taken in December 1913, shortly after the YWCA was opened on West Third Street, near the county prison. The YWCA is the oldest and largest women's membership movement with 312 facilities representing 2 million people. Since its inception in 1893, the YWCA services allow women and their families to live in dignity and peace.

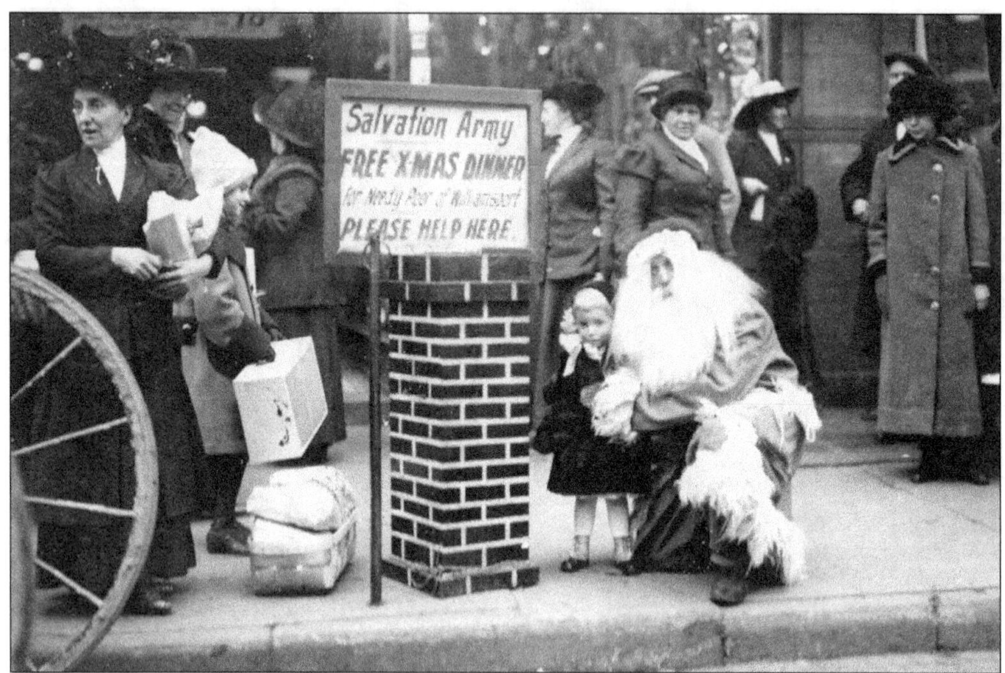

Santa Claus and some of his admirers gather around a Salvation Army collection pot on December 21, 1913, on Pine Street. Passersby are urged to donate to the charity's "free X-Mas dinner for needy poor of Williamsport." The Salvation Army still collects money and goods and distributes its resources to people in need.

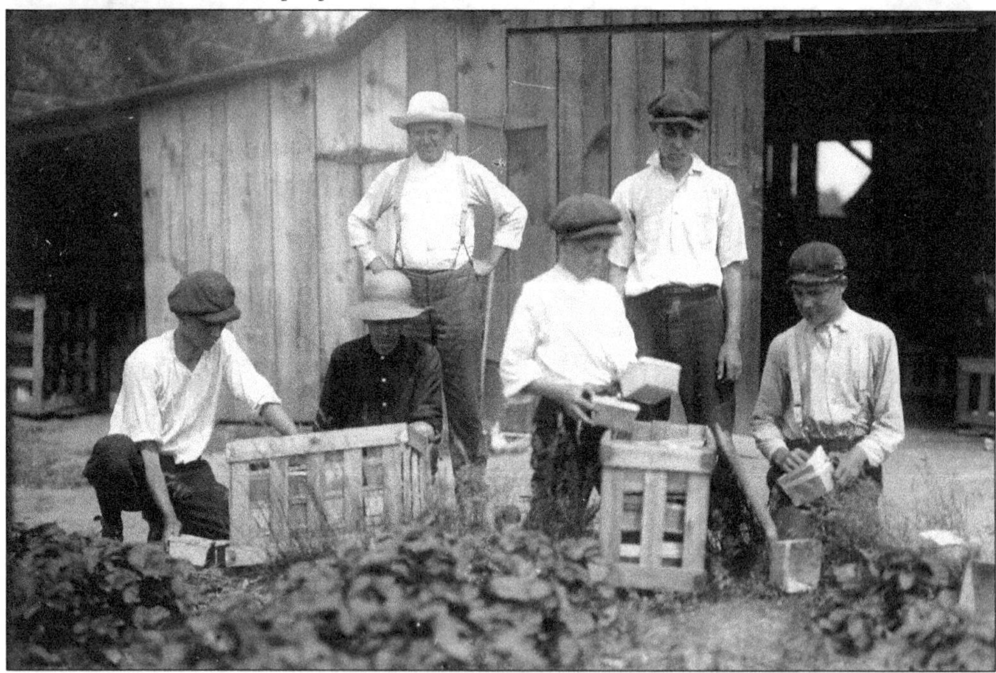

Boys earn a summer's wage picking strawberries on the King and Nuse farm in Montoursville. Picking strawberries is still a popular summer outing, but for the farm worker it is labor that can make backs and knees ache, causing a permanent distaste for the red berry.

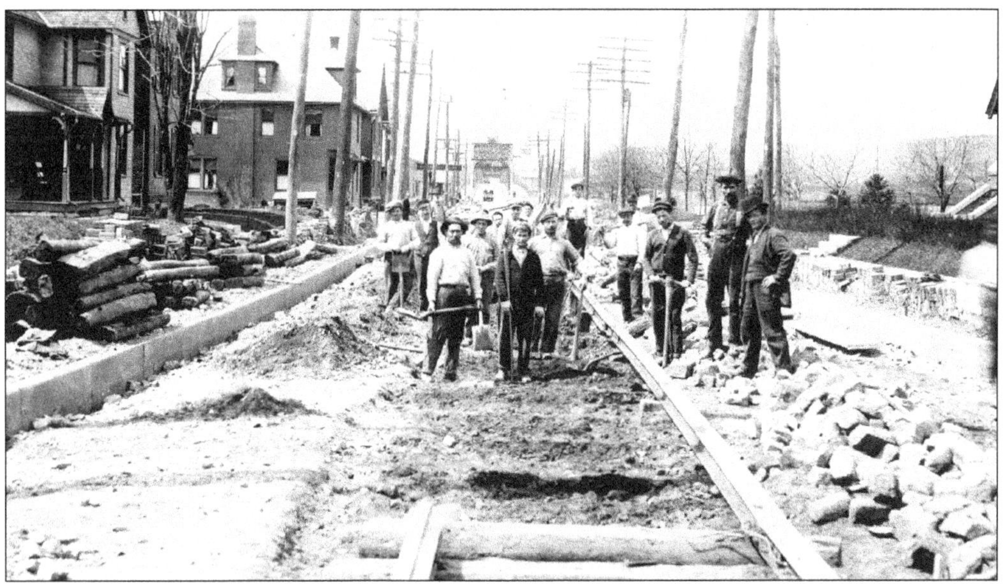

Market Street in South Williamsport was given new brick pavement, as this photograph from May 17, 1914, shows. The construction crew is tearing up trolley tracks to make way for the brick pavement. Behind them is the bridge into Williamsport. Market Street is better known as U.S. Route 15, which traverses Pennsylvania and leads into New York.

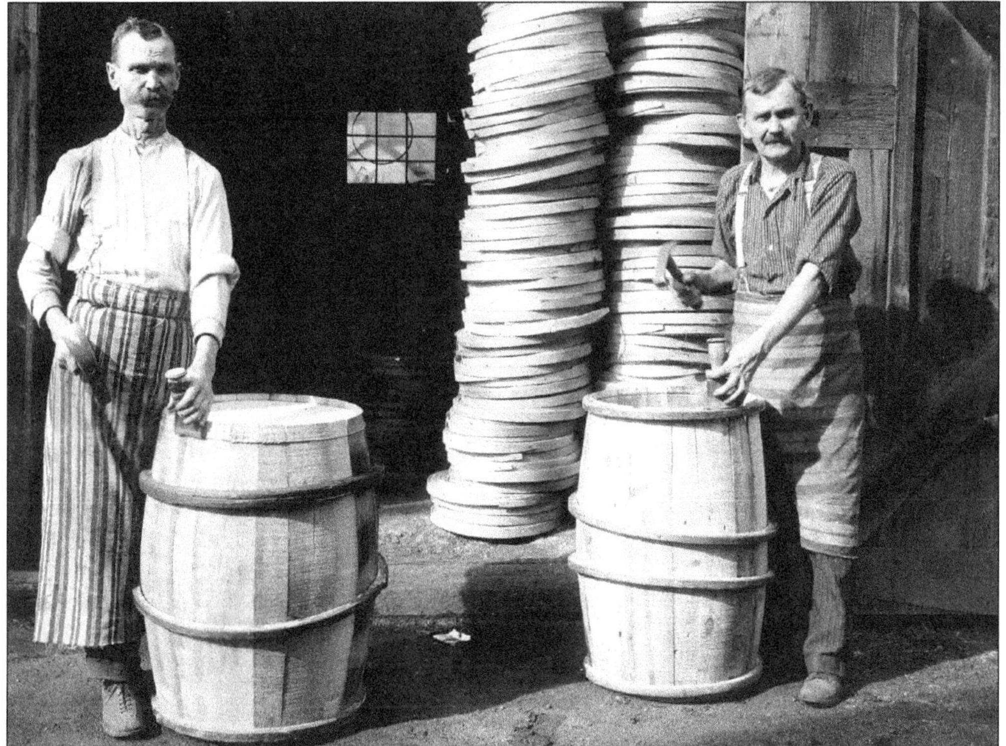

A barrel is ready for heating at the Case Cooper Shop on Fifth Avenue in Williamsport, in October 1914. Thousands of barrels were made in Williamsport shops and factories during the World War I era. At least 50 to 60 barrels a day could be made at this shop.

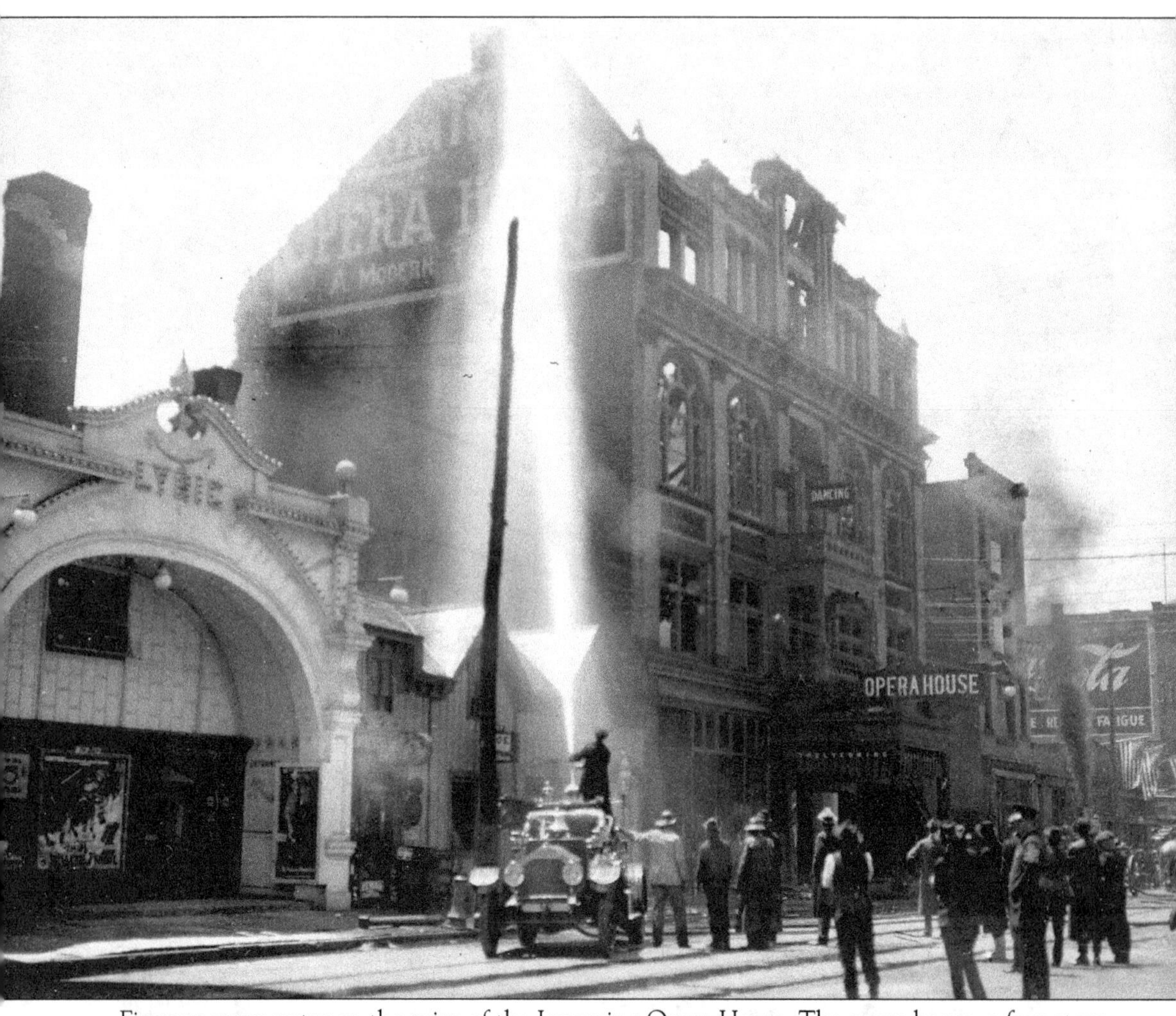

Firemen spray water on the ruins of the Lycoming Opera House. The opera house, a four-story, $85,000 structure, opened on September 8, 1892, on the southwest corner of West Third and Laurel Streets. It was a major entertainment center for the Williamsport area until a spectacular fire gutted it on May 31, 1915. Despite the fact that the firefighters had a motorized fire engine (purchased in 1911), a motorized, triple-combination pumper, and a chemical and hose wagon (purchased in 1914), the theater was lost. The historic Repasz Band, which played at Gen. Robert E. Lee's surrender at Appomattox, Virginia, lost all its instruments, music, and historic artifacts in the fire. The opera house was a major Williamsport cultural institution and featured many famous entertainers. John Philip Sousa's band performed a composition by a local resident, Cora Elwest Vandersloot, at the Lycoming Opera House on October 7, 1897. It was the only non-Sousa composition played at the concert.

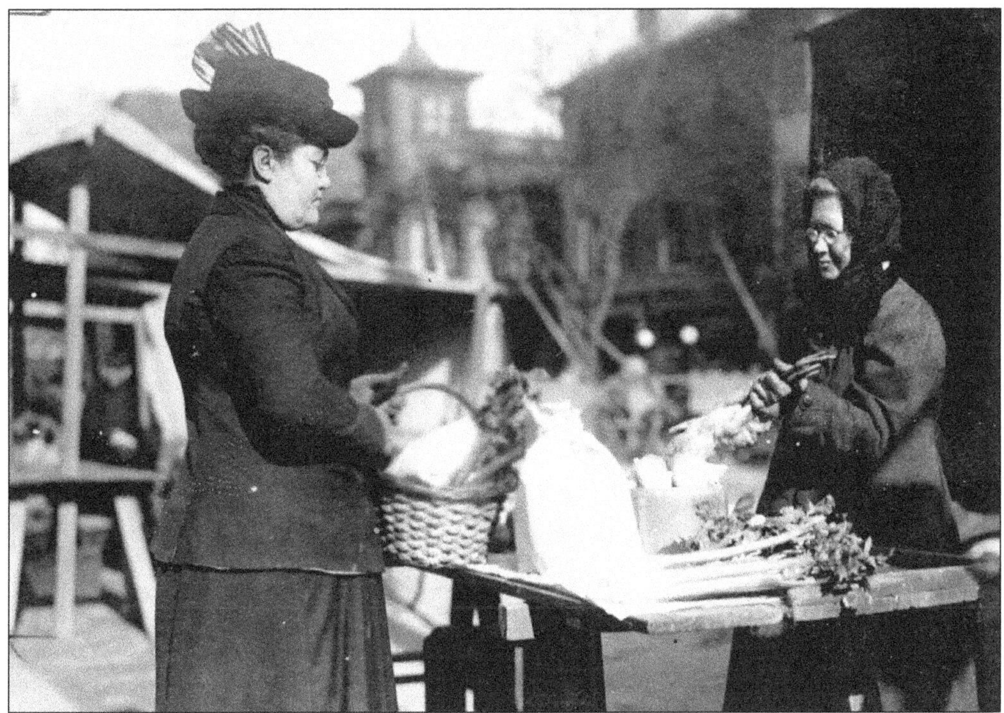

This local market scene, photographed in November 1913, shows the progress of goods from producer to consumer. The curbstone market was filled with fresh produce (when in season), meat, fish, dry goods, and all of the necessities of life during the turn of the century. In Williamsport, the curbstone market once was a million-dollar industry.

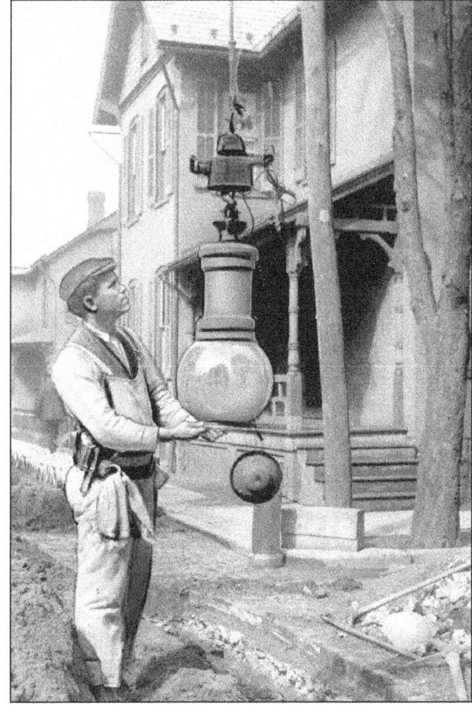

Harry B. Winner is pictured repairing an old carbon arc street light in 1915. Winner made his rounds and carried his tools on a bicycle. He was a common sight on Williamsport streets. The arc light replaced the old gaslights shortly before this photograph was taken.

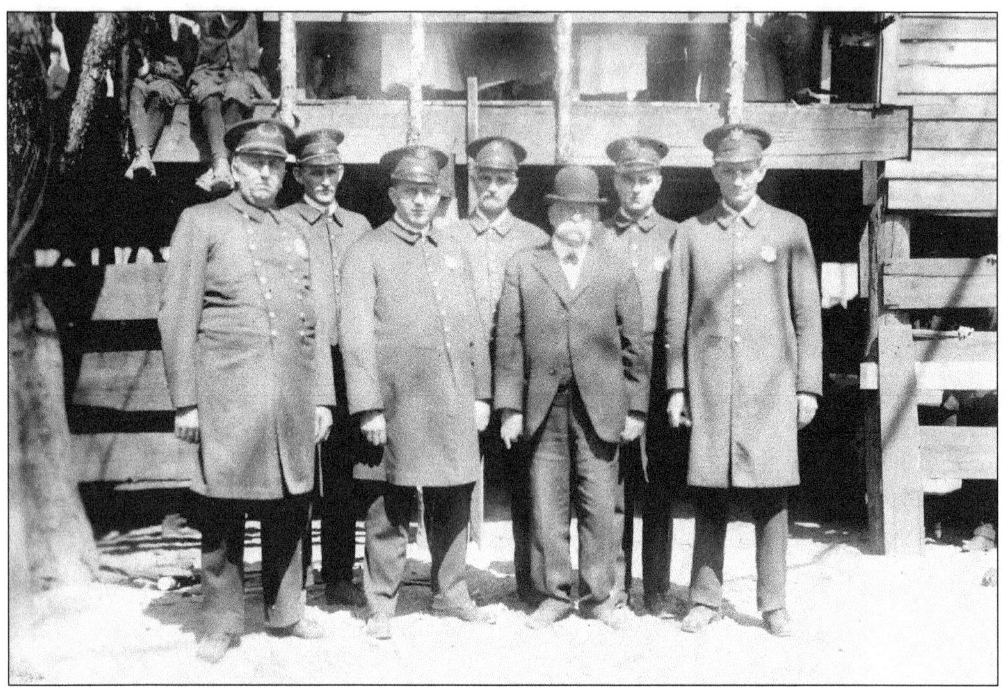

Several Williamsport police officers and Mayor Jonas Fischer are pictured at Fischer Park in May 1916. From left to right are Jasper Fincher, Jim Fenstemaker, Pete Coleman, John Mahaffey, Mayor Fischer, Lee Brooks, and Jack Peters. These officers assisted in keeping order at the huge ox roast at the park. Fischer's Park was located at the foot of Susquehanna Street.

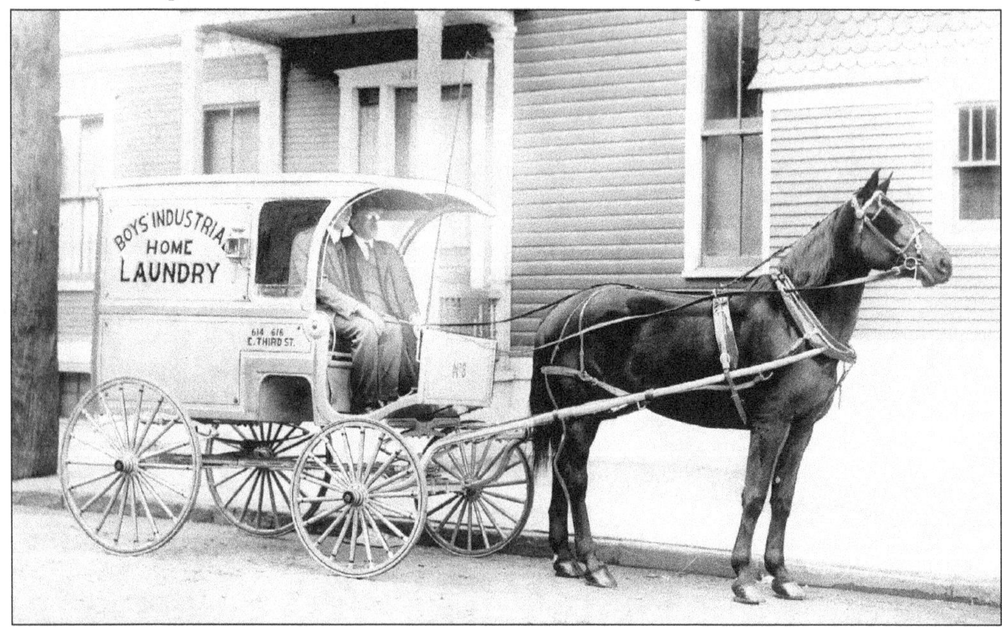

A laundry wagon was presented to the Boys' Industrial Home of Williamsport as an early Christmas gift in 1916. Augustine and Frank Bosch, well-known liverymen in the eastern end of Williamsport, provided it. The school for homeless boys was established in 1898 and was associated with the city mission.

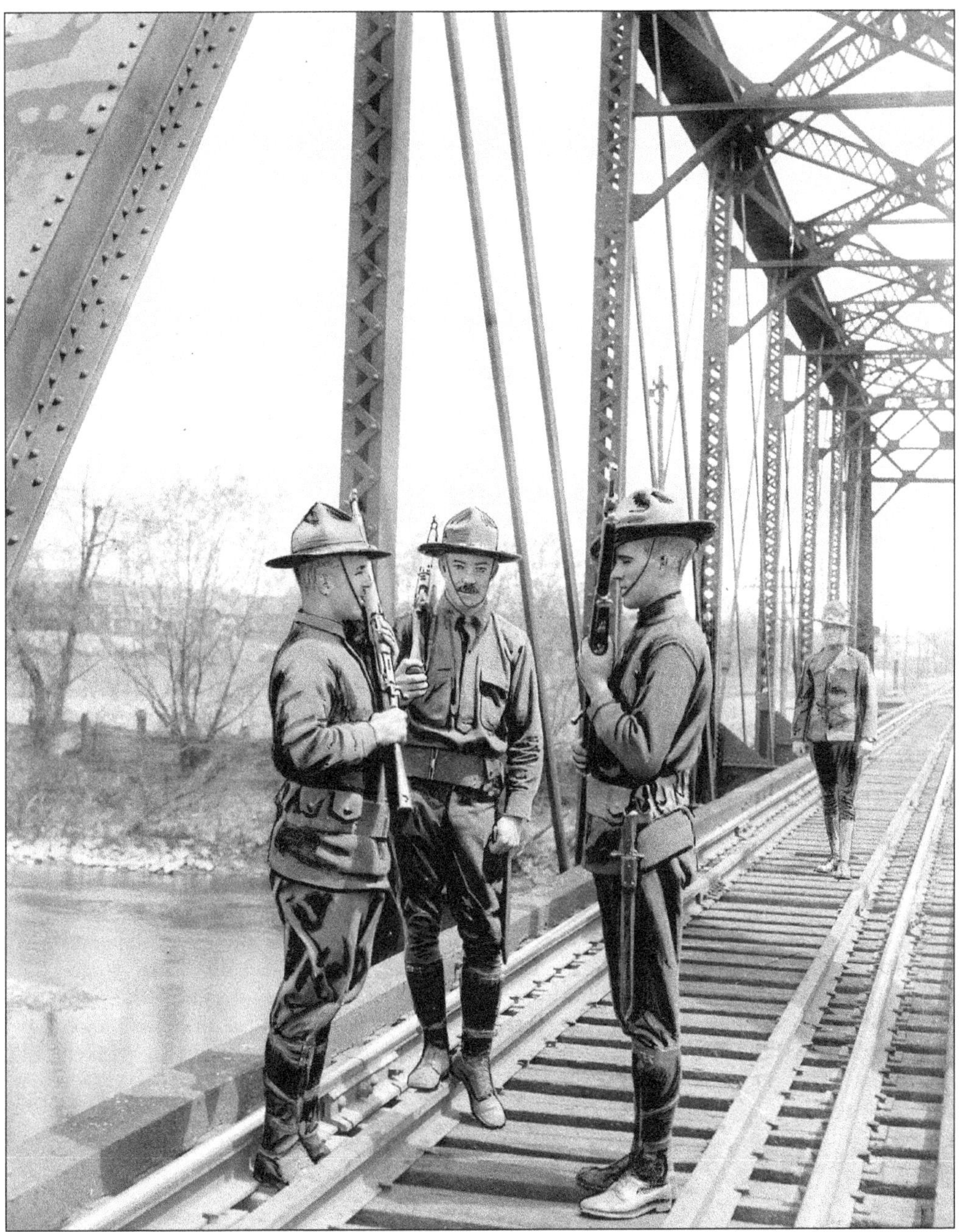

A soldier from Company D of the 13th Regiment of the Pennsylvania National Guard relieves another soldier guarding a bridge on Lycoming Creek in this photograph from May 1917. There were other guardsmen securing various rails and bridges against possible German saboteurs soon after the United States entered World War I. Camps were set up throughout the area, guarding these bridges 24 hours a day. The mission of the Pennsylvania Army National Guard, when summoned by the governor of the commonwealth, is to provide trained personnel and units organized and equipped to function effectively in saving lives, protecting property, and maintaining law and order and public safety when emergencies are beyond the capability of civil authorities.

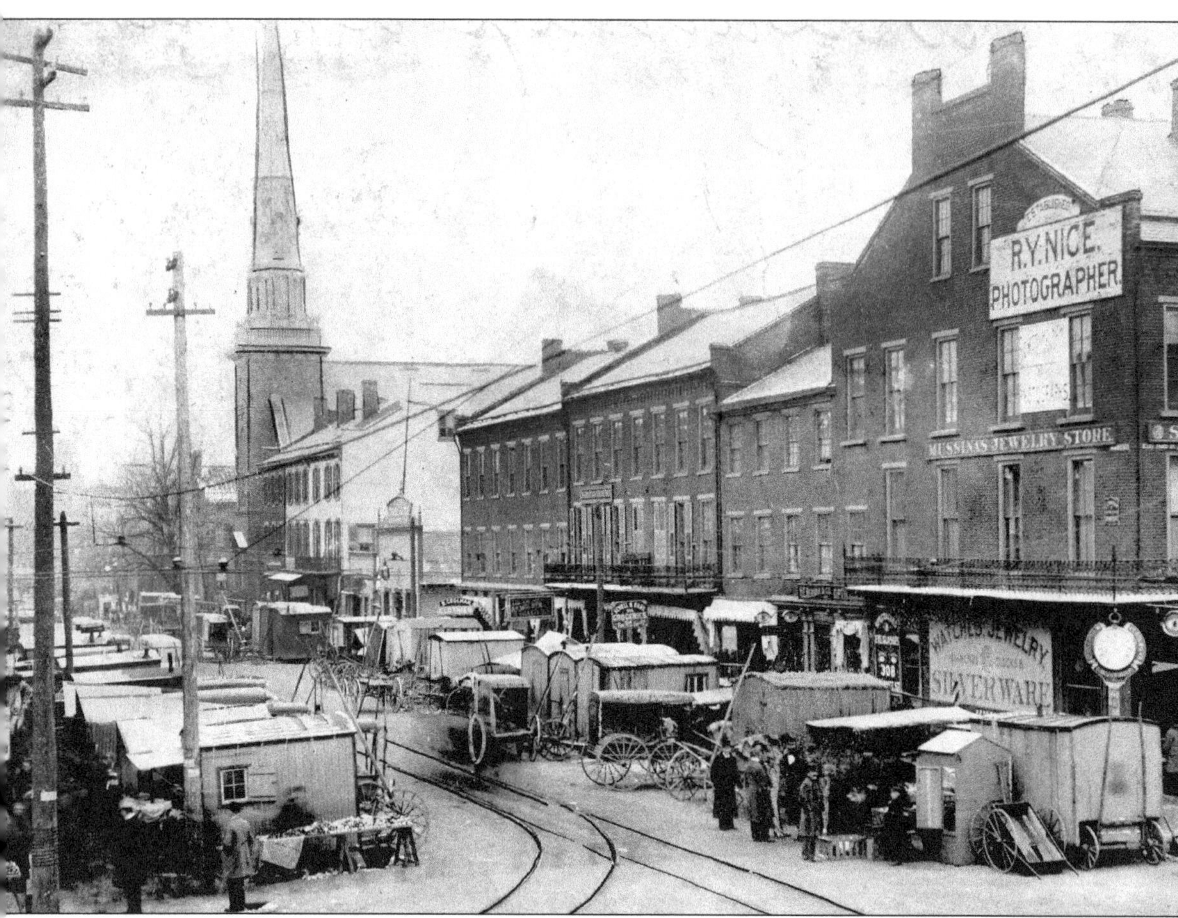

From *c.* 1860 to 1930, the curbstone market in downtown Williamsport dominated the city's economy. According to a *Grit* article from December 31, 1899, "almost a million dollars change hands at Williamsport's curbstone market every year." This photograph shows the market in the early 1900s. Wagons would park along the street, and vendors would display their wares and produce to passersby. Not only did the wagons transport goods, vendors used them to make camp until they sold out. The space cost $2 per month to lease, and the primary market days were Wednesdays and Saturdays. At its zenith, the *Grit* reported, more than 230 dealers sold at the market, including 34 farmers, 34 gardeners, 25 hucksters, 19 merchants, 108 butchers, and 2 florists.

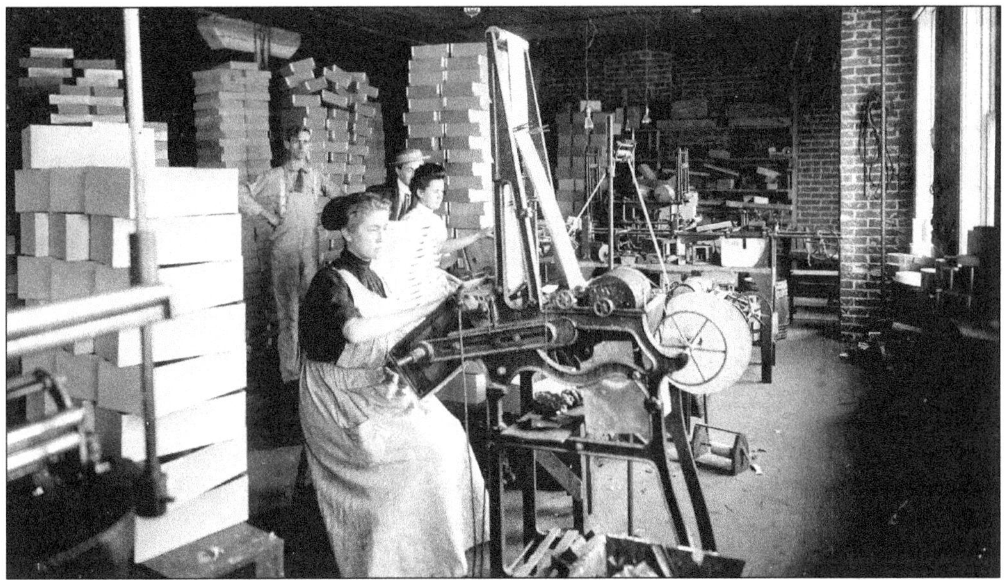

Two women are pictured here making paper boxes while two young men wait to stack them in piles at the J. W. B. Reese factory, formerly located at 51 East Third Street. The machines in the factory used a treadle to stitch fabric binding to create the boxes.

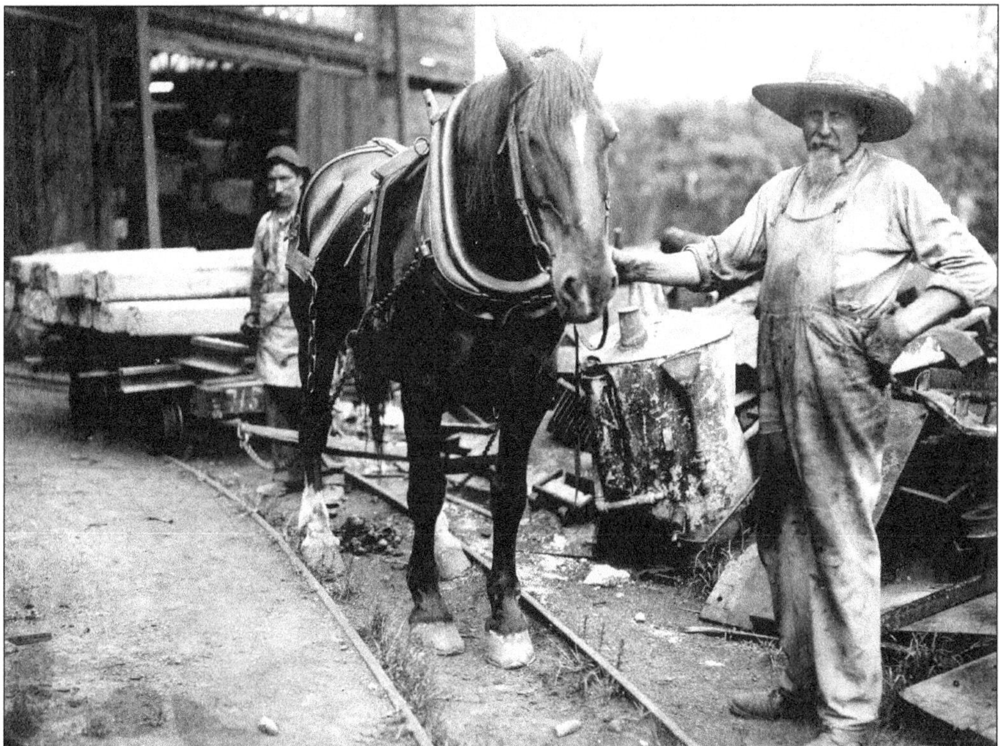

Enoch B. Gamble is pictured here with his horse at the Sweet Steel Plant in Williamsport. Sweet Steel, a Newberry industry formerly of Syracuse, New York, even sponsored a local baseball team. For many Newberry residents, the smoke stacks of Sweet Steel, Armour Leather Company, and the Mosser Tannery were longtime familiar sights.

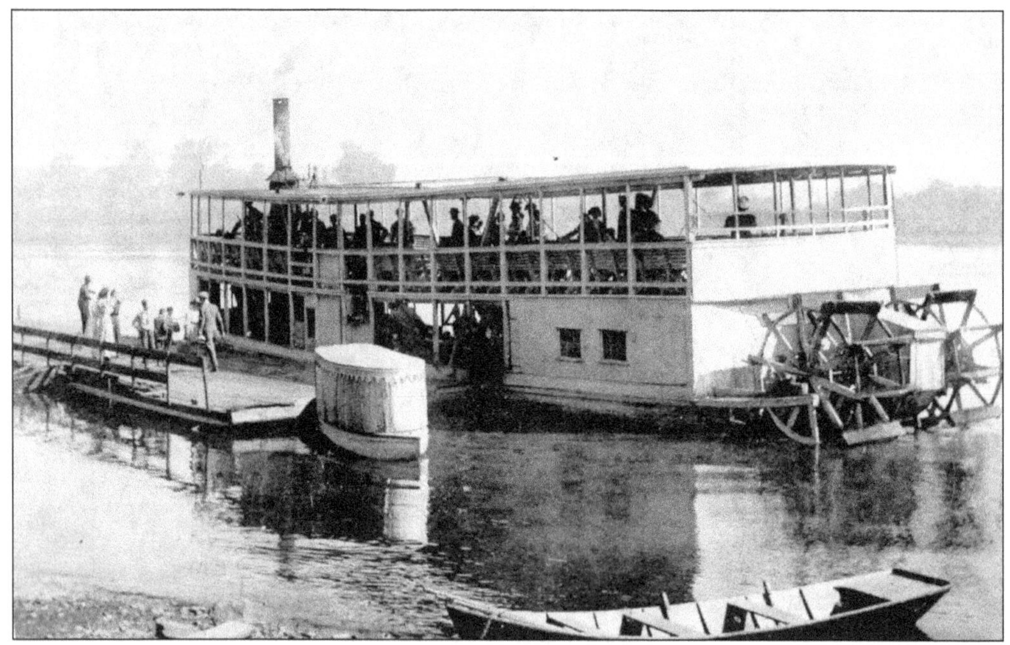

The passenger steamboat *Hiawatha* originally forged the waters of the West Branch of the Susquehanna River near the Sylvan Dell area of South Williamsport in the first decade of the 20th century. In this photograph, taken in the early 1900s, a group of passengers is ready to board the recreational ferry.

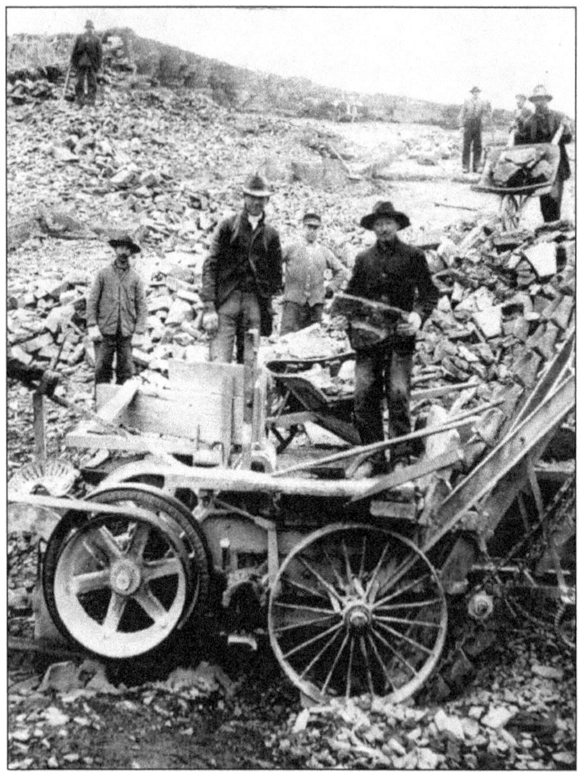

Workers are pictured around a stone crusher at the limestone quarry near Montoursville. All that is left of the outcrop is a springhouse along East Third Street, the Golden Strip. The limestone was used for roads, houses, and construction. In prehistoric times, the quarry provided Native Americans with flint and chert for tools and weapons.

Three

Smiling through War and Depression

The Great Depression—the most serious economic crisis in the nation's history—occurred during the 1930s. Although many Americans had prospered during the 1920s, many Pennsylvanians had not. Three major segments of Pennsylvania's economy already were depressed: farmers were afflicted with low prices, coal miners were experiencing unsteady employment, and textile workers were losing jobs as mill owners shifted operations to the South. By 1933, 40 percent of the state's work force was unemployed. People lost their homes because they could not pay rents, or mortgages, and many could not buy sufficient food. In Williamsport, a variety of social services stepped up to the plate to feed the community and to give them jobs. Among these were various missions and the government. Between the Works Progress Administration and Victory Gardens, many Lycoming residents performed honest labor and fed their families. The WPA was a relief measure established in 1935 and supplied with an initial congressional appropriation of $4,880,000,000. It offered work to the unemployed on an unprecedented scale by spending money on programs, including construction of highways and buildings, slum clearance, reforestation, and rural rehabilitation.

The WPA included a provision for unemployed artists and writers too: the Federal Art Project and the Federal Writers' Project. Qualifying musicians, actors, directors, painters, and writers could work directly for the government. The New Deal arts projects made a lasting impact on American cultural life, and none contributed more than the Federal Writers' Project. At its peak, the writers' project employed about 6,500 men and women around the country, paying them a subsistence wage of about $20 a week. In 1939, the Pennsylvania Writers Projects of the WPA published *A Picture of Lycoming County*. Many of the area's brightest scholars worked on the project and created an enduring literary tribute to the history of the region.

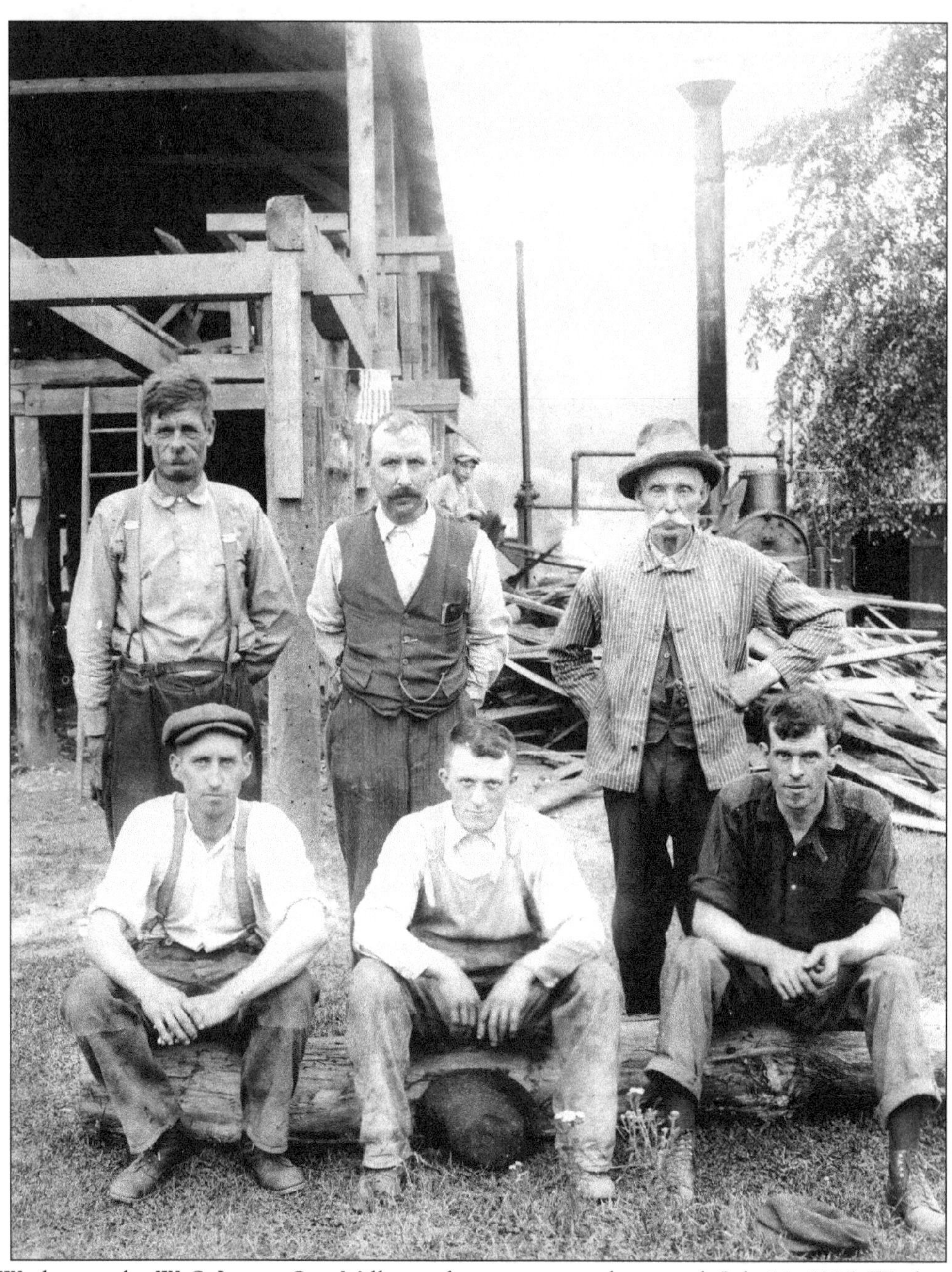

Workers at the W. S. Larson Saw Mill pose for a company photograph July 11, 1915. Working in a sawmill was a dangerous occupation, and a sawmill was usually a family business. The father would build the mill, and his sons would work in it. Usually the wife and daughters stayed home, prepared the meals, and cleaned the clothes and rooms of the employees. The prospering nation needed finished lumber, and the sawmills were erected. In Williamsport, booms to trap the sawn timber were built to divert the logs down the West Branch of the Susquehanna River. Williamsport, the lumber capital of the continent from 1862 to 1894, supplied more than one and a half million logs annually. Transportation evolved from rafts to canal boats, which soon were replaced by the railroad.

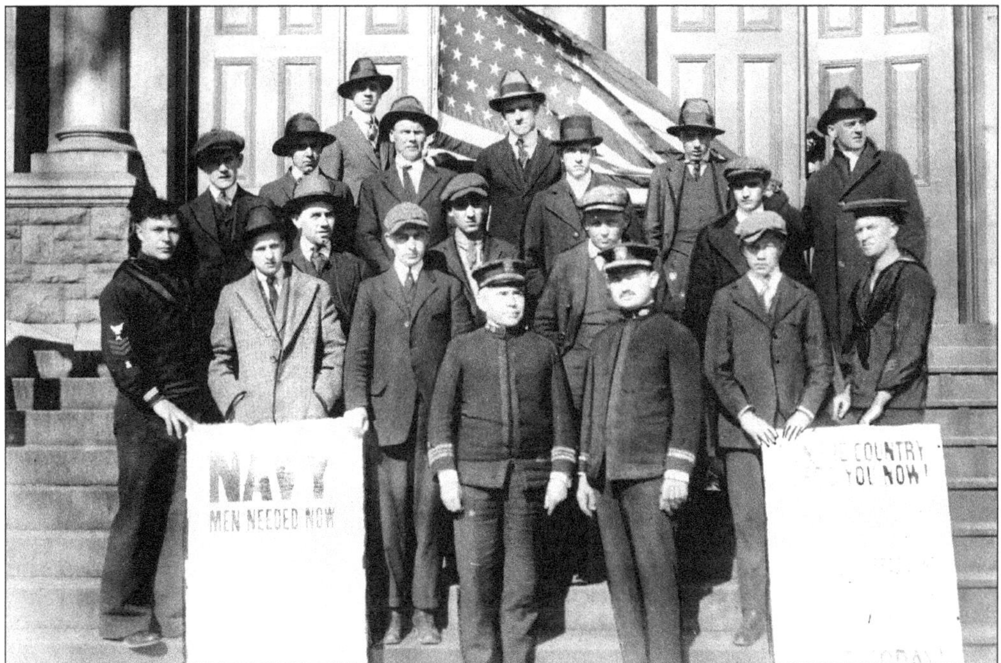

"The Navy needs men," read the posters, and when the men of Lycoming County answered the call to the colors after the United States entered World War I in April 1917, they did so enthusiastically as this photograph from May 1917 shows. In Williamsport, the U.S. Army and U.S. Navy accepted 124 out of 154 who enlisted during the first week of April 1917.

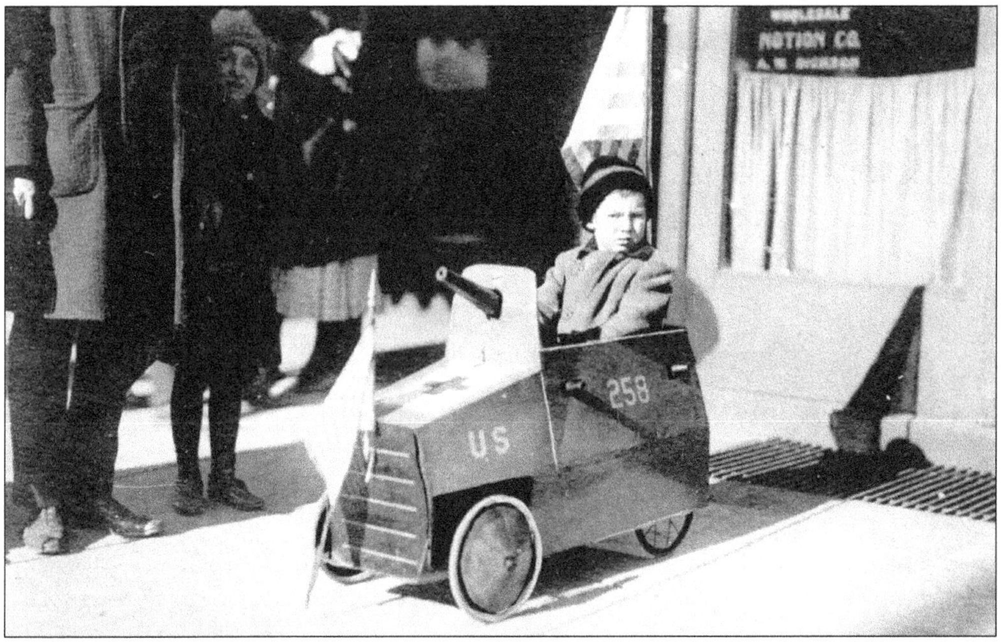

As part of the victory parade in downtown Williamsport celebrating the end of hostilities in World War I on November 11, 1918, little John McKenna Jr. is seen getting ready to join the parade in his little homemade tank made from a wagon. The news of the armistice was met with the blowing of fire whistles and the honking of horns, and thousands took to the streets in celebration.

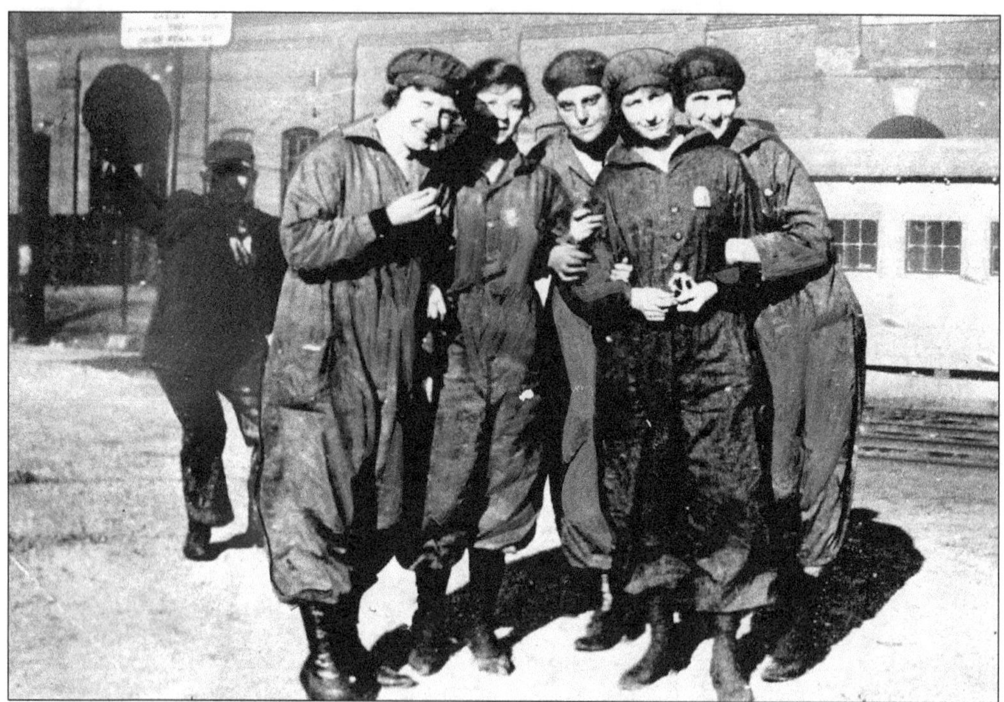
A woman working in war industries was nothing new for Williamsport. During World War I, the production army of the Lycoming Division of the Aviation Corporation included women. Above, a group of employees model the streamlined factory uniforms. The photograph was republished in *Grit* in 1943 to encourage women to work and the industrial population to accept them.

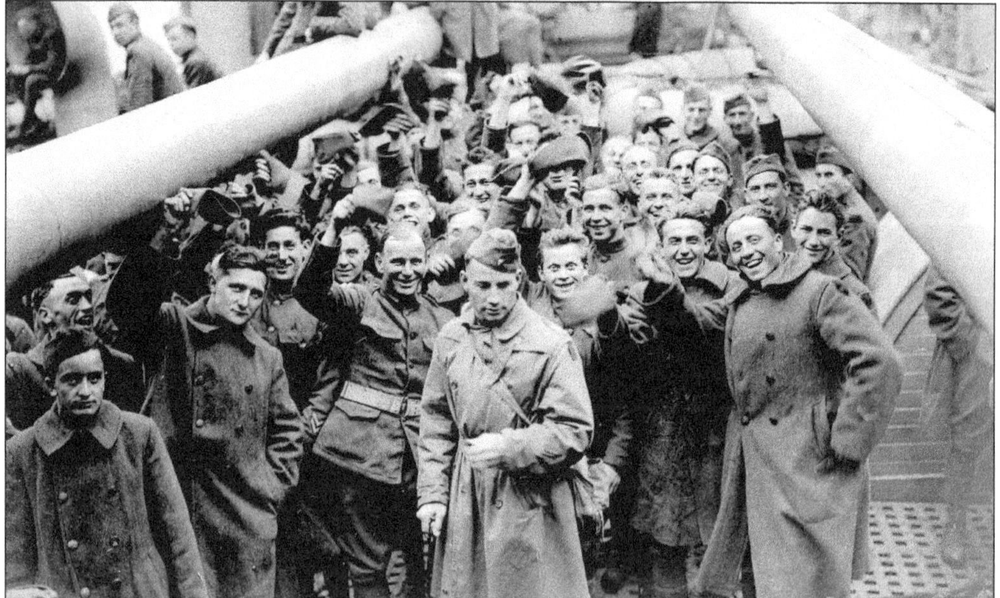
These local boys from Williamsport's Battery D, 107th Field Artillery are pictured here singing "Hail, Hail, the Gang's All Here, What the Hell Do We Care," as they return from France and disembark at the port of New York after the end of World War I.

Officer Charles Clay poses with Beppo, his Belgian police dog on Christmas Day 1921. Clay trained the dog to be a member of the police force and aid in catching robbers and such. This was the first K-9 unit the Williamsport Police Department used.

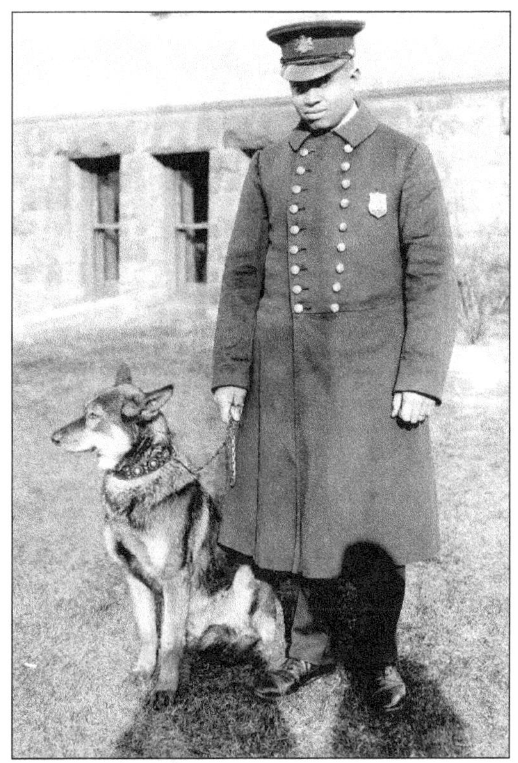

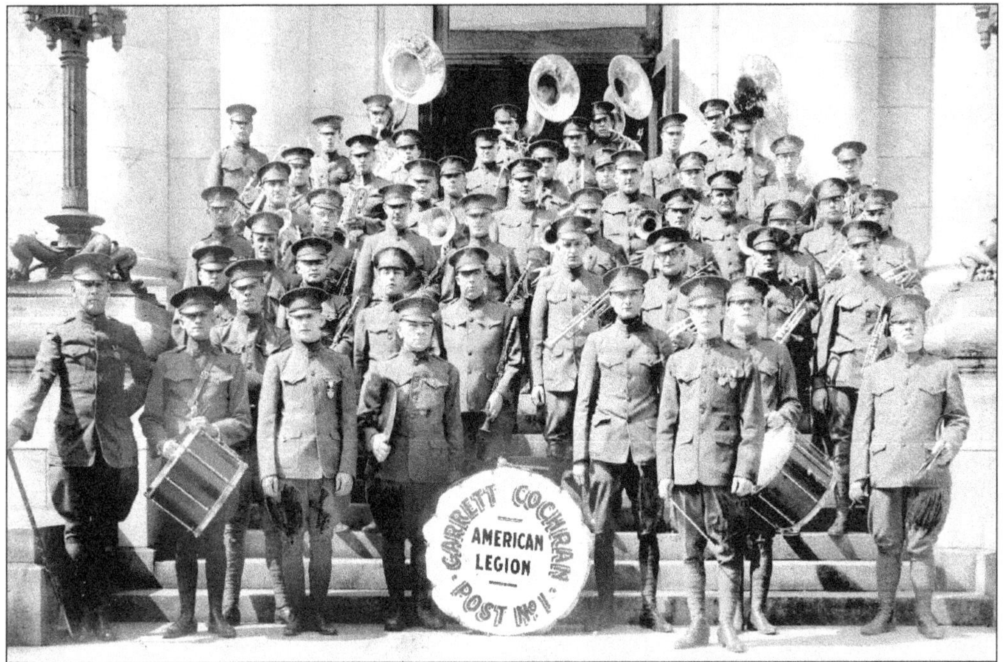

The band of Garrett Cochran Post 1 American Legion pictured here won first prize at the American Legion Band Contest in Williamsport on September 9, 1922. Nine American Legion bands participated in the competition. This band won the right to represent Pennsylvania at the National American Legion in New Orleans, Louisiana.

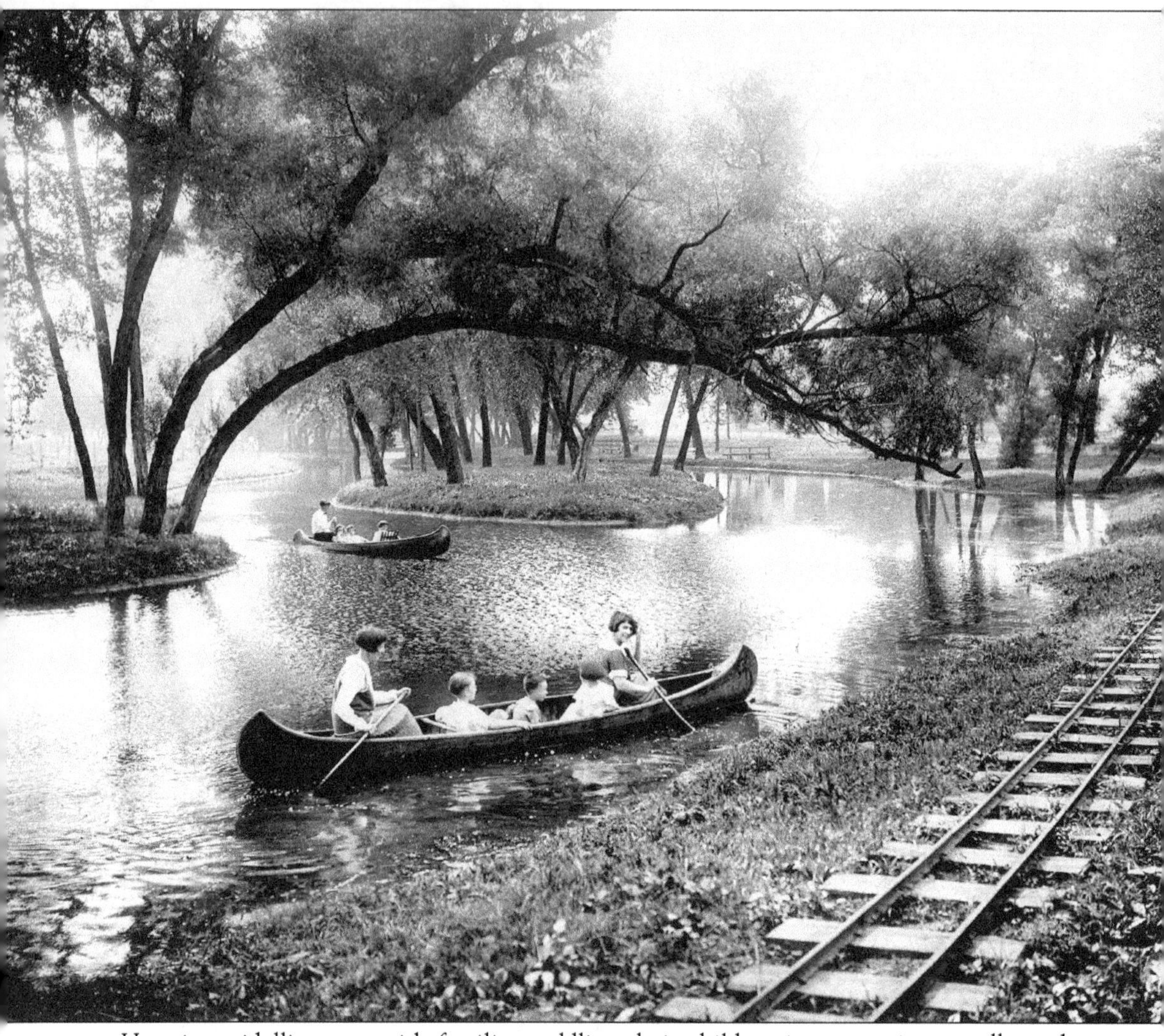

Here is an idyllic scene with families paddling their children in canoes in a small pond at Memorial Park. Also seen in the picture are tracks for a miniature railroad that once served the tourists. Memorial Park was one of the most popular recreational venues for Williamsporters during this time period. Louise L. Chatham, a public-spirited citizen and the city's first woman lawyer, used her professional advantage to render service to her fellow citizens. She became the moving spirit in the civic club, conceived the idea of Memorial Park, and energetically carried out that idea as a further tribute to the boys who went "over there." She also secured the renaming of Erie Avenue to Memorial Avenue.

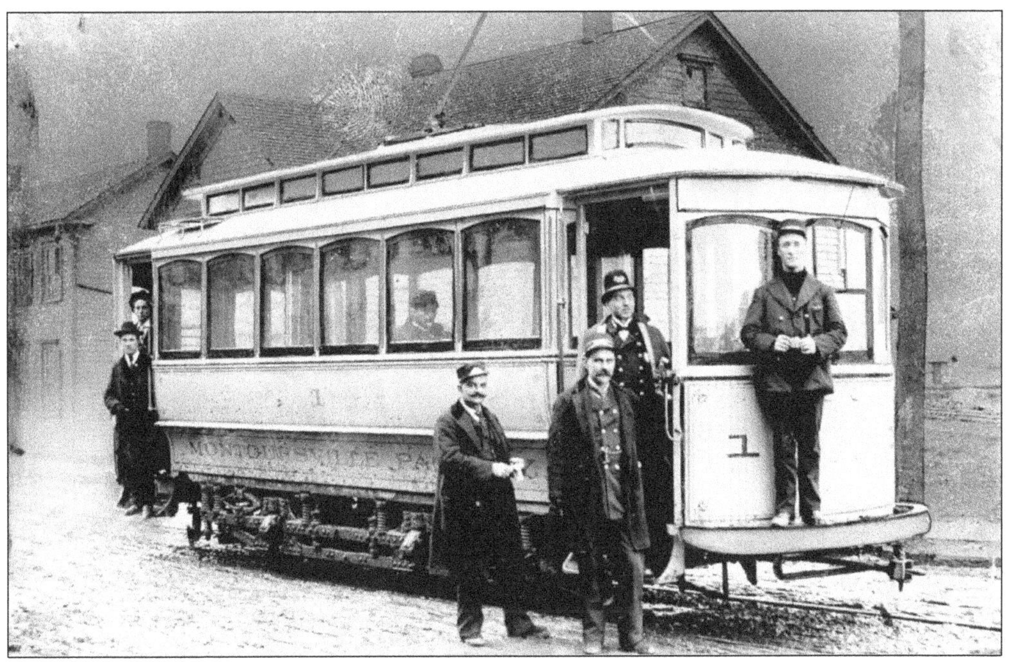

Shown here is one of the streetcars that formerly traveled from Williamsport to Montoursville in the early 1900s. Until the advent of the passenger bus and the automobile, streetcars were a major mode of transportation. The carbarn for many of the streetcars was in the Vallamont area of Williamsport at the corner of Glenwood Avenue and Cherry Street.

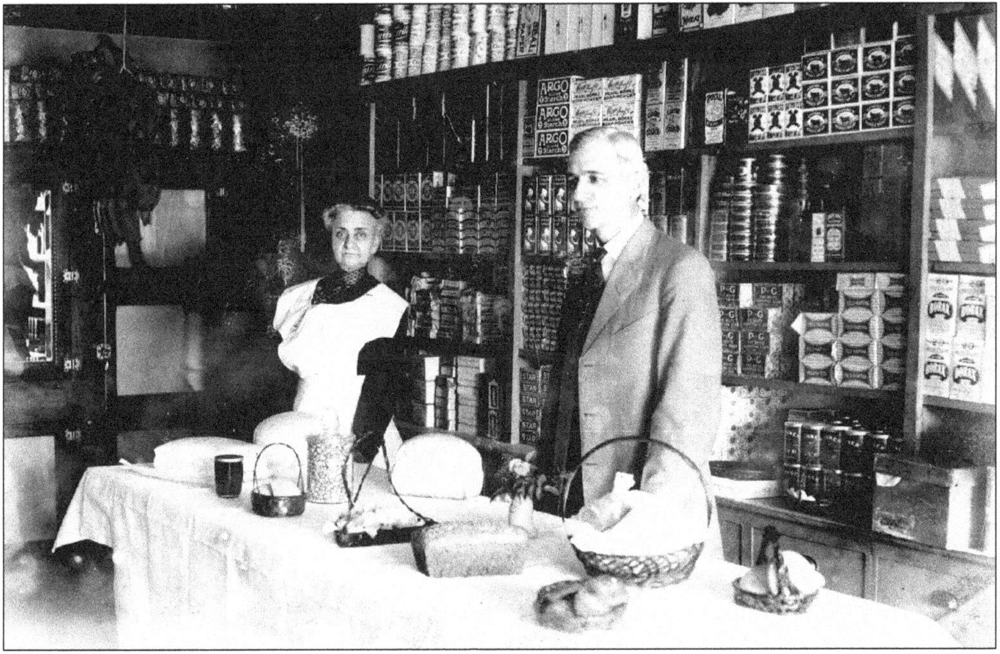

Family businesses, such as this general store, were a major component of small-town America. This couple's shop catered to the community by supplying food, hardware, and clothing. Often, credit was extended to all who needed it and payments were often made in trade (a chicken for a sack of flour, and so on).

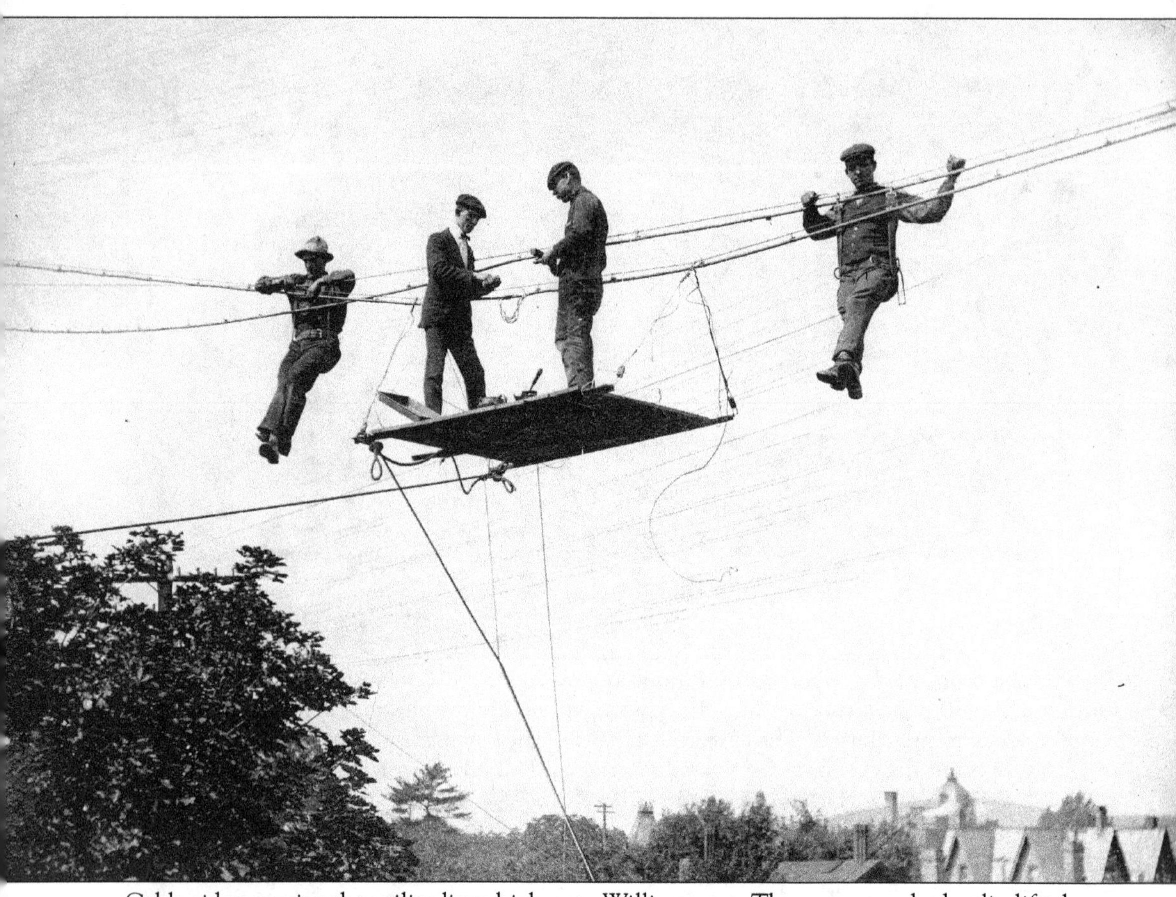

Cable riders service the utility lines high over Williamsport. There were no hydraulic-lift cherry pickers to help these brave men perform their maintenance work. A person working on these lines had to be surefooted and have a steady hand. Williamsport started early in the use of the telephone. Hiram R. Rhoads established the first exchange on May 1, 1879. It was well received because of the many wealthy Williamsport residents who wanted the latest technological gadgets. The new telephone exchange consisted of 385 miles of wire, with 107 residences and 445 businesses involved for a total of 582 telephones in the city. Later, the exchange added 23 phones in Jersey Shore and 20 in Muncy. Rhoads also was founder of the Lycoming Electric Company.

A baby sleeps in comfort in a makeshift hammock (which is actually a padded kettle hanging from a tree) at the tourist court in Memorial Park in August 1928. This allowed the inventive mother a chance to relax while her husband entertained their toddler. Memorial Park, with its creek, zoo, carnival-type rides, and picnic areas, was a popular tourist destination during the early half of the 20th century. Most of the attractions were destroyed in the devastating 1936 flood.

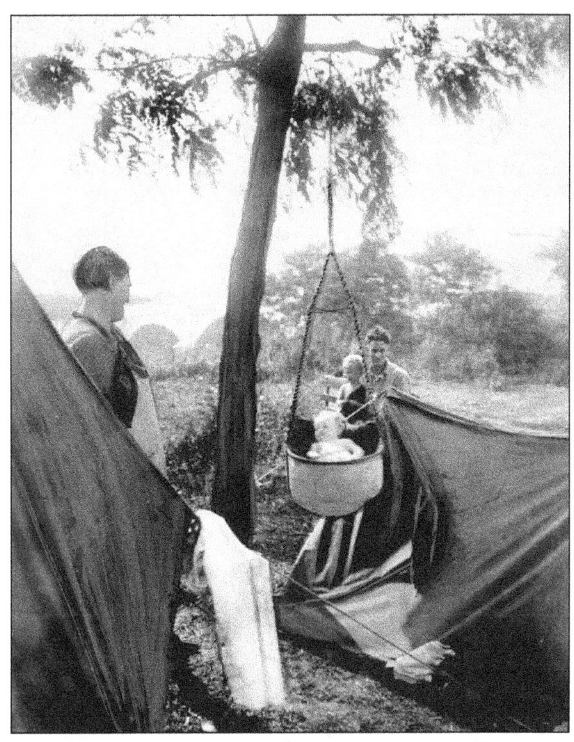

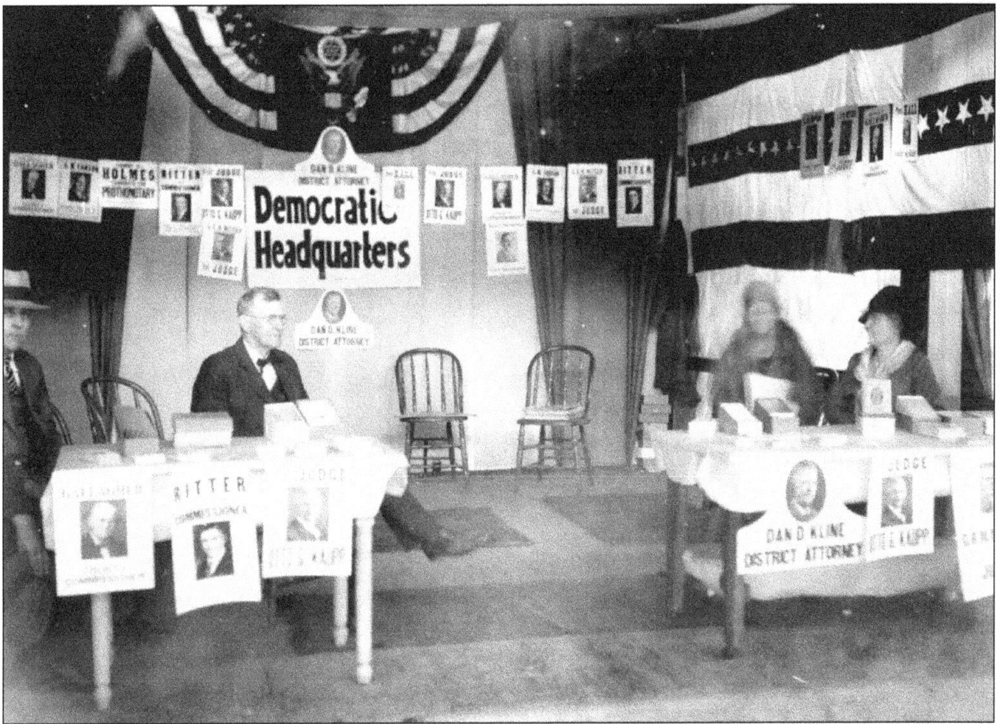

Williamsport party hopefuls staff the Democratic Headquarters booth at the Lycoming County Fairgrounds in Hughesville during the 1920s. One of the candidates, Judge Otto Kaupp, was the delegate to the Democratic National Convention from Pennsylvania in 1912.

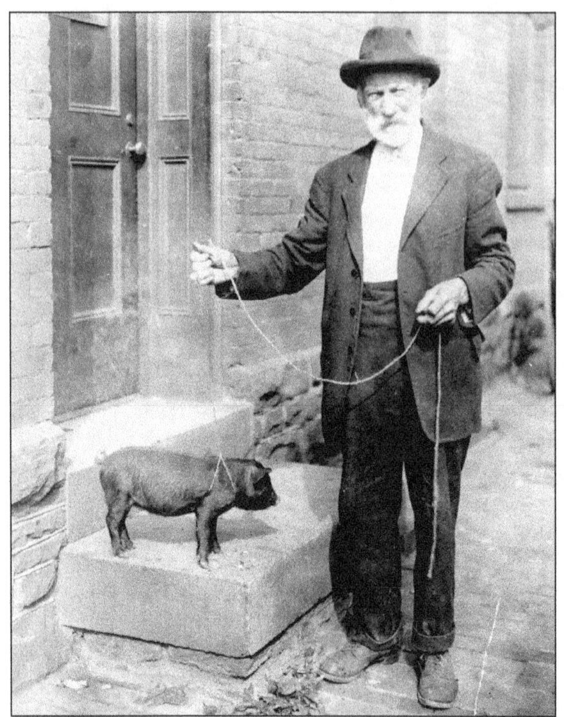

This turn-of-the-century photograph features C. F. Deane and his pig, a curiosity because of its solid hoof. Deane often walked the pig around his neighborhood on a string. Here, he poses outside of the *Grit*'s office as a staff photographer snaps his portrait.

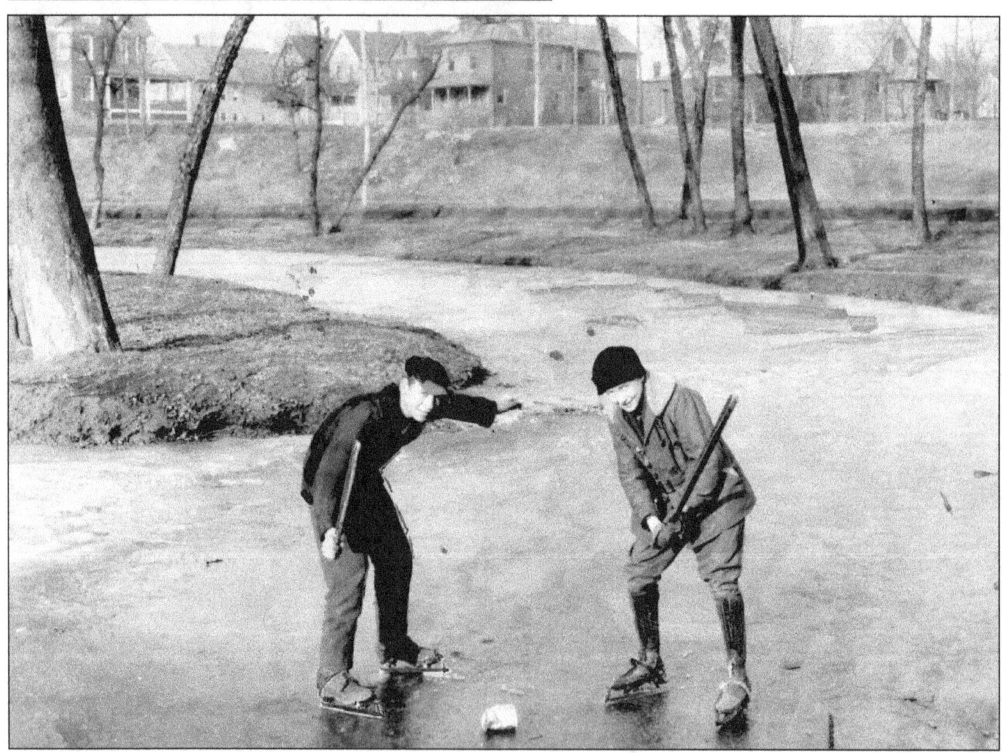

Two unidentified boys are enjoying a pickup game of ice hockey (using a crushed tin can as a puck and tree limbs as hockey sticks) at Memorial Park in January 1924. Memorial Park was not just a summer recreation venue but a winter one as well.

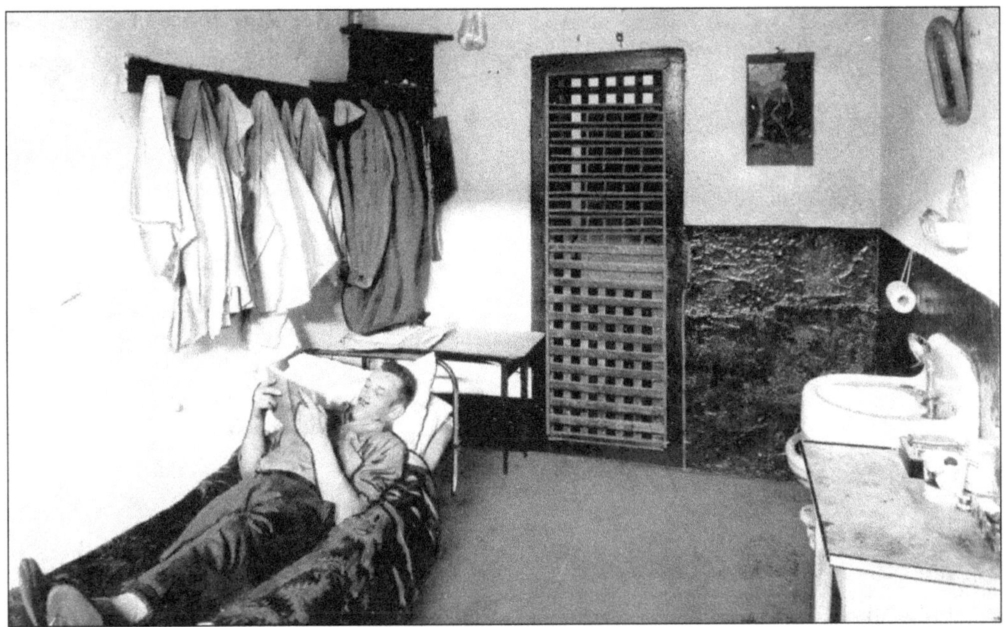

Pictured here is a typical jail cell under normal conditions at the Lycoming County Prison in March 1929. The prison population at this time was 82 inmates, causing doubling and tripling in some of the cells. The jail had just undergone a renovation and remodeling. There were three cots in many of the cells.

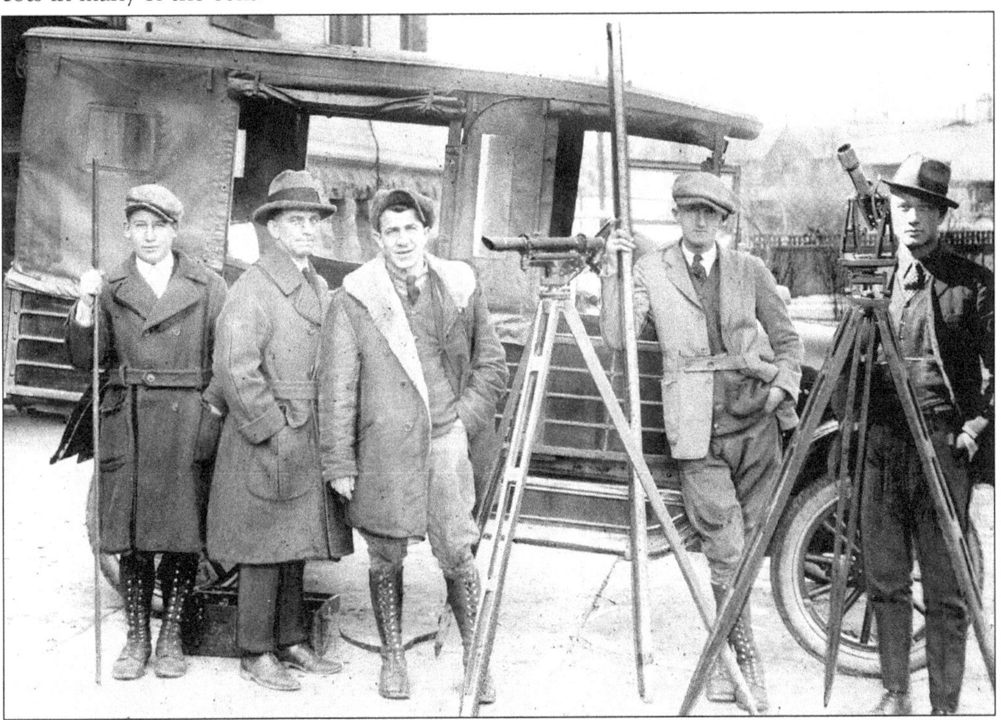

The surveying staff of the Williamsport Bureau of Engineering is pictured in April 1924. From left to right are J. W. Monroe, M. D. Edwards, Carl Sebring, and John G. Good. The city engineer at the time was Lyons Mussina. Good later became Williamsport's police chief.

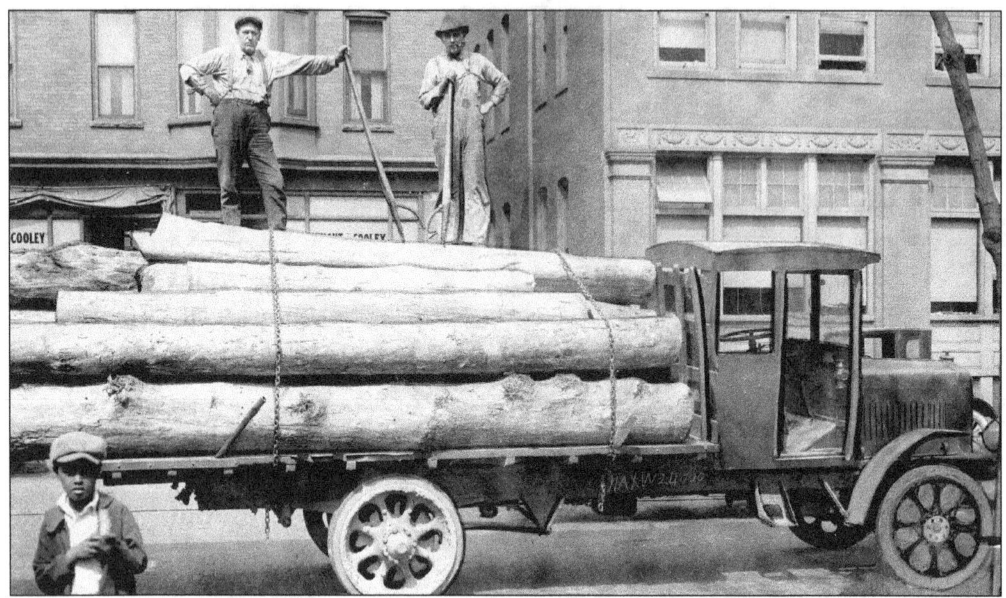

Thick logs are cut at Wolf Run for wood pipe manufacturing in November 1924. Pictured on top of the logs, from left to right, are Danny W. Wright and Collins Yeagle. Wolf Run is below Trout Run in northern Lycoming County. The Standard Wood and Pipe Company used the logs. The 17 logs in this load weighed about seven tons.

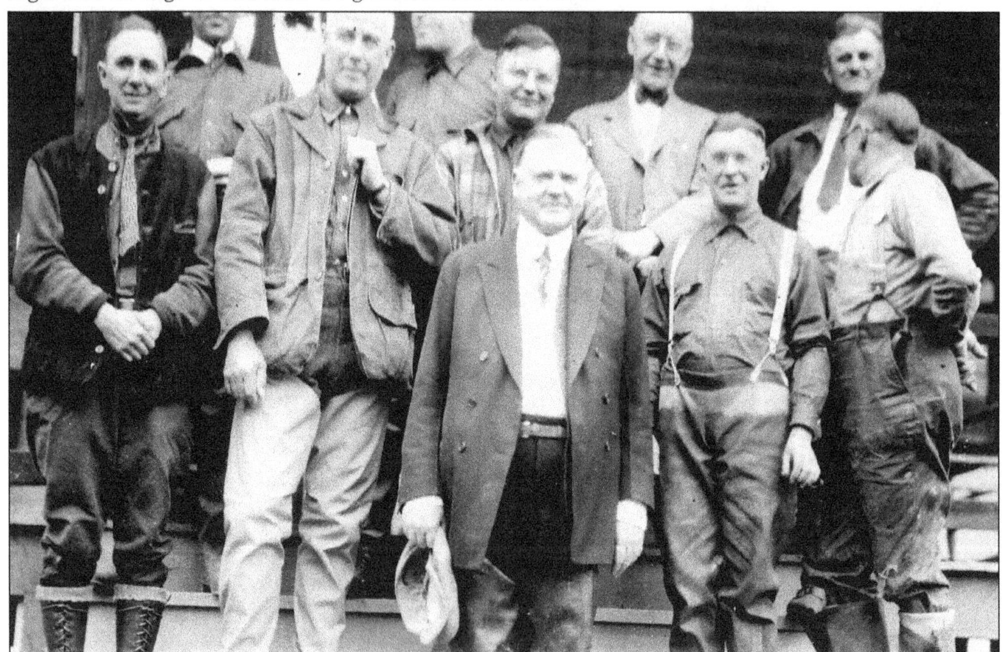

Future president Herbert Hoover, then secretary of commerce, is pictured at the Texas Blockhouse Fish and Game Club on May 16, 1928. He spent May 14 and 15 as the guest of the Ogontz Fish and Game Preserve, near Salladasburg. On the last day of his visit he motored to Texas Blockhouse, where he fished until noon. After dinner, he motored to the Park Hotel and boarded a sleeper to Washington, D.C. In November 1928, he was elected the 31st president of the United States.

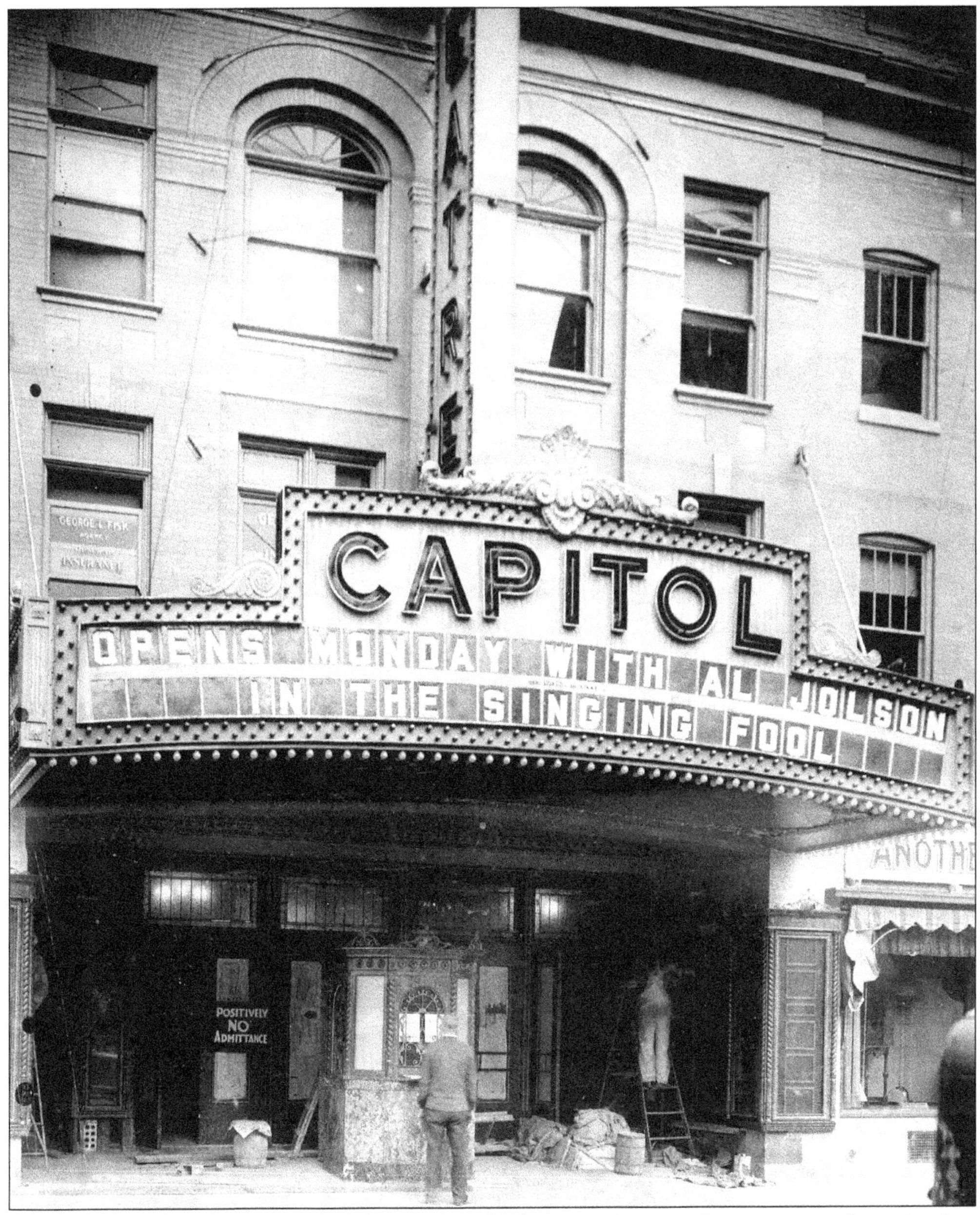

The Capitol, Williamsport's magnificent new playhouse and movie theater, opened on October 22, 1928. The first feature shown was *The Singing Fool*, starring Al Jolson. M. E. Comerford, president of the Comerford chain that owned the theater, attended the opening. In the early 1990s, the theater underwent a multimillion-dollar restoration and is now the Community Arts Center. Painstakingly restored to its original 1928 grandeur, the arts center has entertained more than 650,000 patrons since 1993 with such sell-out attractions as Bill Cosby, Barry Manilow, Anne Murray, Chicago, B. B. King, *Cats*, *Grease*, Tori Amos, Foreigner, Willie Nelson, David Copperfield, Michael Bolton, Kenny Rogers, and many more.

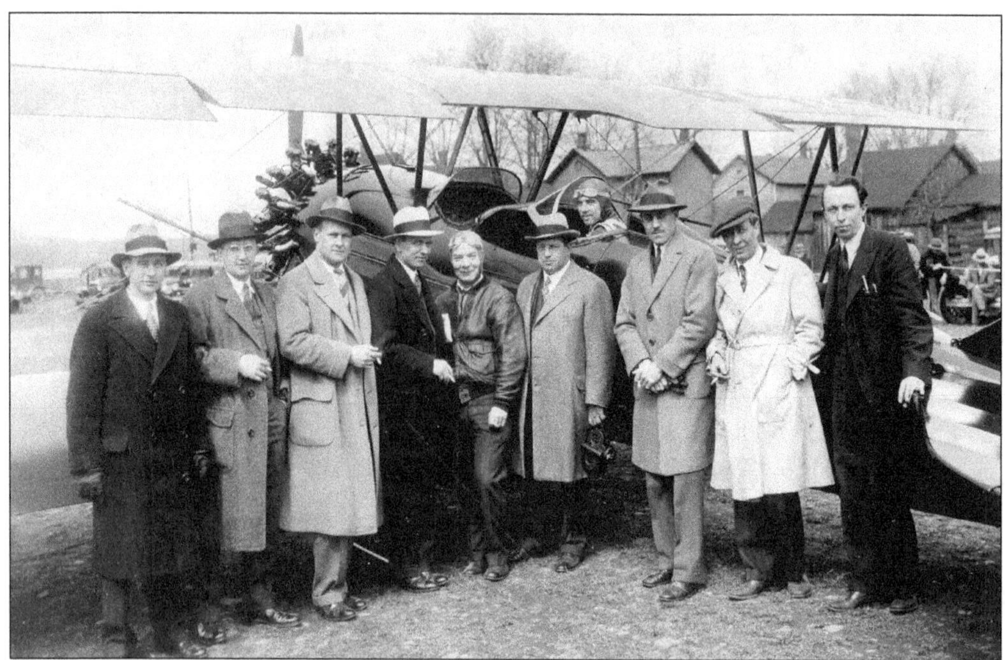

Officials of Lycoming Motors Company are shown at the first flight of a Lycoming Aero engine in April 1929. Pictured from left to right are F. M. Kender, L. B. Manning, E. L. Cord, "Doc" Kincade, J. H. McCormick, John G. Kelly (pilot), E. M. Herrick, Val Cronstadt, and L. Dickinson.

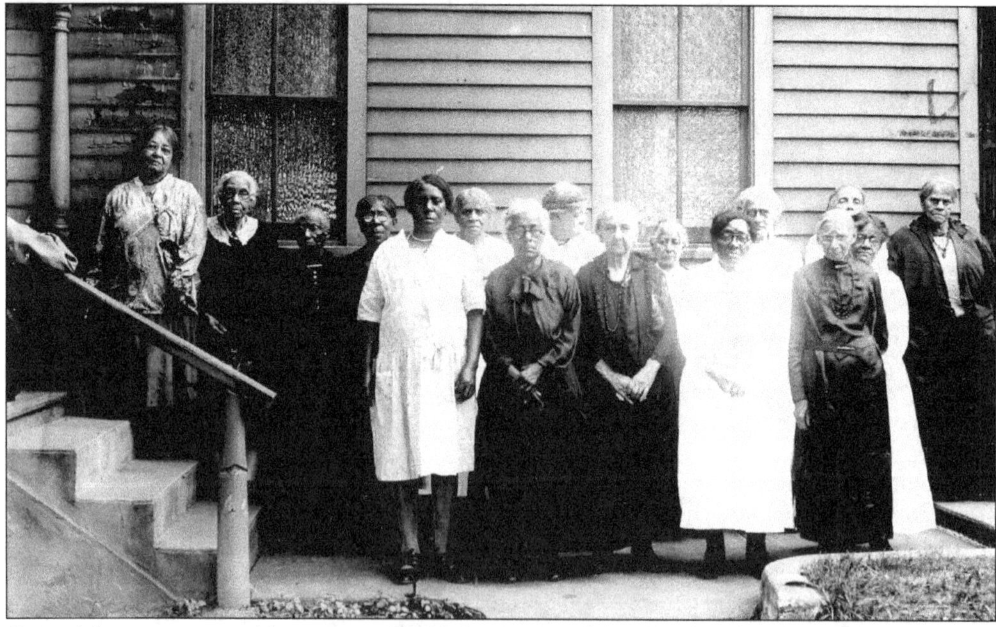

One of the most enjoyable events of 1929 for guests of the Aged Colored Women's Home at 124 Brandon Avenue, Williamsport, was the annual picnic in August. Many friends called during the afternoon, and a dinner was given in the evening. Established by ex-slave Mary Slaughter in 1889, the home was a place for indigent, elderly African American women to live out their last years in a dignified, caring setting.

Caretaker and manager Ralph McCullin of the Memorial Park Zoo transfers a groundhog to a heated building in November 1929. Home to many exotic animals, from monkeys to panthers, the zoo was a popular tourist attraction. The amusement park also had a 1924 Philadelphia Toboggan Company, Herb Schmeck Comet Coaster. Most of the park's attractions were destroyed in a 1936 flood.

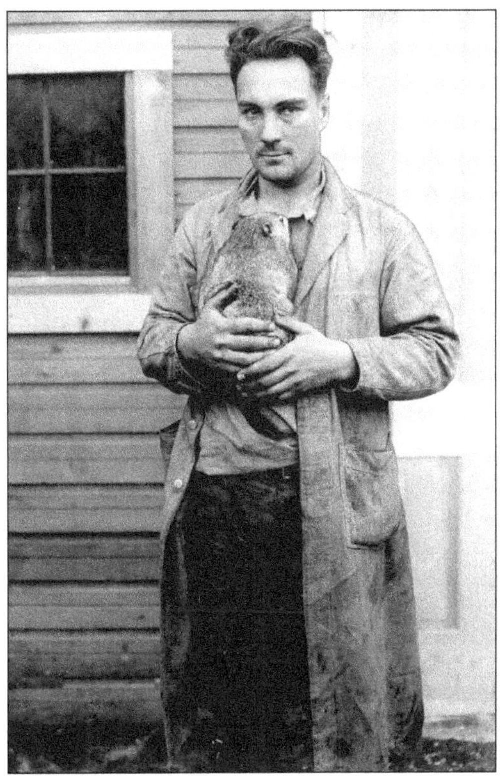

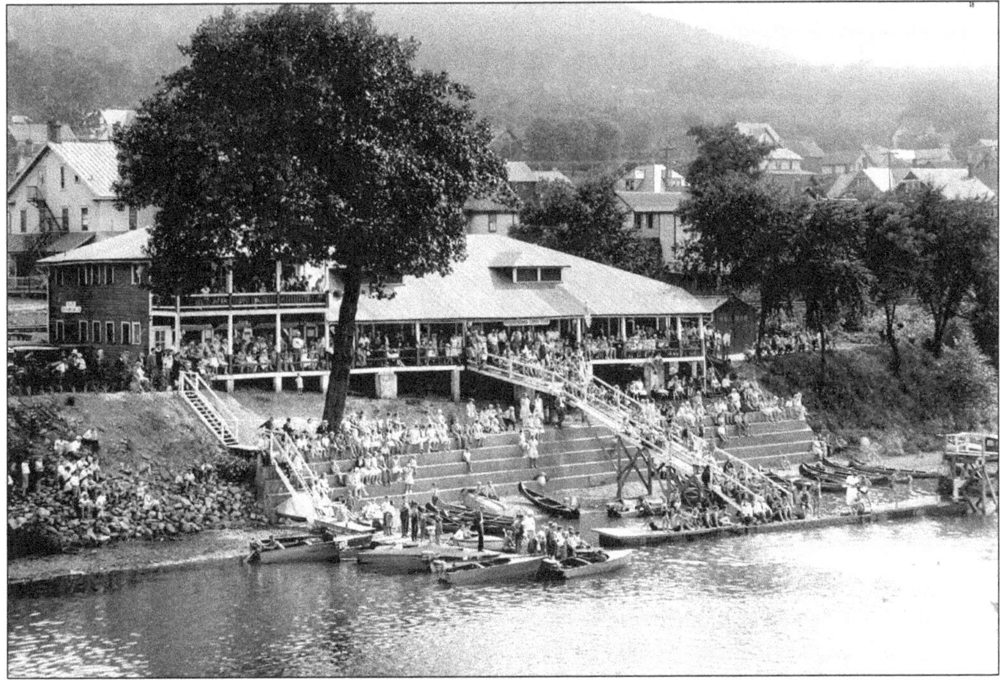

People gather for an event at the Susquehanna Canoe Club, near the Maynard Street Bridge, in August 1930. A trendy and popular club, the building featured steps to the river and canoes and boats for rent. Many dances and dinners at the club brightened the south-side neighborhood.

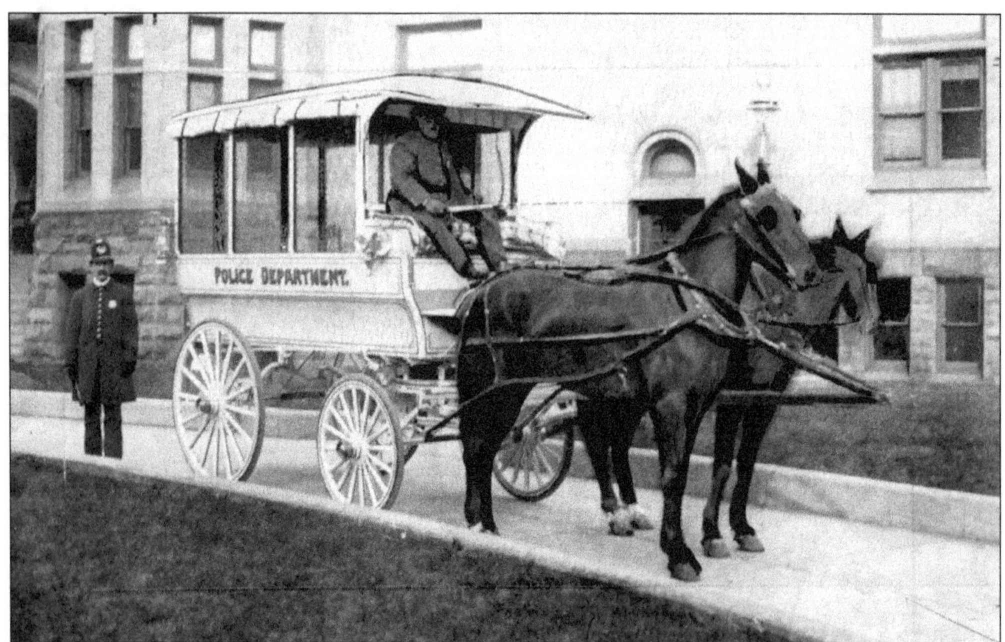

Inebriates now ride to city hall in comfort; it was not so years ago. Overly intoxicated persons of years ago rode in this conveyance, which was known as a Black Maria. It is seen here parked in front of city hall sometime during the first decade of the 20th century.

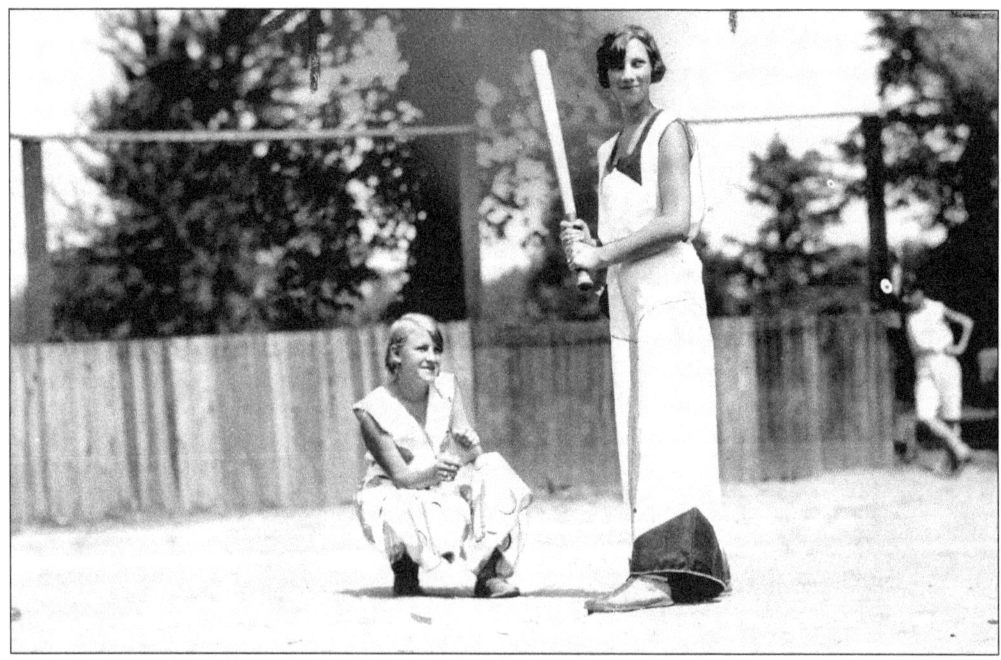

"Batter up," is the call for this girl as she takes her swings during a baseball game at one of the city's playgrounds in the summer of 1931. In the style of a flapper, these young girls have cut their long, lush hair for the more popular bob.

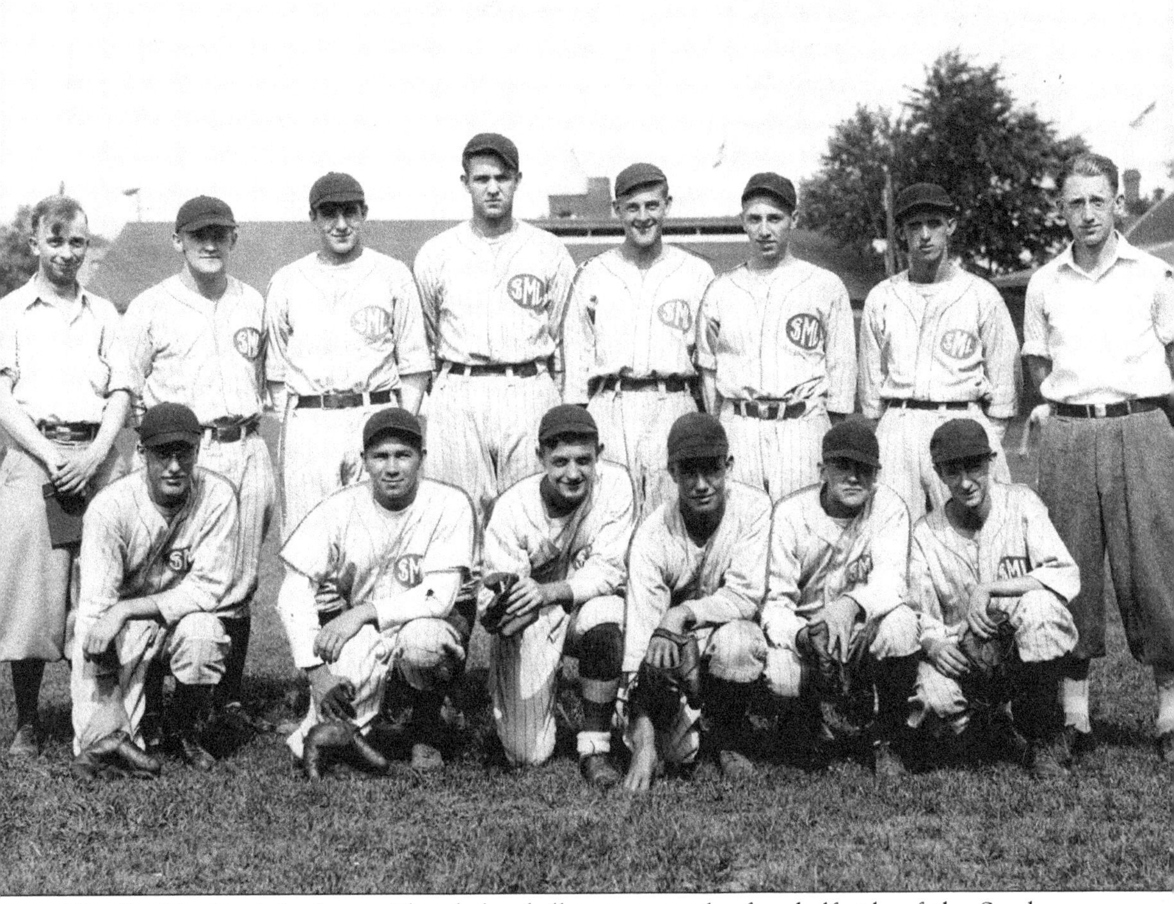

The St. Matthew's Lutheran Church baseball team won the first half title of the Sunday School Baseball League, defeating DuBoistown 3-1 on July 18, 1931. From left to right are the following: (first row) G. Updegraff, C. Nuss, Robbins, J. Updegraff, E. Patt, and M. Kurtz; (second row) Beach, Sassaman, Chrisop, Wascher, Billig, Fry, Hill, and I. Sassaman. Sunday school leagues were part of the impetus for the creation of Little League Baseball by Carl E. Stotz. A former baseball player, he sympathized with his young nephews, too small to play ball with the bigger boys. Stotz dreamed of a baseball program that he could scale down to their size. He enlisted George and Bert Bebble, Williamsport brothers involved in their own Sunday school leagues, to help him manage the first three teams. Little League Baseball became the largest youth sports program in the world.

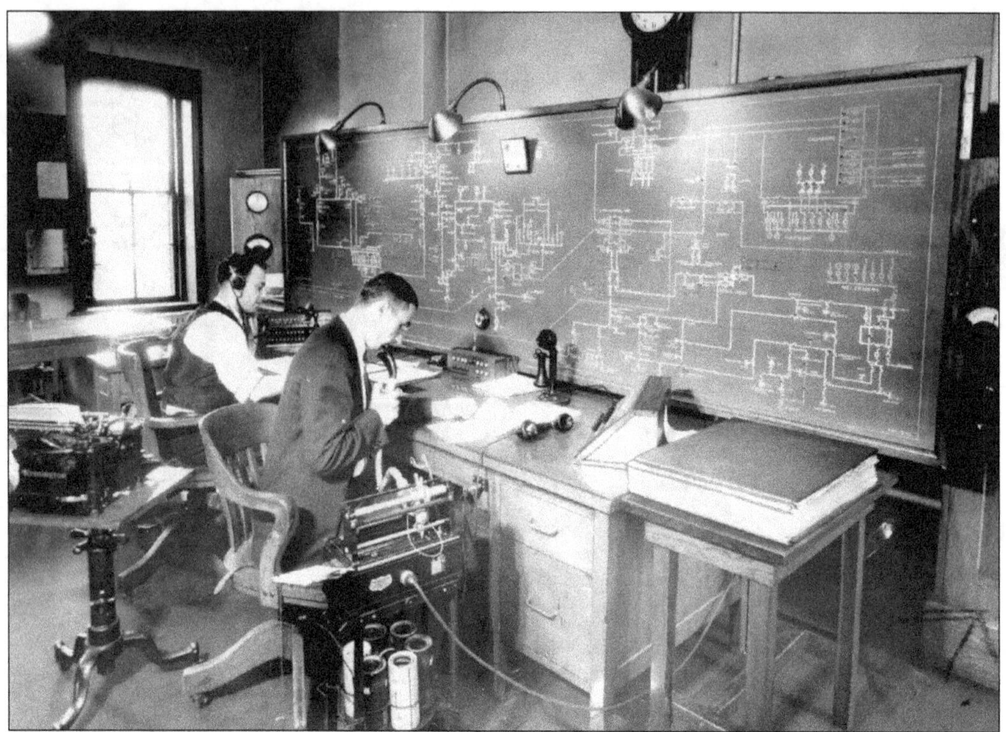

A control board pictured here in October 1931 monitors weather reports at the Williamsport office of the Pennsylvania Power and Light Company. Electric officials monitored weather to help make sure service was not interrupted for their customers. Weather changes such as sleet, hail, and violent and heavy storms all could interrupt electrical service.

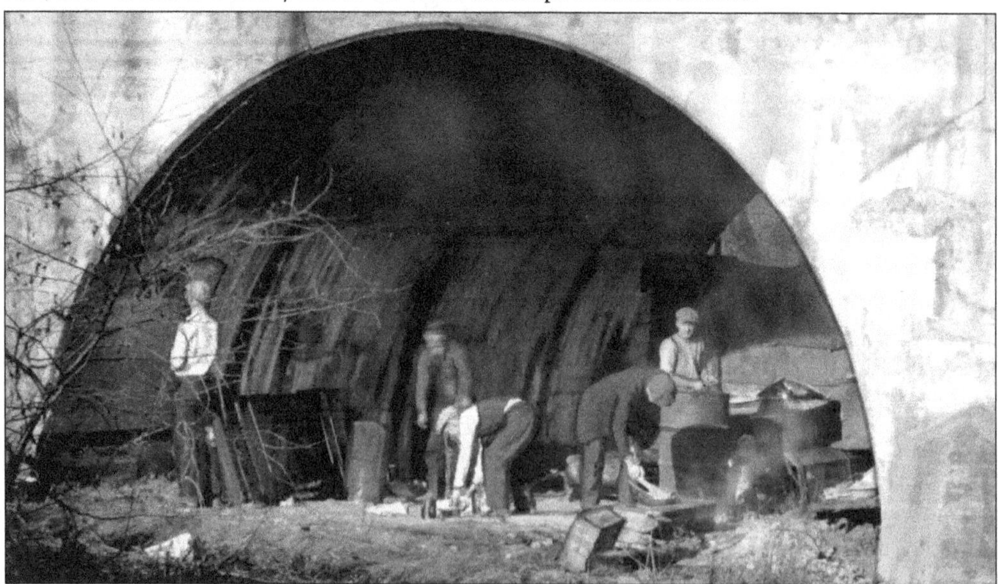

Unemployed men make a no-frills home for themselves underneath a culvert near DuBoistown in December 1931. The unemployed men's camp held about a dozen men and boys. At the height of the Great Depression, more than 250,000 teenagers were living on the road in America, many crisscrossing the country by illegally hopping freight trains.

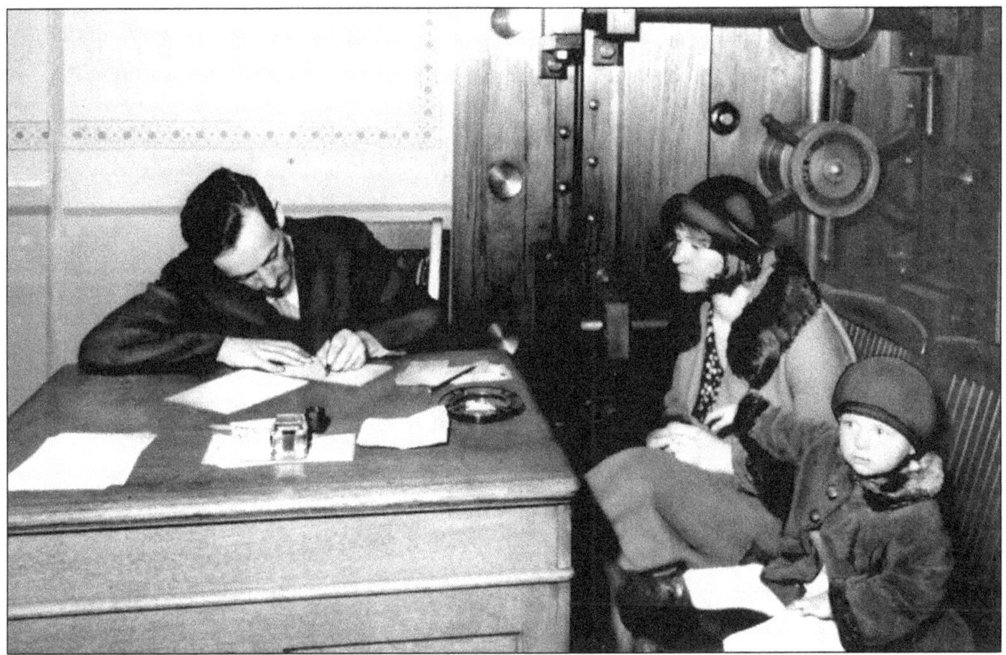

A woman and her small child make application for relief to the Williamsport Relief Committee in December 1931, during the darkest depths of the Great Depression. The family structure for poor Americans did not improve during the 1930s. The father's role as provider and head of household became more challenging because there were fewer jobs. The general expectation was for fathers to work and support their families. When they could not, relief was available from the government.

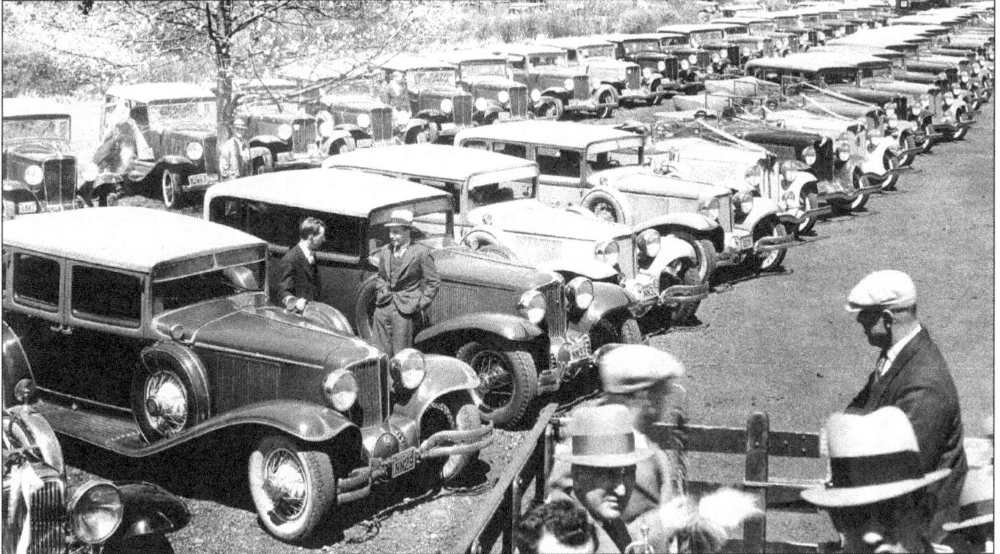

Eighty automobiles, all powered by engines produced at the Lycoming Manufacturing Company plant, made up a "boost business caravan" that moved on the principal streets of the city and South Williamsport in May 1932. While the cars, including many Auburns owned by department heads and foremen of the company, were on parade, two Lycoming-powered airplanes flew overhead.

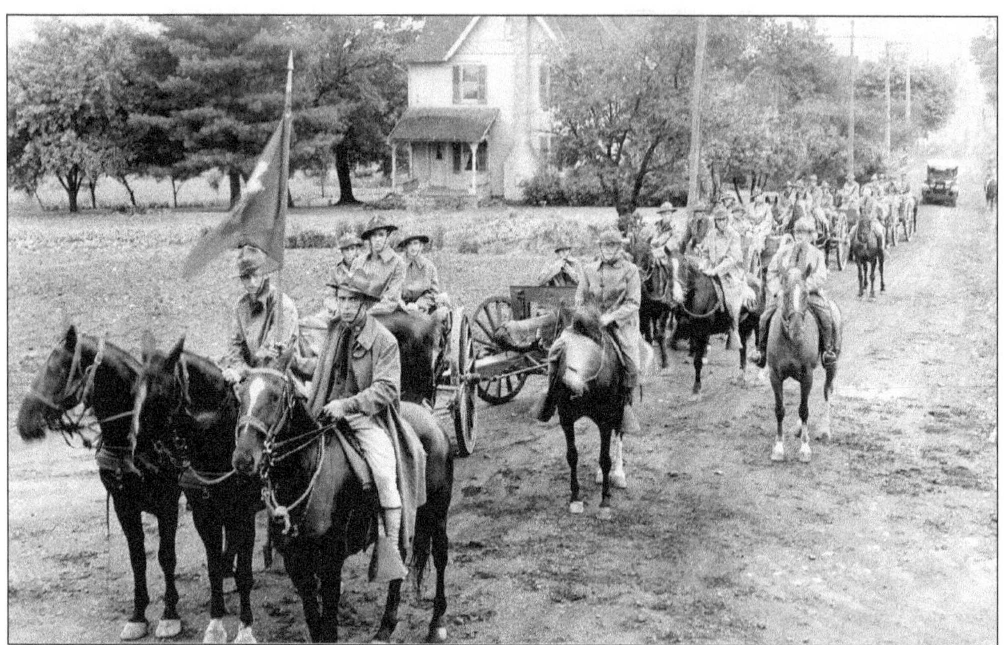

Members of Battery D, a Williamsport unit of the Pennsylvania National Guard, travel to their encampment at the Heim farm along Mill Creek, three miles east of Montoursville, on the first of their overnight marches during 1932.

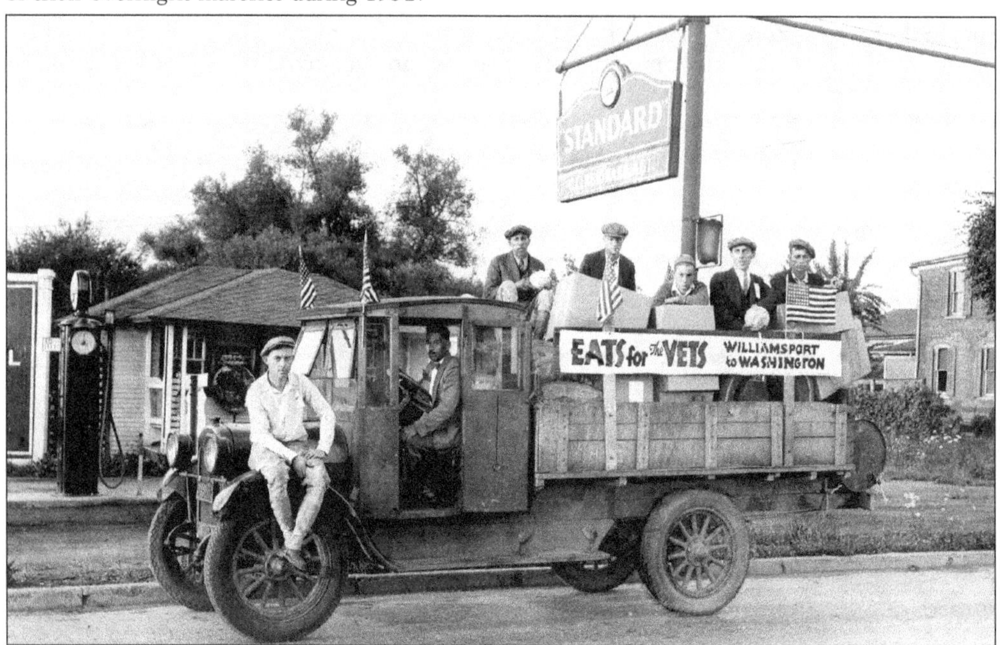

At the end of World War I, the U.S. government passed legislation that authorized the payment of cash bonuses to war veterans, adjusted for length of service, in 1945. However, the crash of 1929 wiped out many veterans' savings and jobs, forcing them into the streets. Groups of veterans began to organize and petition the government to pay them their cash bonus immediately. Two tons of food and clothing were collected in Williamsport for local veterans going to the 1932 Bonus March.

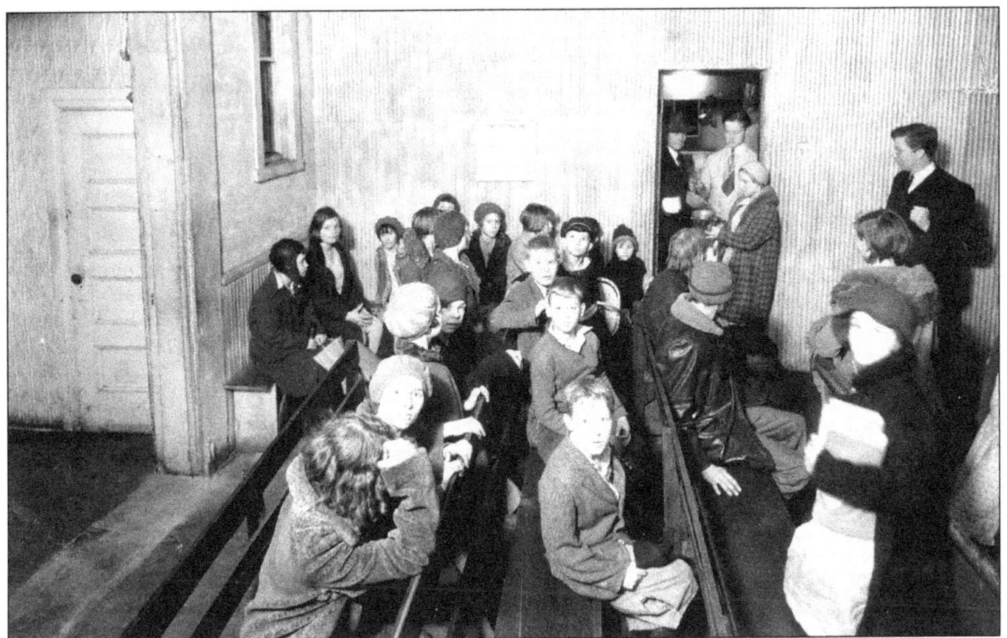

Bread lines formed early every evening at the City Mission on Pine Street. Shown here are children waiting for food in December 1932. The mission dispensed 100 gallons of soup per week. Women and children came each day for a loaf of bread and a bucket of soup that they carried home for other members of their families.

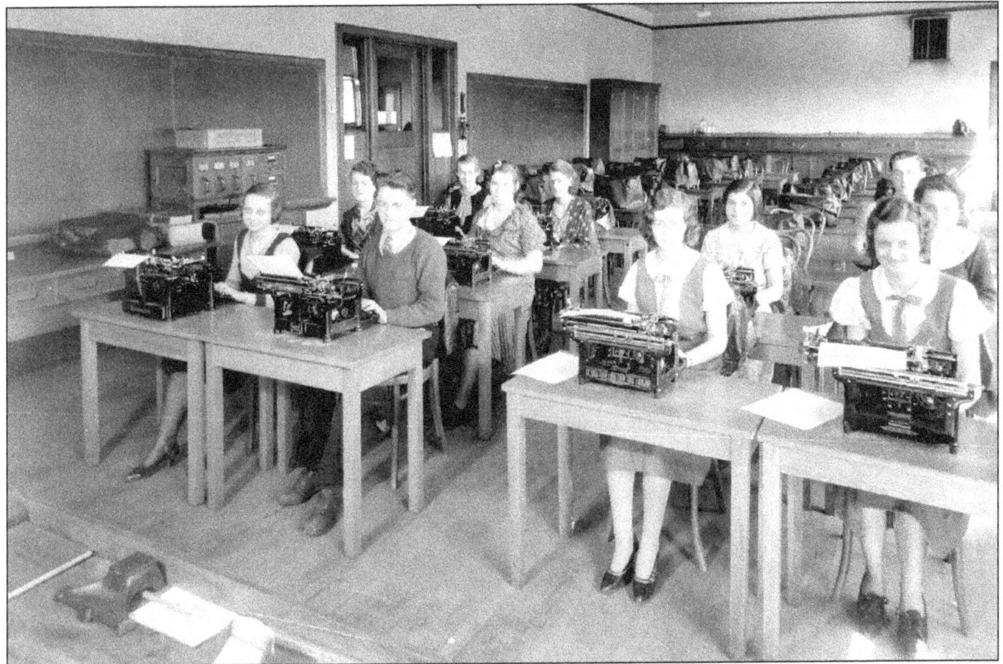

Pupils in commercial education class at the Williamsport High School work to increase the speed of their typewriting. Typewriting experts and effective stenographers were in the making in this class in March 1933. Ezra D. Heyler, instructor of typewriting and office practice, taught the classes.

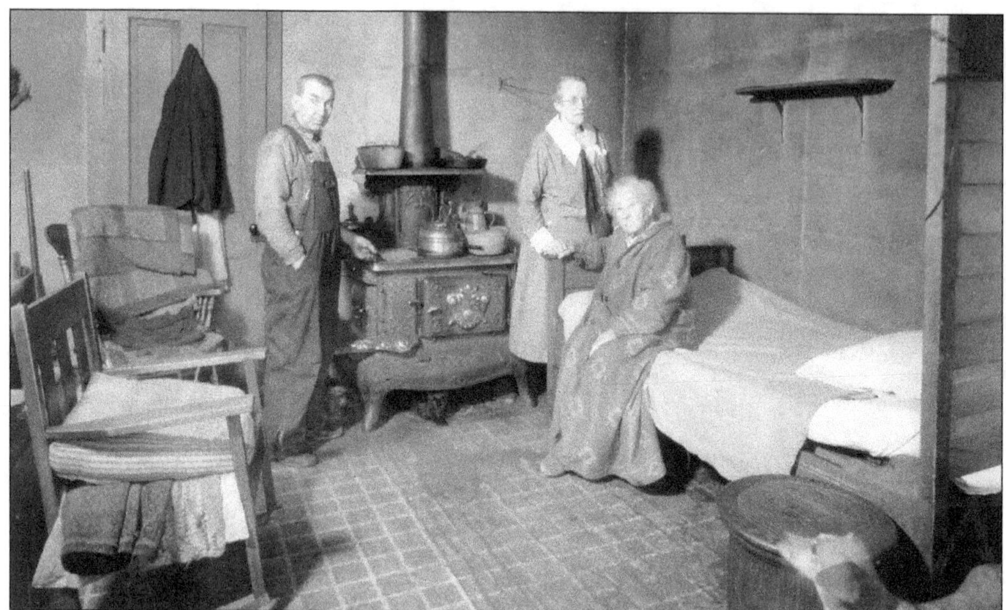

Red Cross nurse Abbie Kent makes a home visit to 92-year-old Mary Meyer, one of the many services the Williamsport Chapter of the American Red Cross offered in October 1937. Like many lower-income Williamsport residents, Meyer lived in a one-room apartment warmed by a wood stove. Note the presence of a dog by the latrine at bottom right of the photograph and the cat warming itself under the stove.

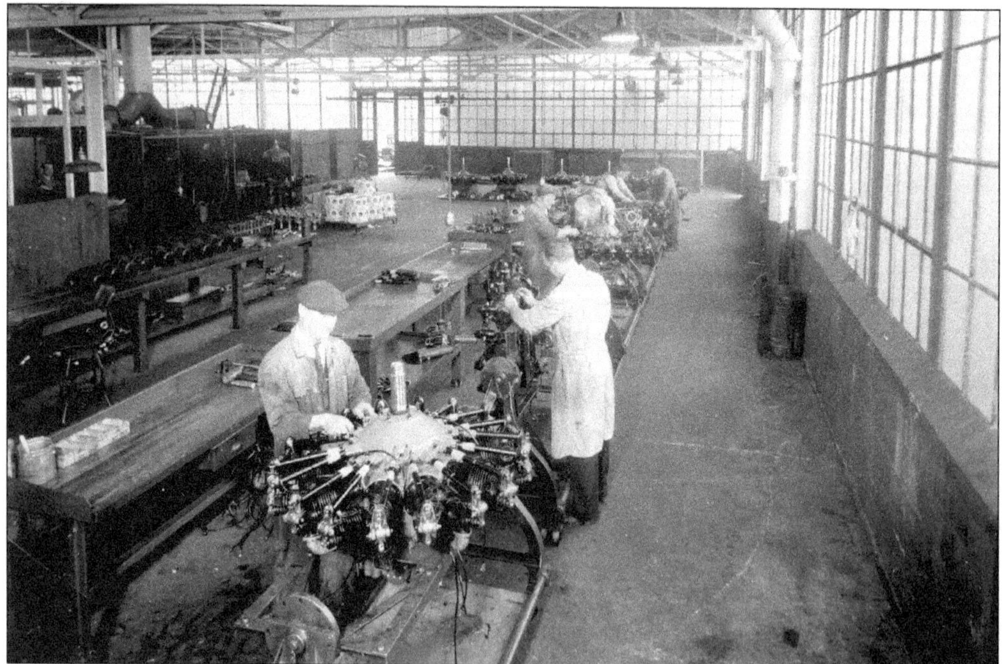

Laborers work on aircraft engines at Lycoming Motors, the forerunner to Textron, in the spring of 1933. The engines later serviced airplanes in World War II. Also in 1933, Lycoming, a division of Cord Corporation, released a sample FA V-8 engine. One sample was built, probably along the lines of Lycoming's earlier model BB V-12, and used by Auburn.

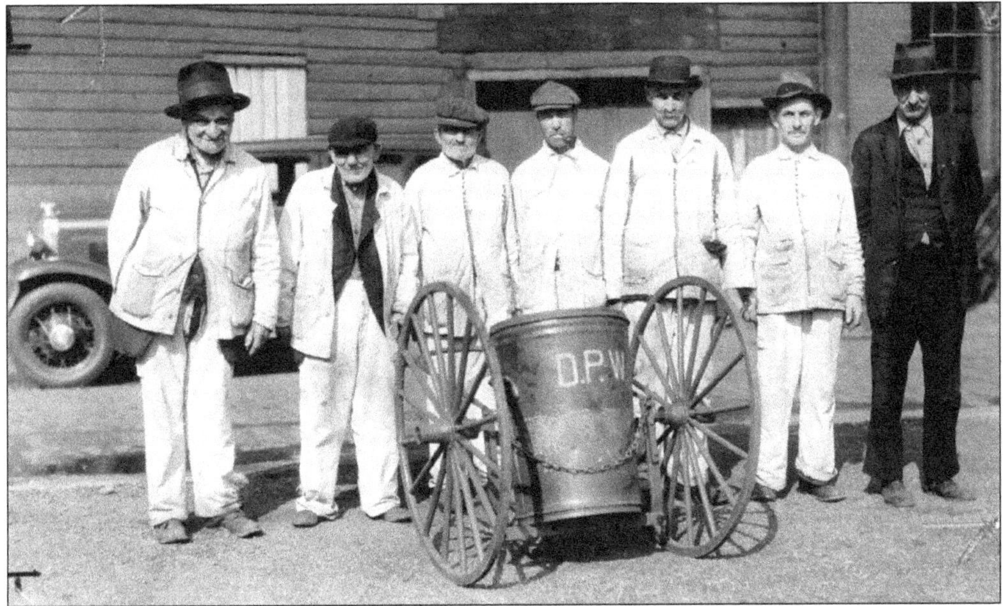

Williamsport's street sweepers were known as the whitewings because they wore white uniforms. Members of the 1933 sweeping crew, from left to right, are Fred Kackenmeister, Jacob Huff, Jim Perrto, Tony Esposito, Jim Bowman, David Bartlett, and John Rehm. Rehm was the foreman of the crew. The day's accumulation of refuse was put in pushcarts like this one.

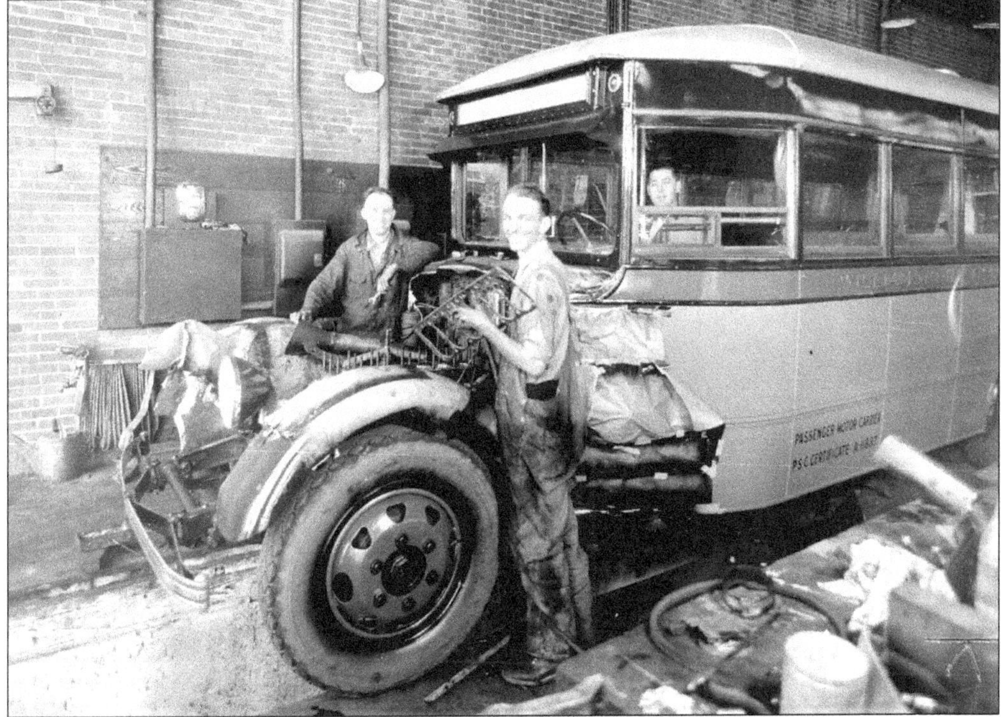

With the heyday of the streetcar and trolley over, buses are readied for replacement. Williamsport Transportation Company mechanics prepared 15 buses to be placed into service on June 11, 1933. Mechanics are seen working at the company's garages in this May 1933 photograph.

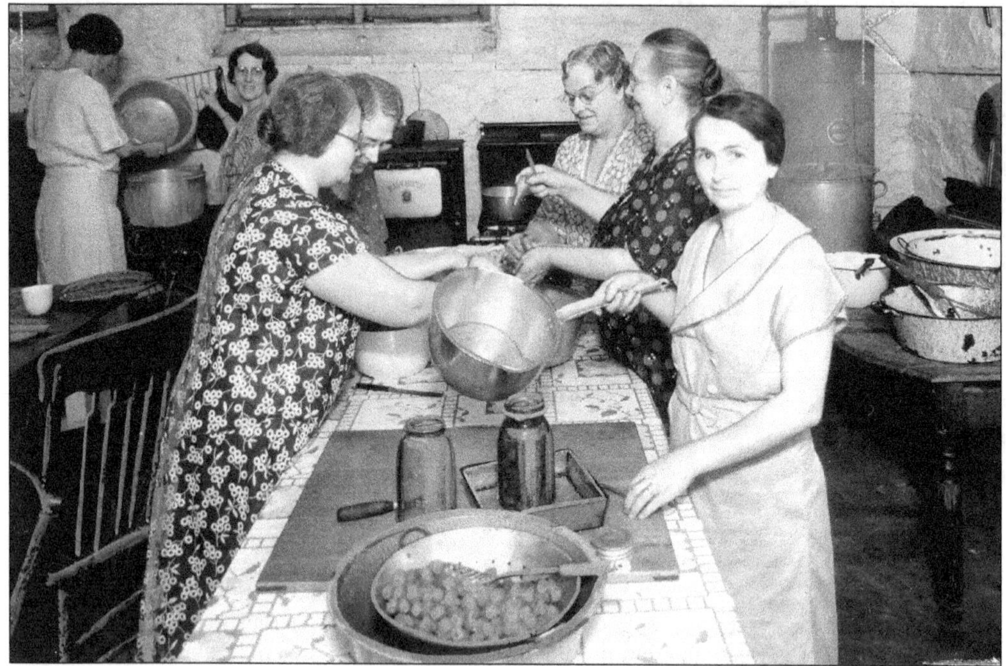

Between Victory Gardens and government surplus, it was important during the Great Depression that food not be wasted. Here, on July 16, 1933, members of an emergency relief organization demonstrate canning berries to city women. Victory Gardens supplied 40 percent of the vegetables consumed on the home front.

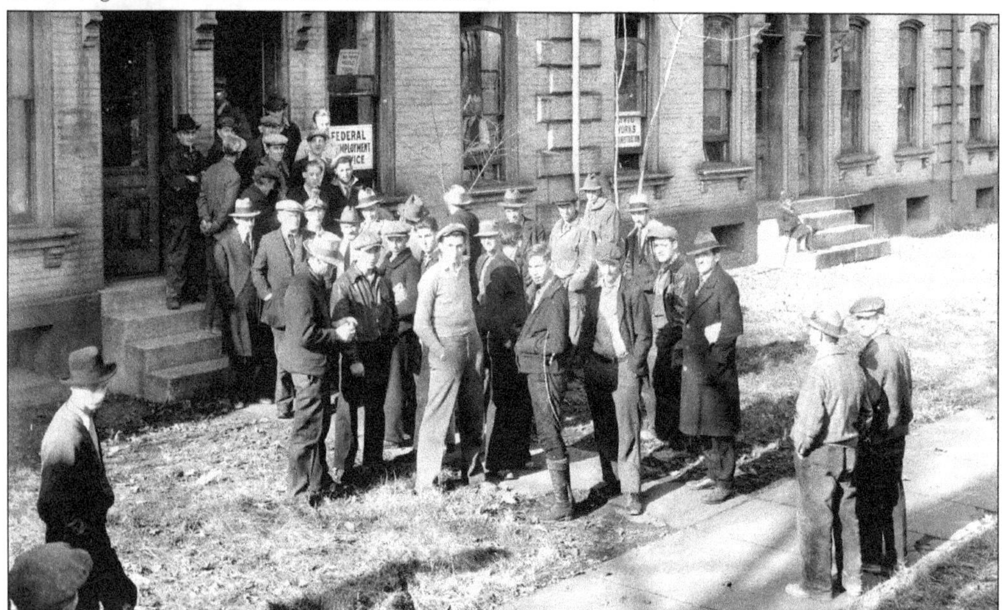

Men wait in line to receive pay for work done in November 1933 for the Works Progress Administration, a New Deal work program to put the unemployed back to work. With the inauguration of Franklin Delano Roosevelt on March 4, 1933, the federal government's response to the economic emergency was swift. The legislation, which came to be collectively called the New Deal, was designed to halt suffering and put the country on the road to recovery.

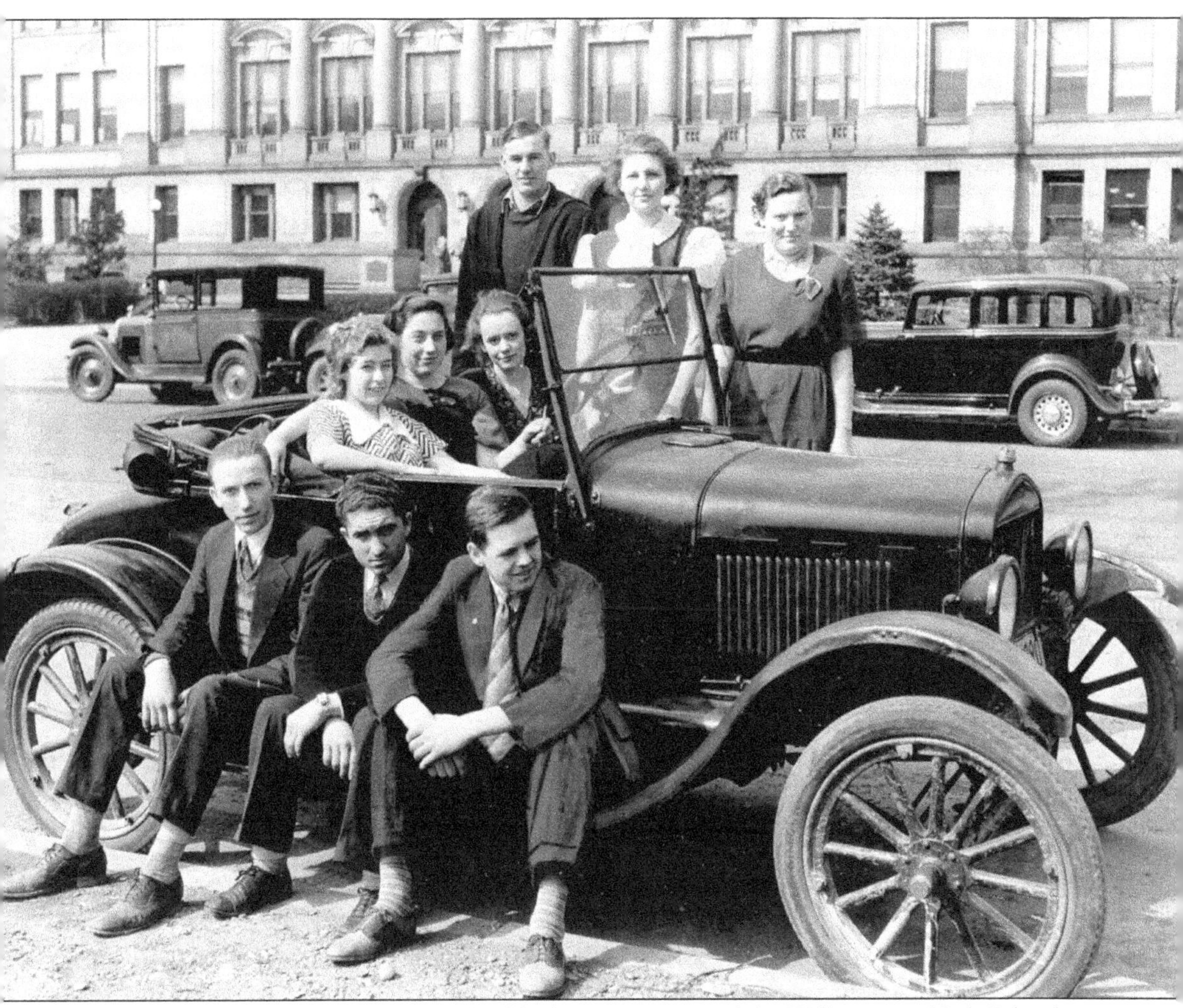

Young men and women traveled considerable distances to attend the Williamsport High School and often carpooled. In this March 25, 1934, portrait, are, from left to right, the following: (first row) Reno Clark, Harry DePolis, and Charles Null; (second row) Marie Dieffenderfer, Marguerite Bonnell, and Mable Hopkins; (third row) Clyde Brass, Helen Stroble, and Anna Henninger. Samuel Transeau was a leader in establishing Williamsport's high school. Born on October 1, 1836, in Northampton County, Transeau was encouraged by his parents, William and Elizabeth Schnabel, to take an interest in education. His family moved to Lycoming County so their son could continue his studies at a more advanced school. Transeau himself moved to Williamsport in 1869 and taught at the Franklin School. Soon he was entrusted with organizing a high school, which he began with an enrollment of 13 students. By the end of its second year, it had 75 students. He became the superintendent of city schools in 1875 and oversaw the reorganization of the city school system, as well as the construction of several schools.

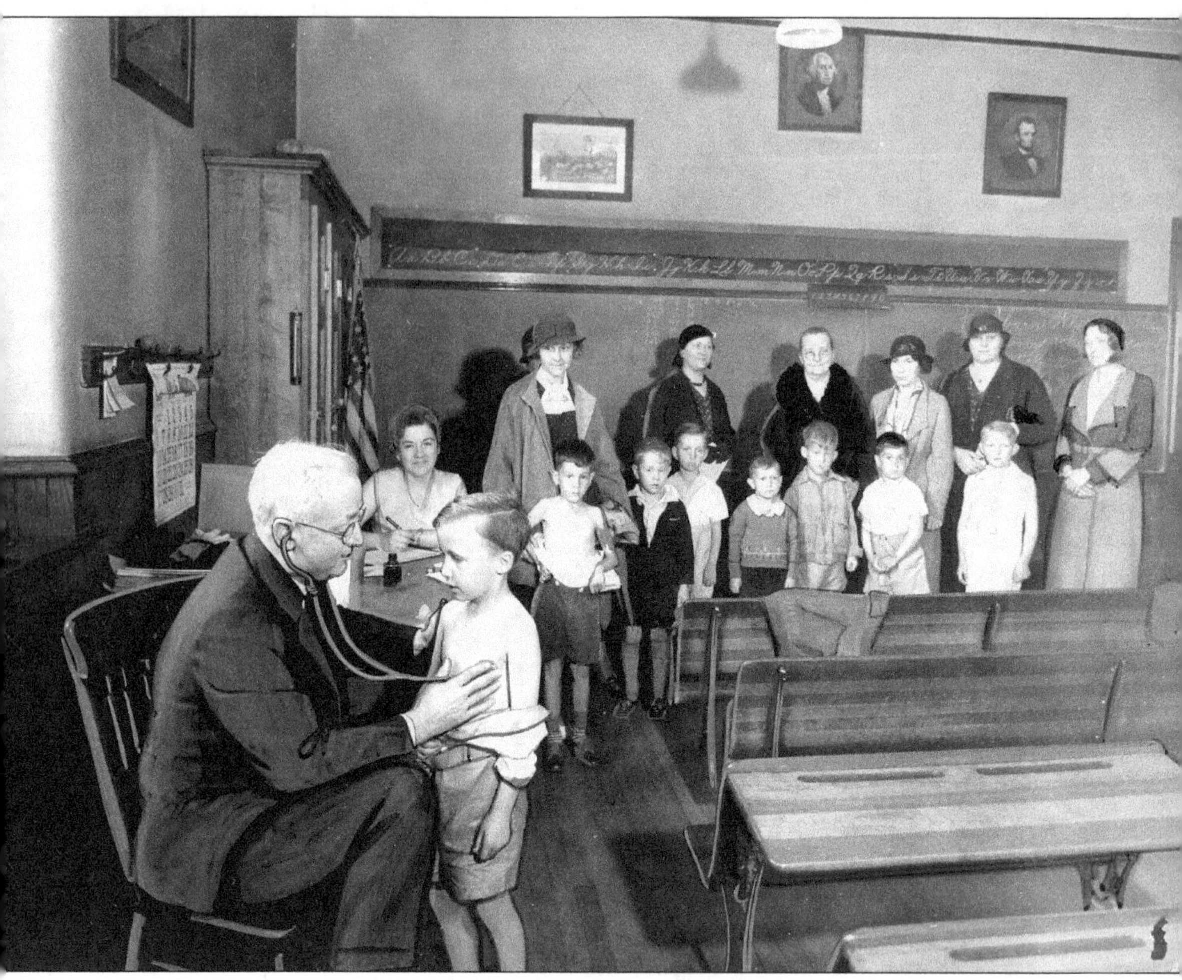

Preschool children receive a checkup from the neighborhood physician in May 1934. With diseases such as tuberculosis and polio on the rise, free clinics were established to ensure health and safety.

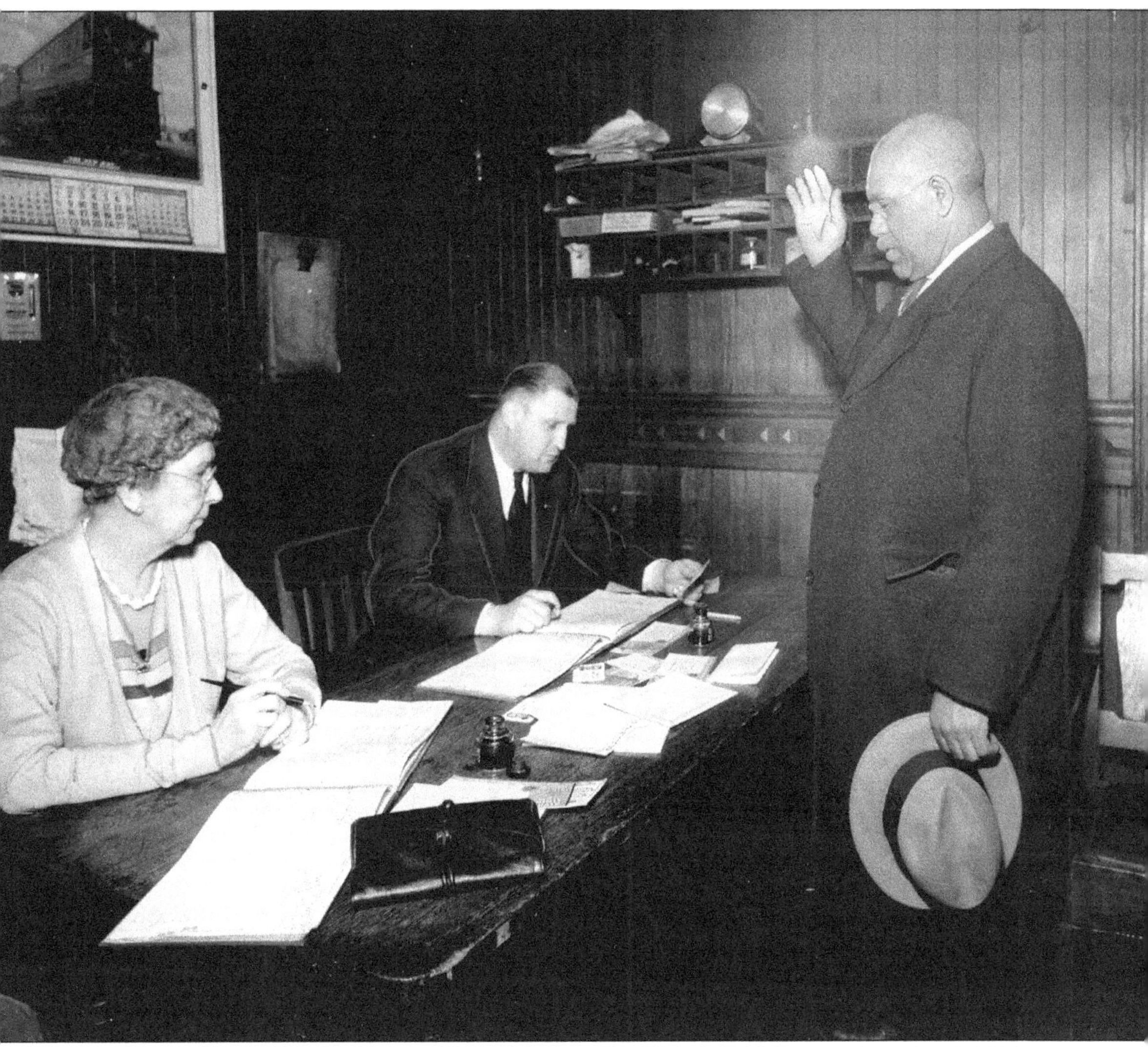

A Williamsport resident registers to vote during a special registration period in April 1934. The total new registrations in Lycoming County at the end of the special registration period were 11,993. Conversely, terror swept the South during an election in 1934 where some black Democratic voters were killed and many were injured. In 1934, President Roosevelt named Dr. William J. Thompkins, a well-known Kansas City physician and politician and the son of a former slave, as recorder of deeds for the District of Columbia, a reward for helping swing black voters in the 1932 Democratic campaign. Roosevelt's black cabinet consisted of William Hastie, Robert Weaver, B. T. McGraw, and Mary Bethume.

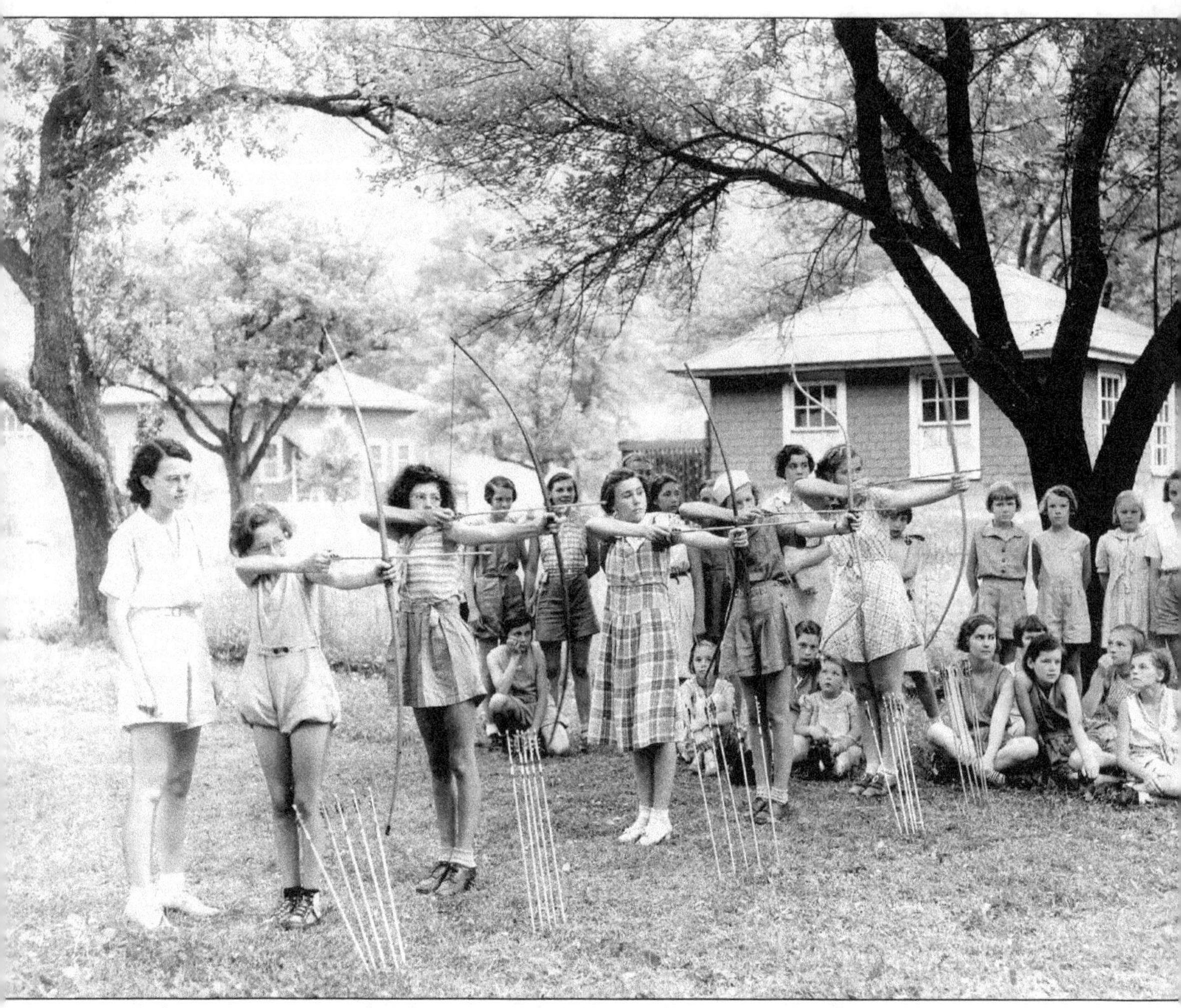

Girl Scouts receive archery instruction at Camp Kline. More than 90 Lycoming County Girl Scouts completed a two-week camp at Camp Kline in late June 1934. Also in 1934, the first nationally franchised Girl Scout cookie sale was held. Girl Scouting has a rich history in central Pennsylvania. Harrisburg, Milton, and Philipsburg recorded troops as early as 1917, just five years after Juliette Gordon Low founded the first troop in Savannah, Georgia. The movement grew quickly, as troops formed across the country. Girl Scouting continued to grow and prosper in central Pennsylvania. More and more girls were introduced to the ideals and values of the growing movement. In 1963, 10 independent councils representing all or part of 15 central Pennsylvania counties merged to form the Hemlock Girl Scout Council.

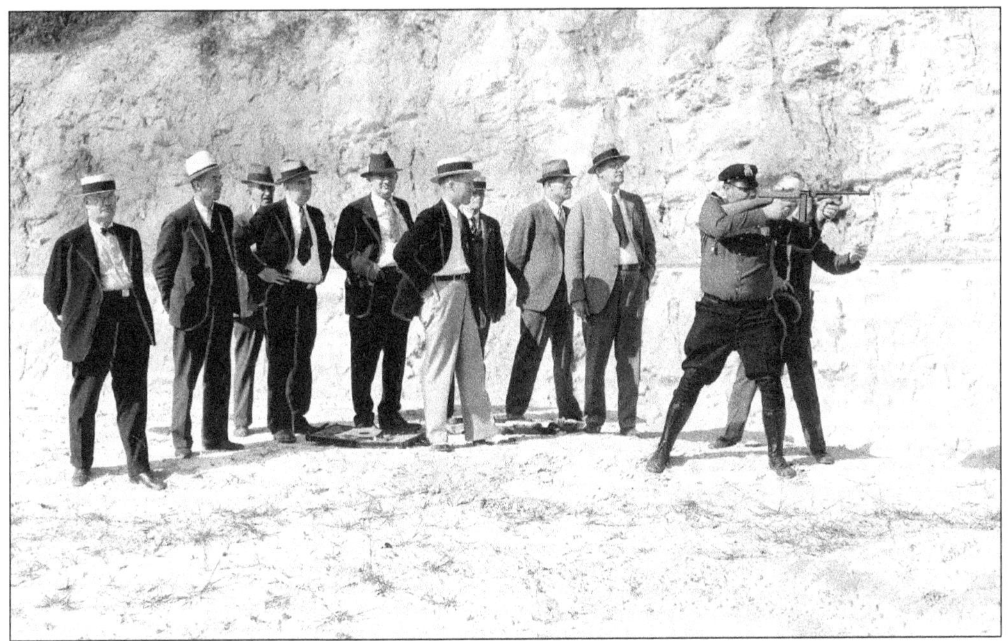

The Lycoming County sheriff, his deputies, the county commissioners, and several other officials saw a demonstration of the use of tear gas bombs and Thompson machine guns near Montoursville on September 6, 1934. The county had just bought a supply of bombs and several guns. At the demonstration the sheriff's force was given instructions in their use.

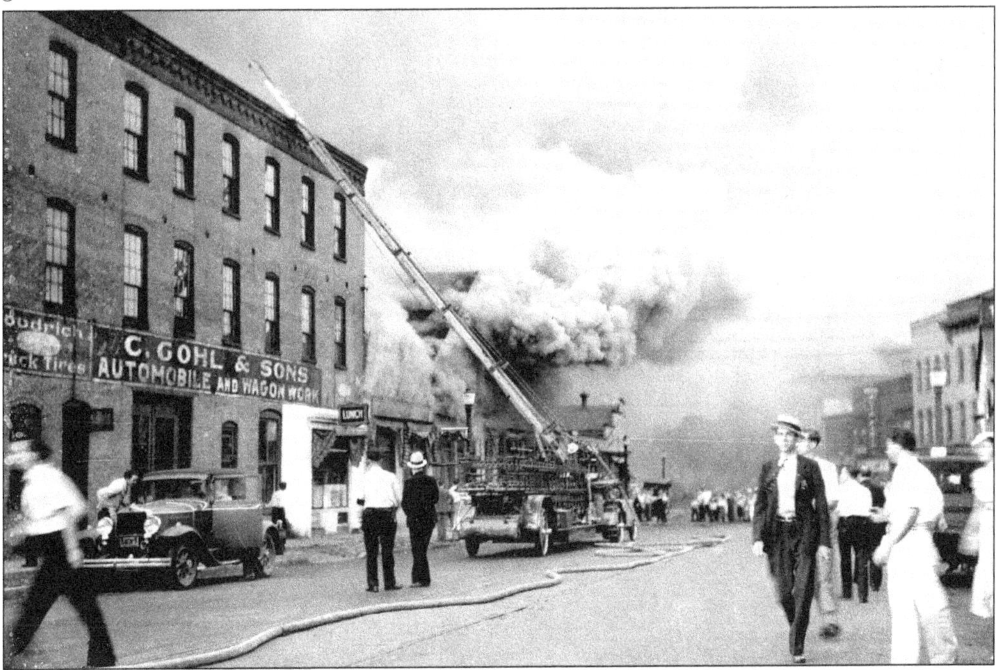

Fire destroyed the Williamsport Grocery building at the northwest corner of West Third and West Streets on August 4, 1934. The damage was estimated at a loss of $150,000. After the conflagration, this business moved to 729 West Fourth Street and later to 439 Walnut Street. The fire department's ladder truck and pumper responded quickly, but the fire was widespread.

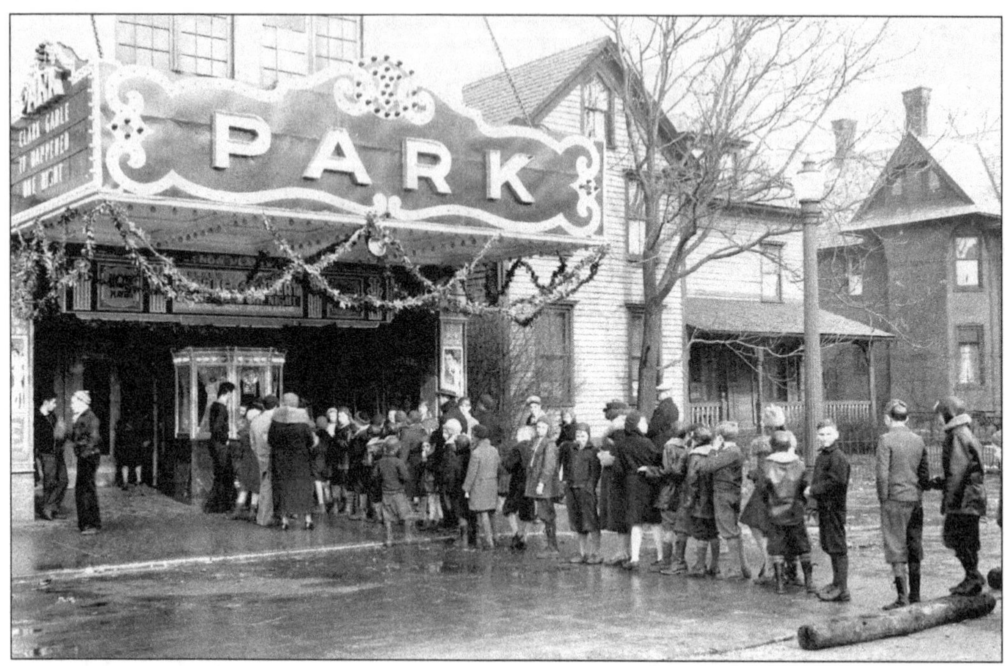

More than 900 children attended the special children's matinee at the Park movie theater on December 22, 1934. Many of the children were wards of the Lycoming County Crippled Children's Society and the Home for the Friendless. Santa Claus sat on the stage and distributed candy to all the children.

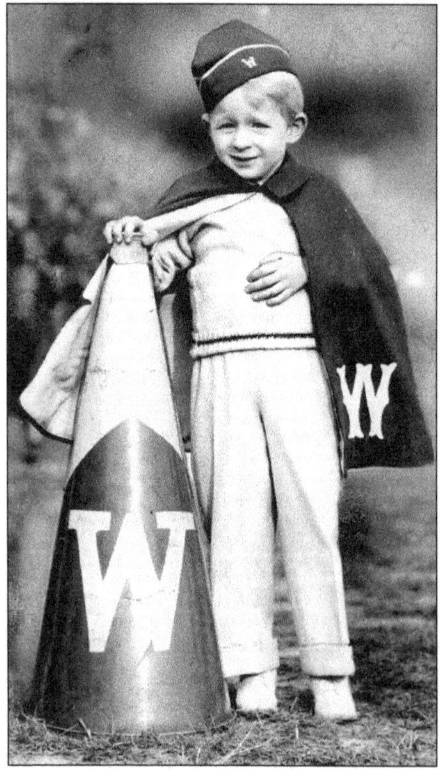

Richard Wettlauffer, four-year-old son of J. Maynard Wettlauffer, director of the Williamsport High School Band, was the mascot for the band and proudly wore his own miniature band uniform. Young Richard and the band paraded through downtown Williamsport on October 26, 1935, along with the John Harris High School Band of Harrisburg before a gridiron clash between the two schools at Williamsport's West Third Street stadium.

Four

World War II

World War II brought out the best in Williamsport as more than 9,000 residents, men and women, joined the armed forces. Those on the home front endured shortages from gasoline and rubber to sugar. Lycoming County provided airplane engines that helped the Allies control the skies of Europe.

One of the most colorful politicians ever to hold office in the area, Leo C. Williamson, led the city through the difficult years of World War II. He helped to get its citizens behind the nation's war effort, using his promotional talent to lead paper, rubber, and scrap drives, as well as war bond drives. When the United States entered World War II, officials at Dickinson Seminary (now Lycoming College) immediately made plans for the college to assist in the war effort by organizing an army education unit, and a Civil Pilot Cadet training program was started with 110 men enrolled. Army Aviation Cadets and the Cadet Nurse Corps also used the college's facilities for training.

In 1941, the Williamsport Technical Institute was established, sprouting from a small high school industrial shop that had become home to adult education and training programs. World War II led to more training to meet defense industry needs. The institute operated on a 24-hour-a-day schedule and part of that training involved disabled individuals and returning World War II veterans. The war production training and special training for disabled veterans led to the institute becoming one of the nation's largest providers of training and retraining for people with physical disabilities. The institute evolved into the Williamsport Area Community College in 1965, and later the Pennsylvania College of Technology, founded in 1989.

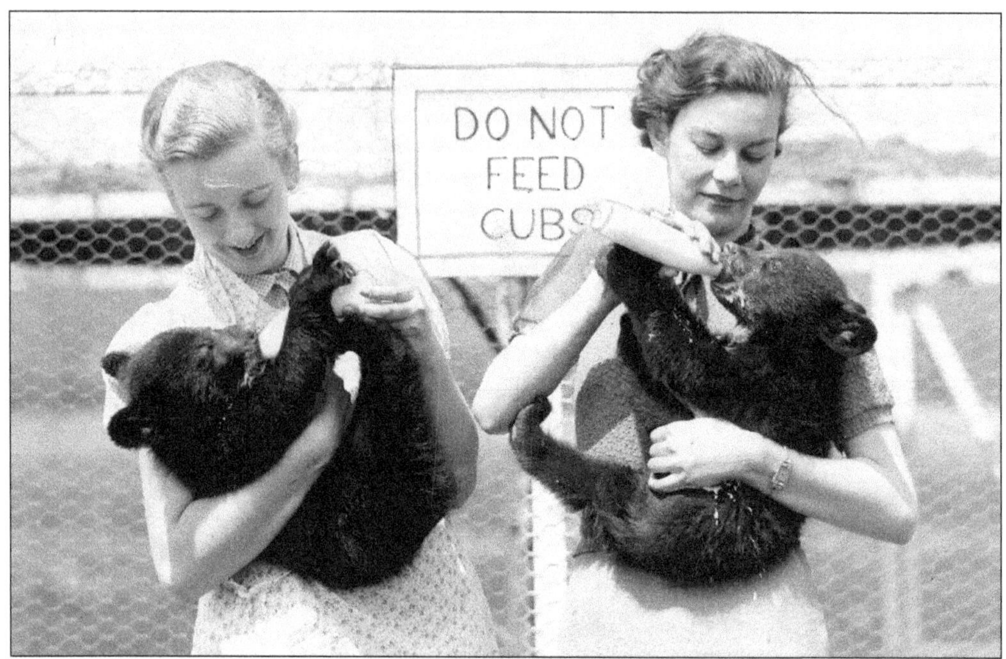

Mary Jane Greenwood and Gracie Soars are pictured with bear cubs at the Loyalsock State Game Farm in April 1935. The cubs' names were Jack and Jill. They were kept in a special pen. The game commission and department of forests and waters purchased 123,256 acres from the Central Pennsylvania Lumber Company in 1930 for the average price of $3 per acre; 51,845 acres became game lands, the rest became state forest.

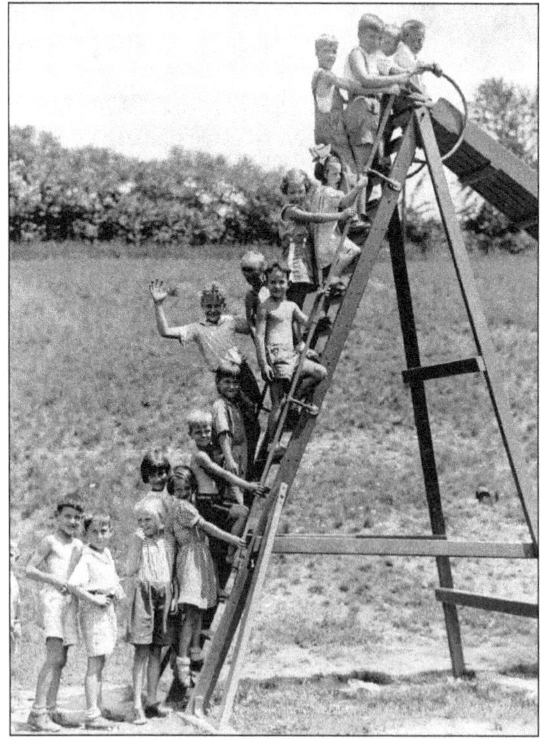

Children anxiously line up to use a sliding board on the playground of Stevens Junior High School in July 1935. Williamsport's schools provided safe playgrounds for thousands during summer break.

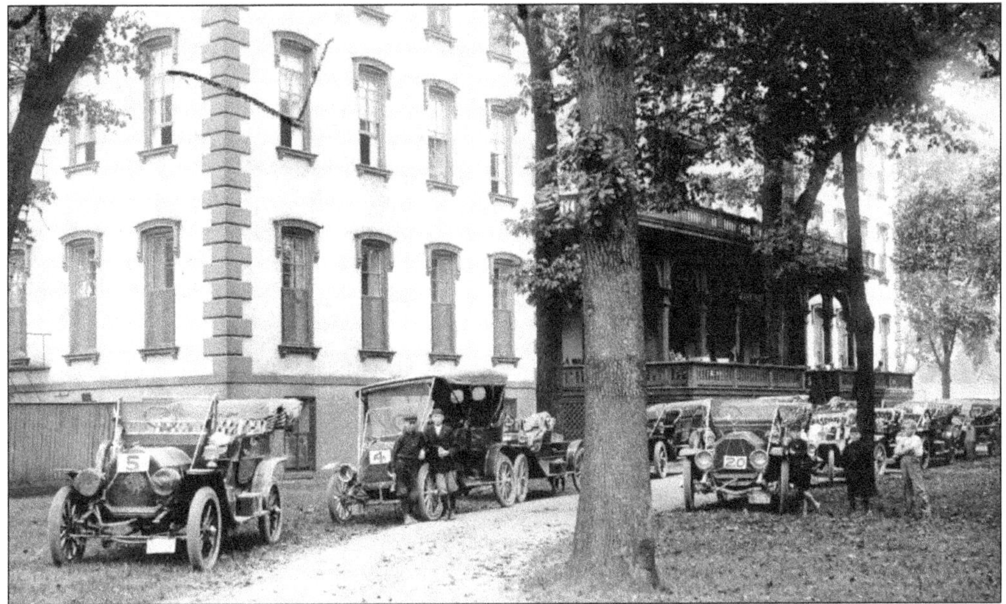

Do you remember when vehicles like this were a positive sensation? These contraptions were lined up in front of the Park Hotel. Each machine bore a number, so eventually they were in a race, although there is no apparent record of just when the event was. Printed in 1936, the picture may have been taken in 1912.

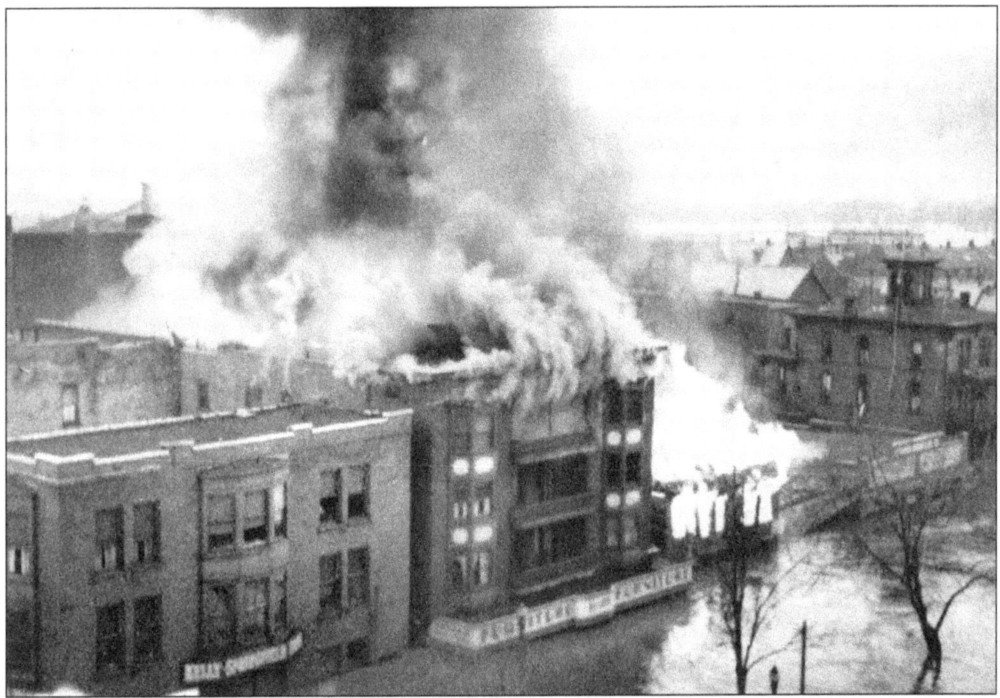

This photograph, taken from the rooftop of the *Grit* building in downtown Williamsport, shows buildings burning across the street during the 1936 flood. After much lobbying, John C. Youngman persuaded the city council to put the dike issue to the voters. In November 1940, the city's voters decided the matter, soundly approving a dike system by a large margin.

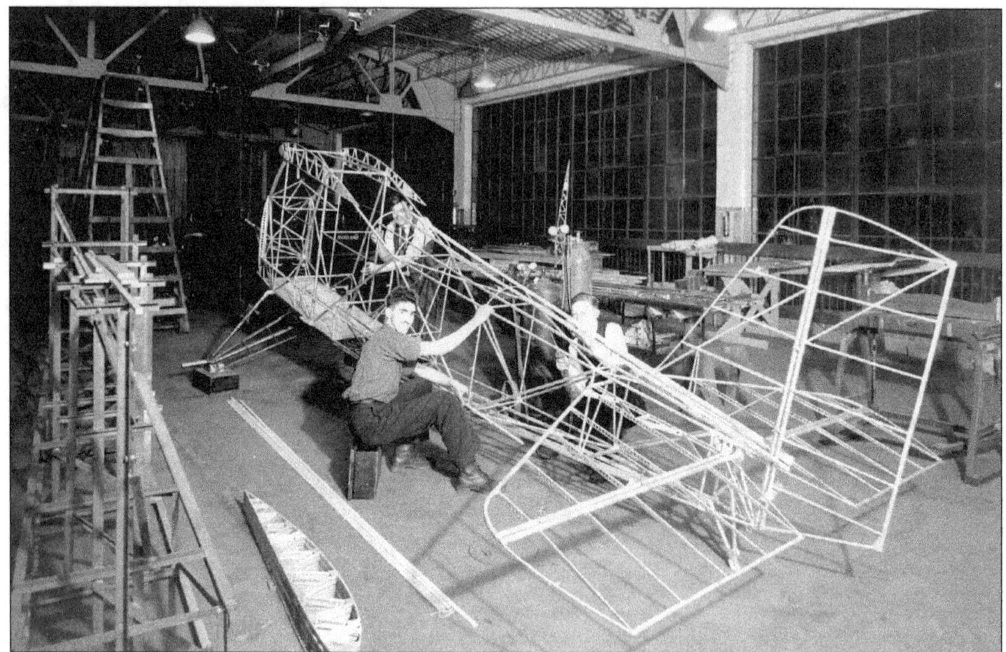

Students construct an airplane at one of the shops at Williamsport High School in April 1937. Showing an ardent interest in aviation are J. H. Jeavon, Charles Morsey, and Joseph Haag. Tony Patterino and several others later joined them. The plane was a two-place, tandem-seated, high-wing monoplane and was capable of a cruising speed of 80 miles per hour.

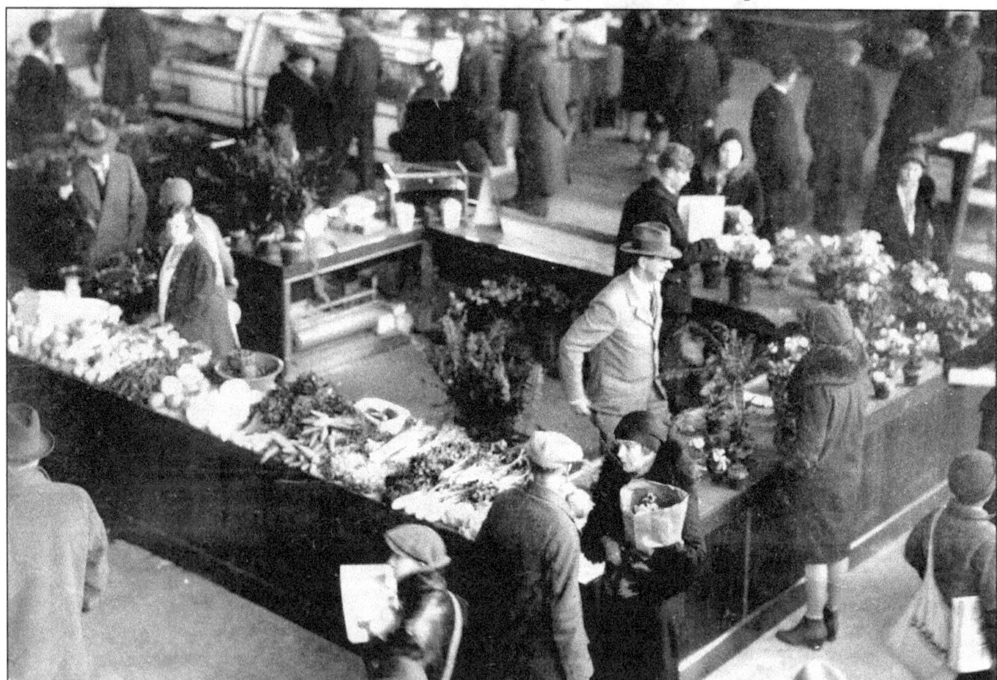

Here is a scene of the Williamsport Growers Market inside the Market House on Market Street, sometime in the late 1930s. The agricultural bounty of the surrounding area was brought to the market, making it possible for consumers to acquire fresh produce.

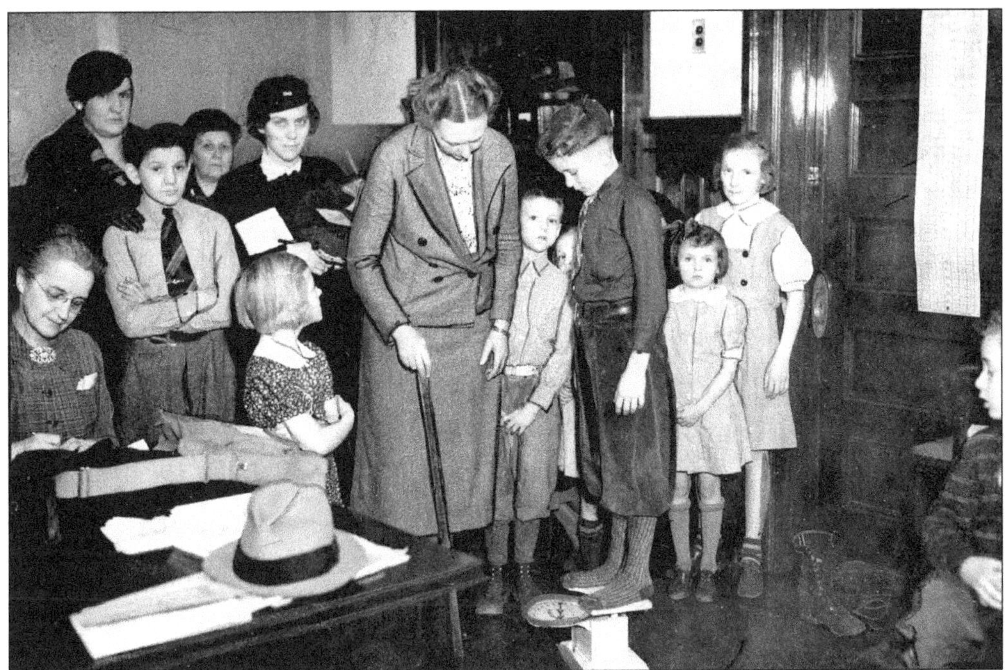

The Lycoming County Tuberculosis Society is seen here in January 1938 weighing and measuring boys and girls during a series of clinics for the purpose of discovering which children in Williamsport and Lycoming County were in need of a three-week camping program at Camp Kiwanis during the upcoming summer.

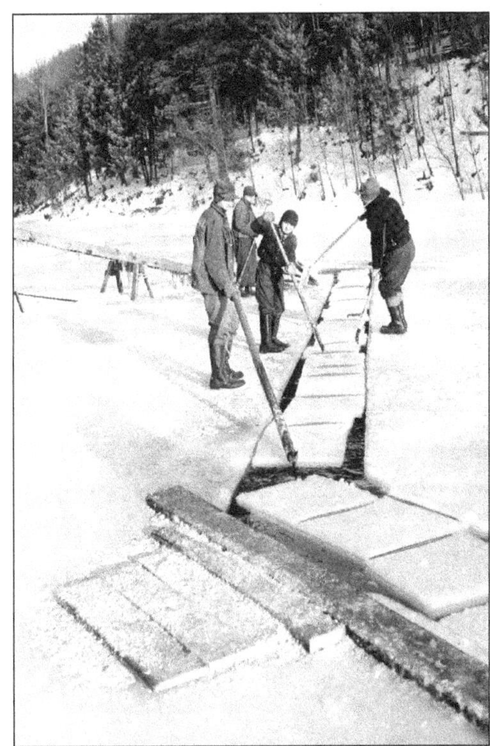

Ice cutters harvest ice in January on Larry's Creek near Salladasburg. The ice was then moved along a lane to a chute. This was done in an era when the refrigerator was literally an icebox. A cubic foot of ice weighed less than 60 pounds.

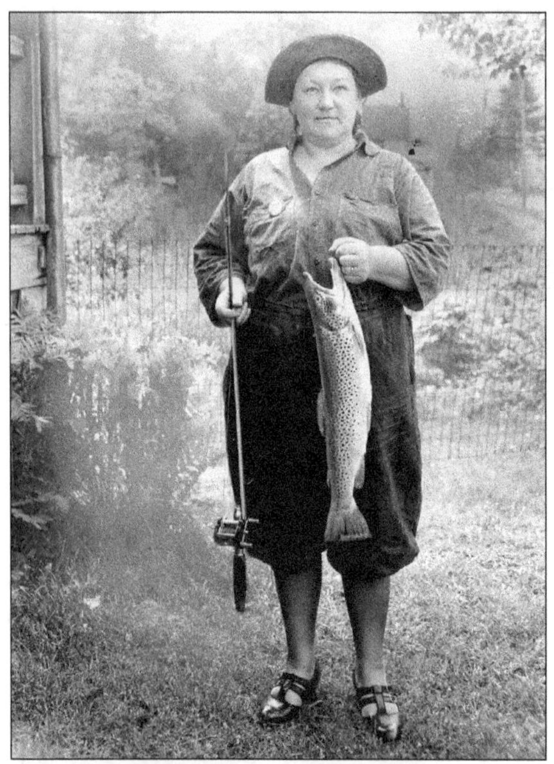

Trout fishing has always been a popular sport in the Susquehanna Valley. One of the largest brown trout caught during the 1939 fishing season was landed by Esther Steinbacher of DuBoistown. Here, she poses with large trout she found in a Mosquito Valley stream.

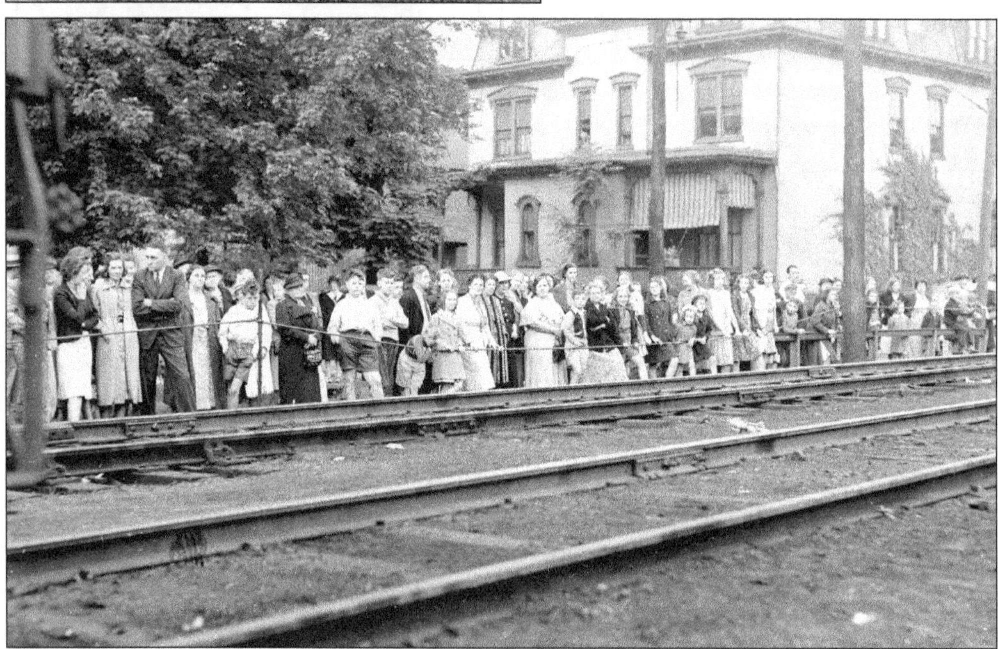

The train carrying King George VI and his wife Queen Elizabeth of Great Britain stopped briefly at the Park Hotel railroad station in Williamsport in June 1939. The royal couple was on their way from Niagara Falls, Canada, to Washington, D.C. Many Williamsporters came to the train station to see the royal train. Many people put pennies on the track to be run over by the train for mementos.

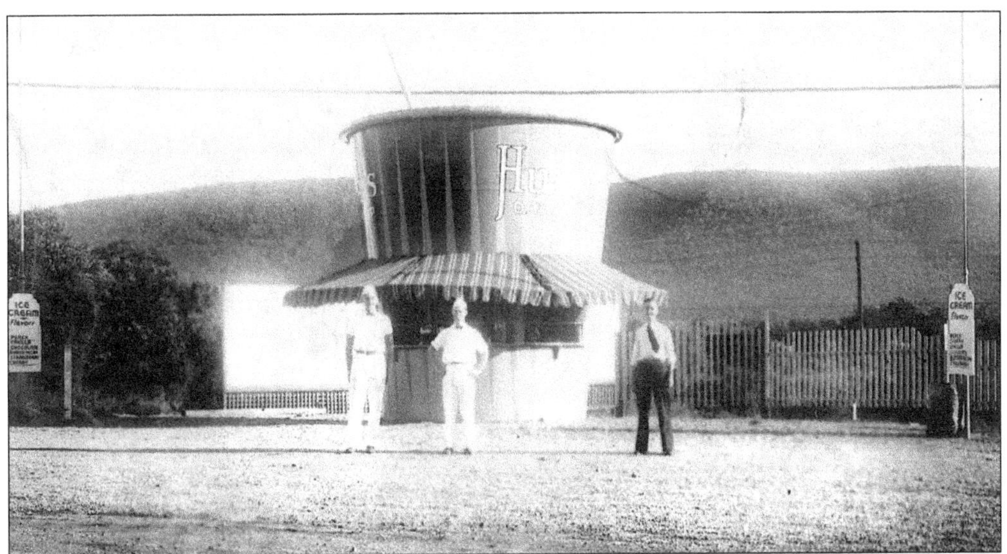

Shown is a unique ice-cream shop operated by Hurr's Dairy along the area that is now the Golden Strip in Loyalsock Township. In the 1930s, when this photograph was taken, the area was very rural with little commercial development around it. This Hurr's Dairy shop is built in the shape of a giant milk shake. Currently, an insurance agency sits on this site.

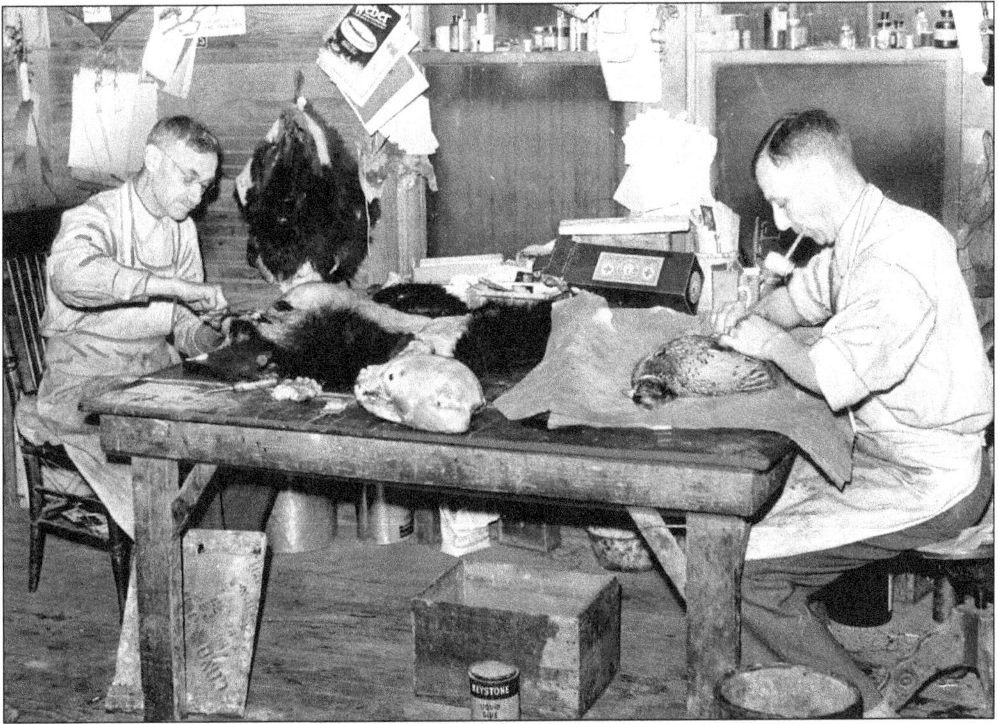

Williamsport taxidermists were busy during the last week of November 1939 mounting specimens brought in by proud hunters. This photograph was taken at a taxidermy shop on Cherry Street. Taxidermy is a method of creating a lifelike three-dimensional representation of an animal for permanent display. In some cases, the skin (including the fur, feathers, or scales) of the specimen is preserved and mounted over an artificial armature.

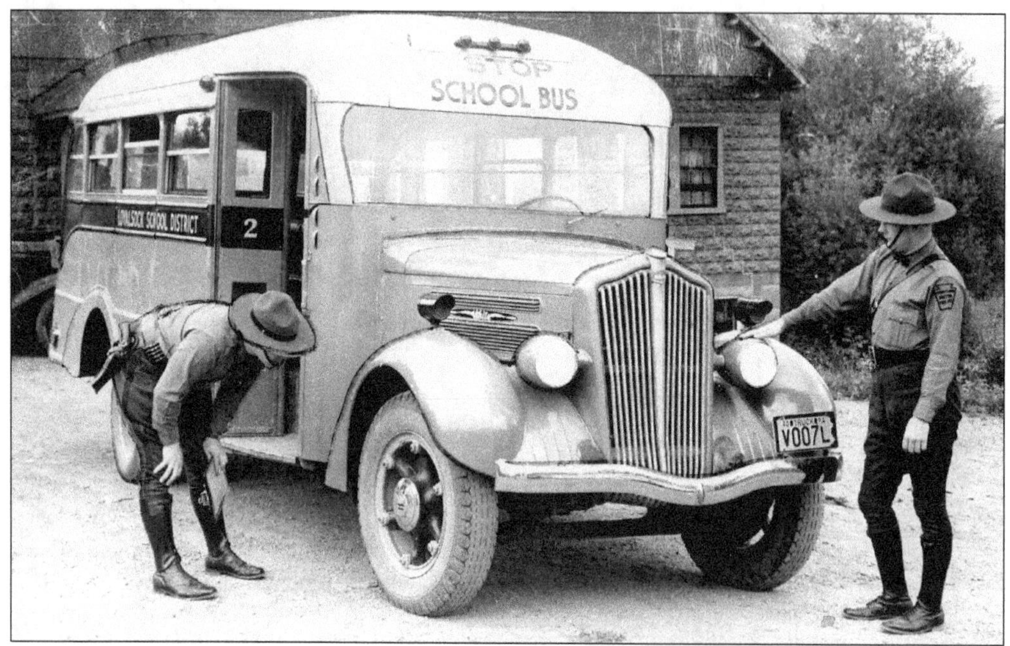

State motor police inspected all buses in Lycoming County in August 1940, preparing for the new school year. Used to transport children to and from schools, this bus from Loyalsock Township is inspected by two patrolmen at the Blackstone Garage in Williamsport.

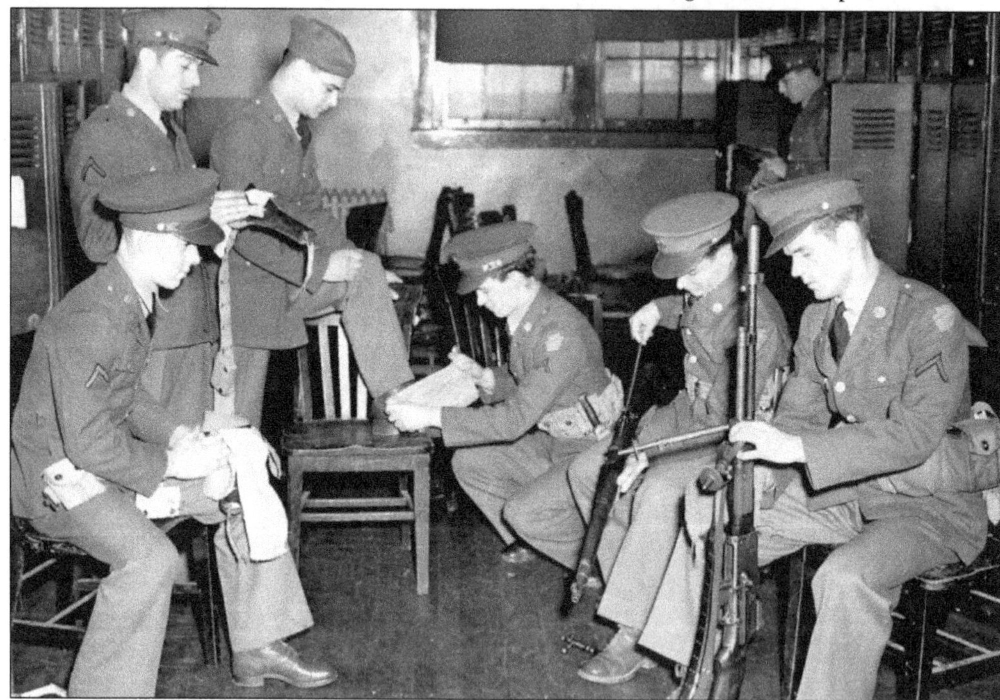
Members of a National Guard unit polish and shine their shoes, equipment, and weapons. This photograph, taken on February 22, 1941, features privates of Company K, which was activated on February 17, 1941, at Fort Indiantown Gap, Pennsylvania. Many of the guardsmen in Company K saw action in Normandy, Rhineland, Ardennes, and Central Europe.

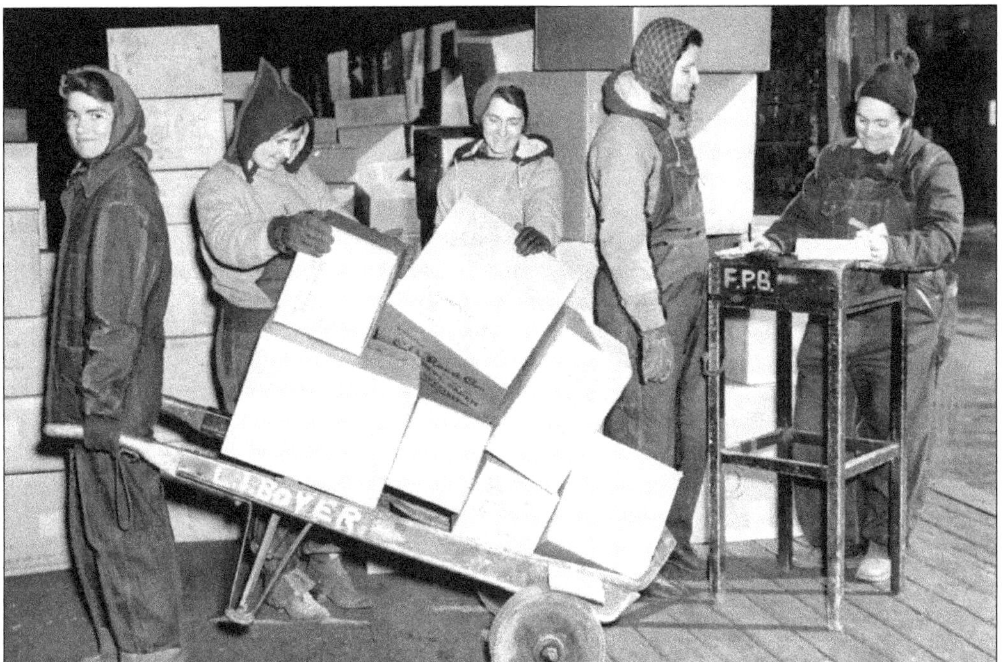

Manpower shortages during World War II put women in various parts of the workplace. This photograph from February 1943 shows women working as freight handlers at the Pennsylvania Railroad Freight Terminal on Hepburn Street. From left to right are Mary Price, Margaret Baier, Hazel Pepperman, Florence Hartline, and Mildred Wise.

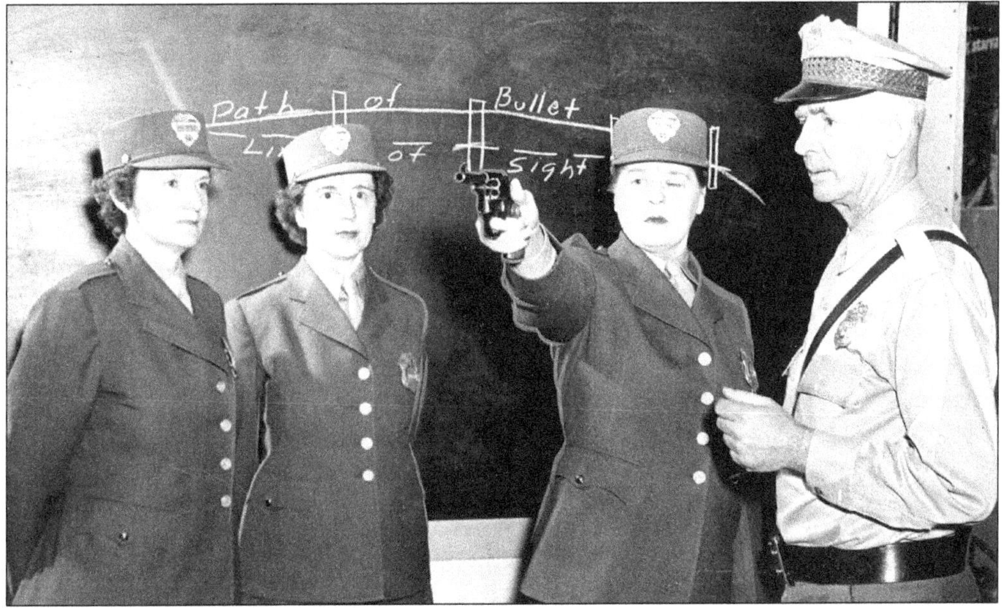

Women join the staff protecting the Pennsylvania Ordnance Works in the White Deer Valley, south of Williamsport, in May 1943. Pictured here are Mildred Hinkle, Beatrice Gramlich, and Margaret Huffman as they study aiming and firing from guard T. G. Townsend. The women guards wore the uniform of the Women's Army Corps. They were part of the Civilian Auxiliary Military Police. They were there to protect this large munition plant against saboteurs.

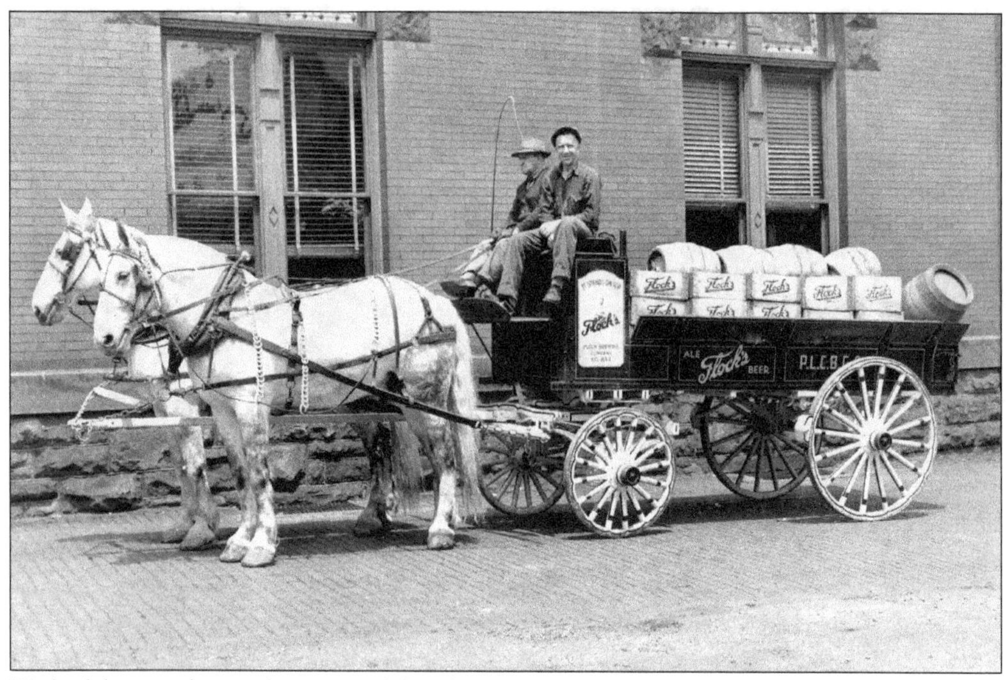

With deliveries by truck restricted by the Roosevelt administration's ban on gasoline for delivery of commodities, the Flock Brewing Company resorted to horse and wagons to deliver its beer. The first load is pictured above as it left the brewery.

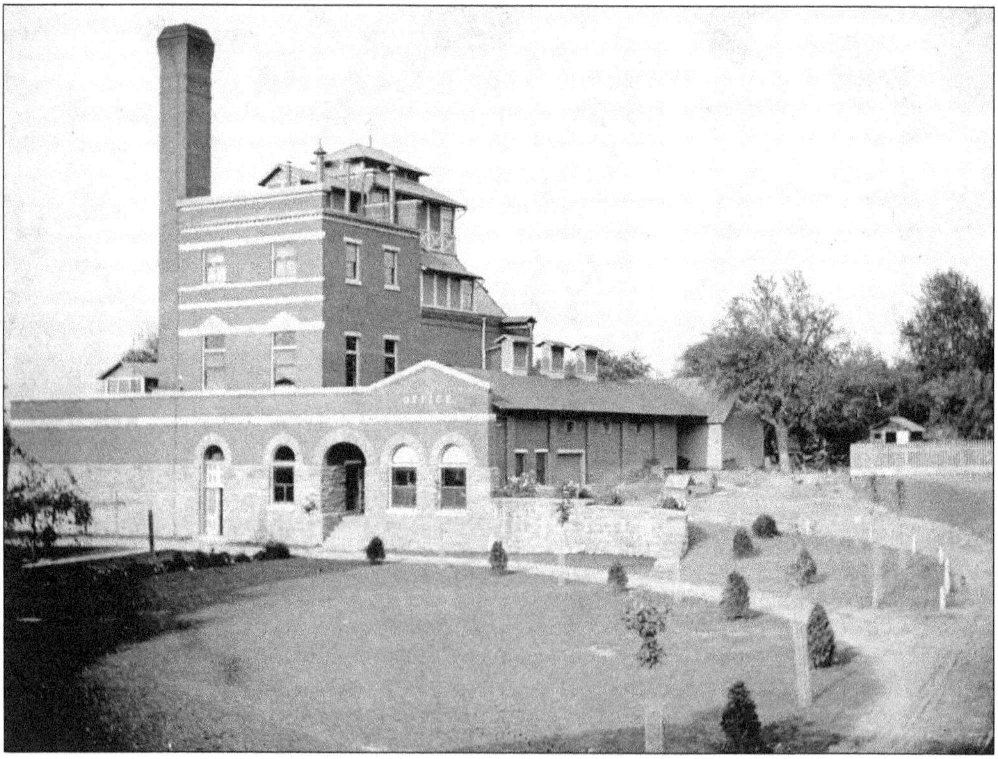

Koch Brewery in South Williamsport is pictured here, date unknown.

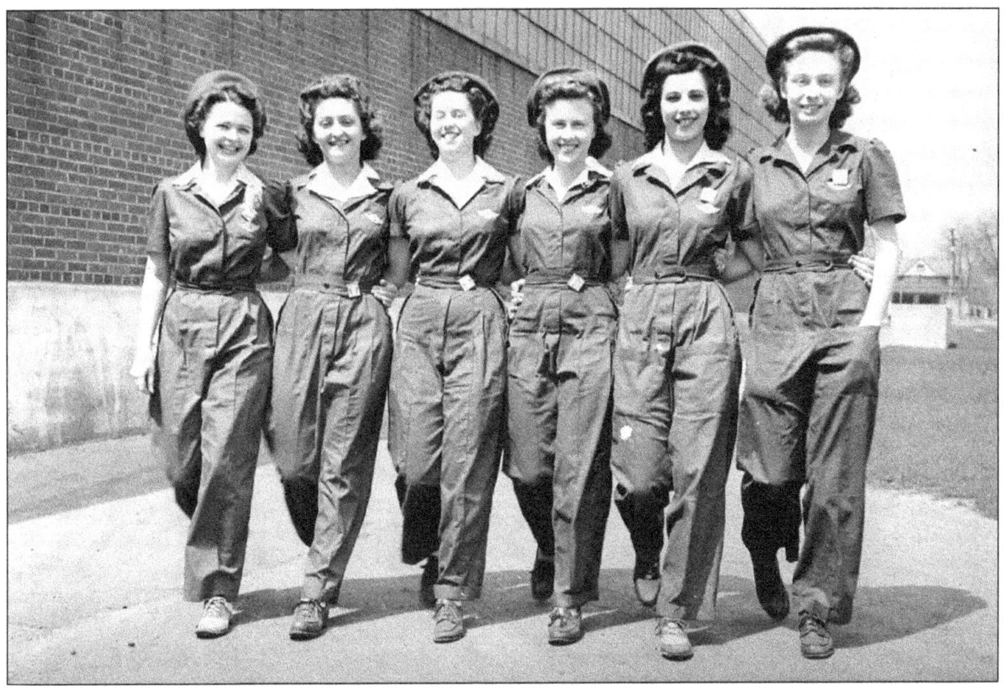

During World War II, women worked in industries typically reserved for men. Here are six employees of the Lycoming Division, Aviation Corporation. From left to right are June E. Schauer, Florence M. Haines, Lois E. Livermore, Marie G. Allison, Shirley Miller, and Lois E. Messick.

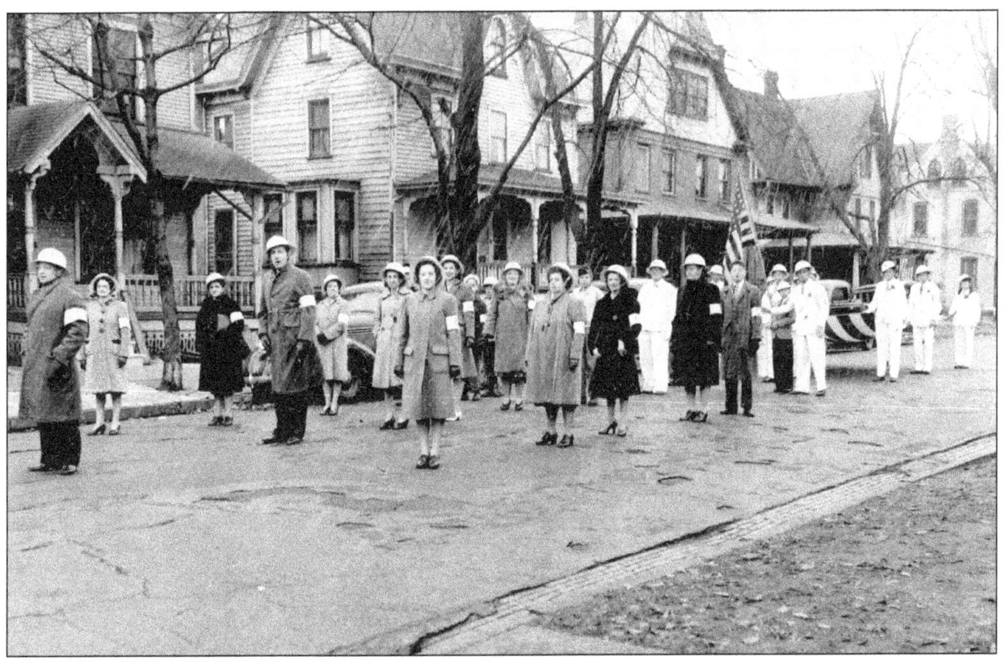

Civil defense workers march in Williamsport's Armistice Day parade on November 11, 1943. Thousands of people lined the streets to view the parade. Numerous military related units participated in the parade as well as various service clubs and high school bands.

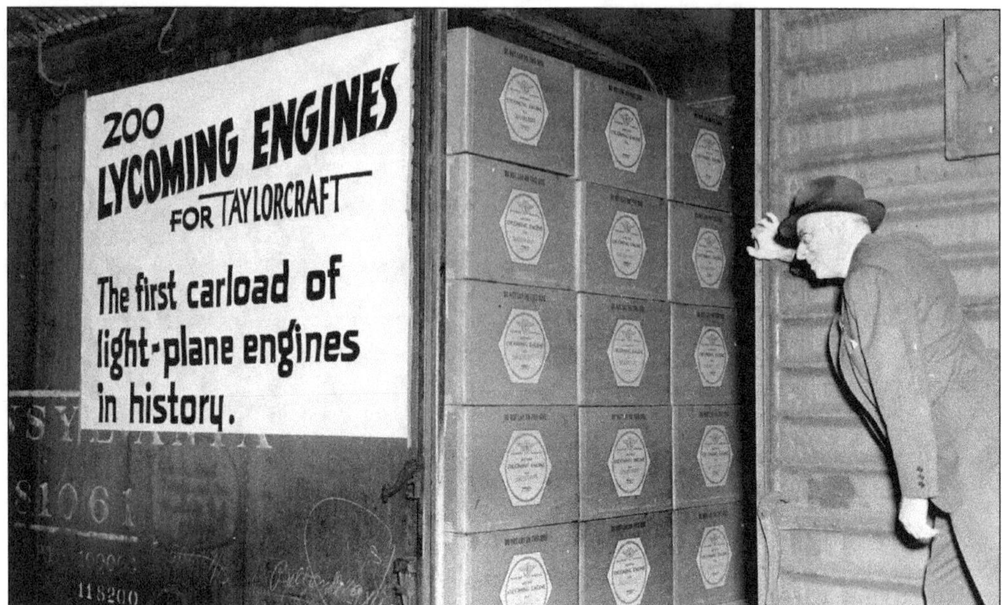

The first shipment of 200 Lycoming engines made at Lycoming Motors (later Avco, and then Textron) for Taylorcraft are shipped by rail car from Williamsport as a Lycoming official looks on, sometime in the mid-1940s. Lycoming engines have been long noted as fine and efficient power plants for use in general aviation. That reputation continues today.

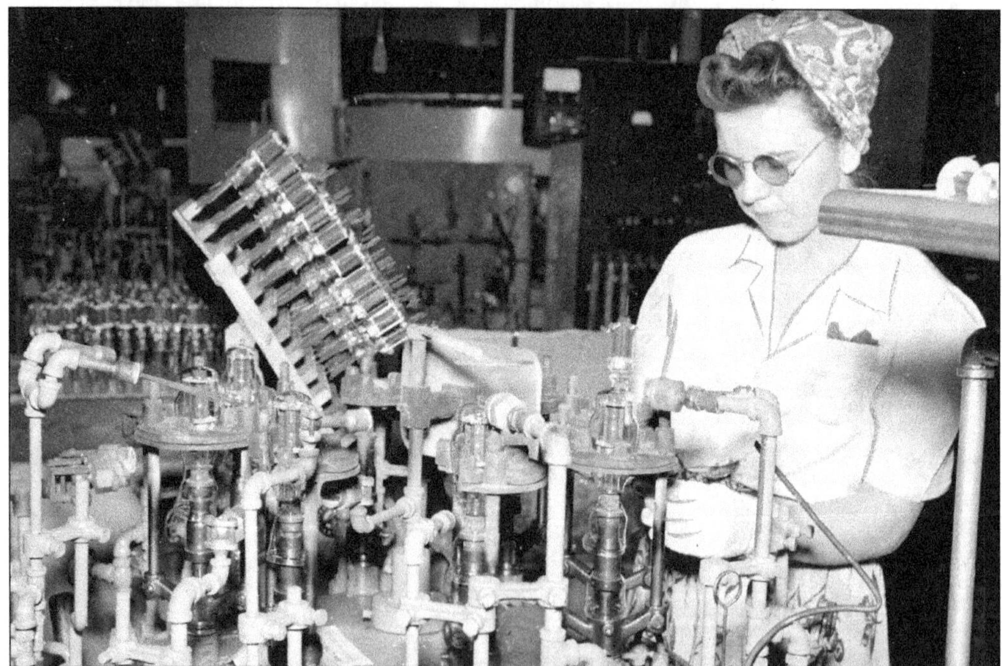
A woman worker at the Sylvania plant places the basic elements of a tube into glass bulbs in February 1944. Radio tubes, the heart of military and naval communications, were made at Williamsport's Sylvania plant. In 1949, the first complete line of television sets was introduced under the Sylvania brand name, and in the early 1960s, Sylvania grew its miniature lighting business, commercializing the first halogen sealed beam in the United States.

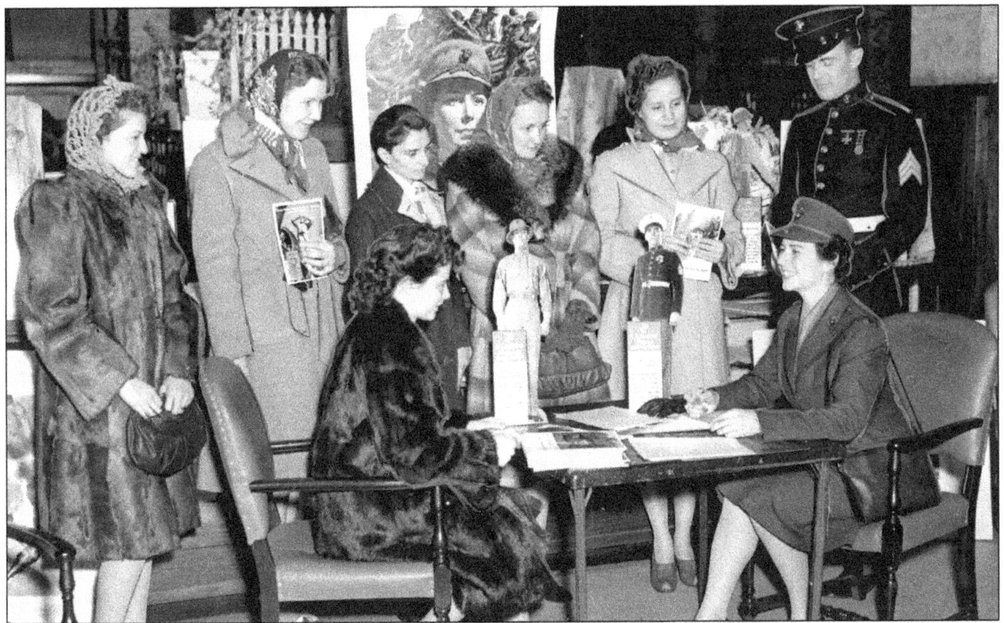

A drive to secure women for enlistment in the U.S. Marine Corps Women's Reserve was conducted by Lt. Helen Perrell, who spoke at the Williamsport High School, the Capitol Theatre, and the L. L. Stearns store in April 1944. Lt. Lieutenant Perrell is shown as she interviews interested women at the store.

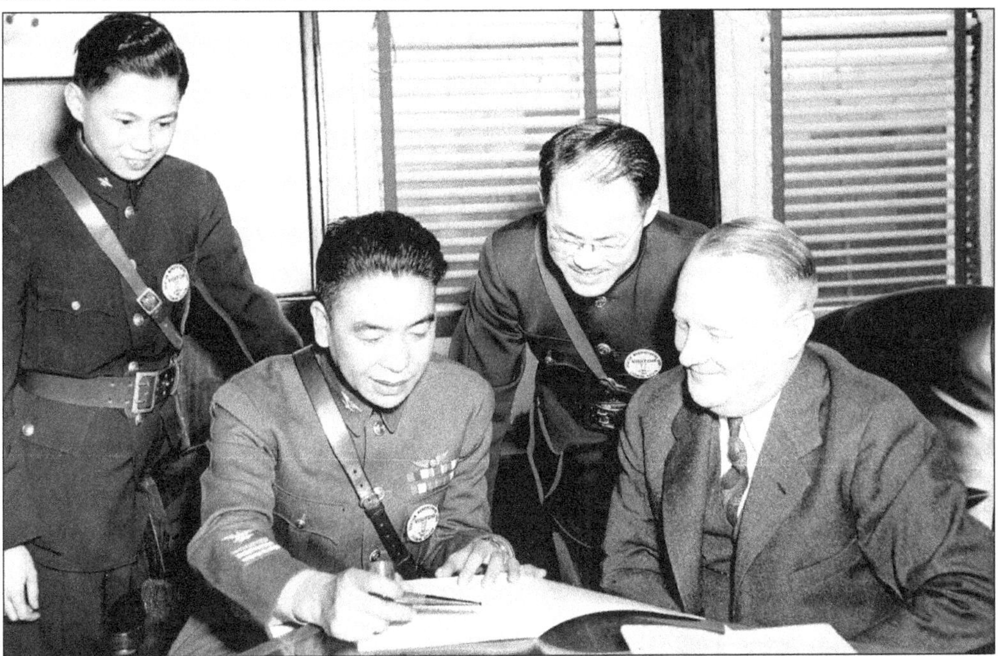

A Chinese military delegation paid a visit in April 1944 to the Lycoming Division of the Aviation Corporation in Williamsport. The group toured the plant and conferred with officials in the company. Shown above at the plant, from left to right, are Capt. William Z. Hwa; Maj. Gen. P. T. Mow, head of the Chinese air forces; Lt. Col. S. C. Wang; and William F. Wise, executive vice president of the corporation.

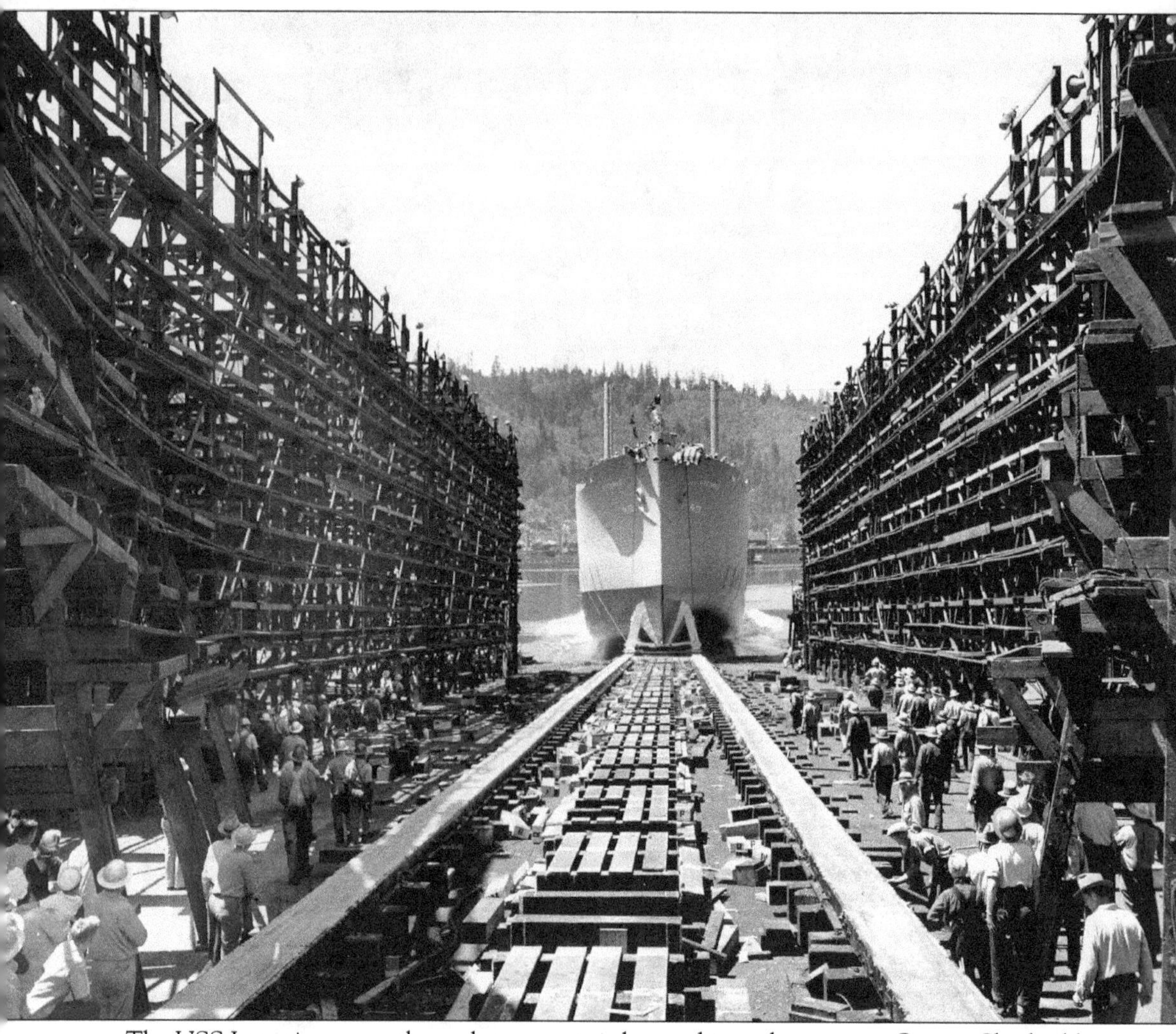

The USS *Lycoming*, a naval attack transport, is lowered into the water at Oregon Shipbuilding Yards on July 25, 1944. This type of ship was named for individual counties. A historic background of Lycoming County was carried in the ship's library. The ship displaced 6,873 tons and was 455 feet in length. It had 56 officers and 1,475 enlisted men. In its war service, the ship dodged fanatical kamikaze attacks to offload 1,300 men of the U.S. Army's 7th Division. Along with 20 other transports, the ship unloaded occupation troops at Nagasaki, Japan, only one month after the atomic bomb was dropped there. David B. Coleman, a 1927 graduate of the U.S. Naval Academy, served as the captain. When the Japanese attacked Pearl Harbor, Coleman was en route from there to Manila in command of the USS *Niagara*, a motor torpedo tender. After his ship was sunk in the Solomon Islands, he was assigned to command the USS *Moe Jack* and operated again with patrol torpedo (PT) boats in the Pacific. The executive officer of the USS *Lycoming* was Lt. Cmdr. D. Dillon. He was called to active duty in the Merchant Marines in January 1941. He previously served as the executive officer of the USS *Kaula* and was commanding officer of the USS *Rio Grande*. The USS *Lycoming* was decommissioned in March 1946.

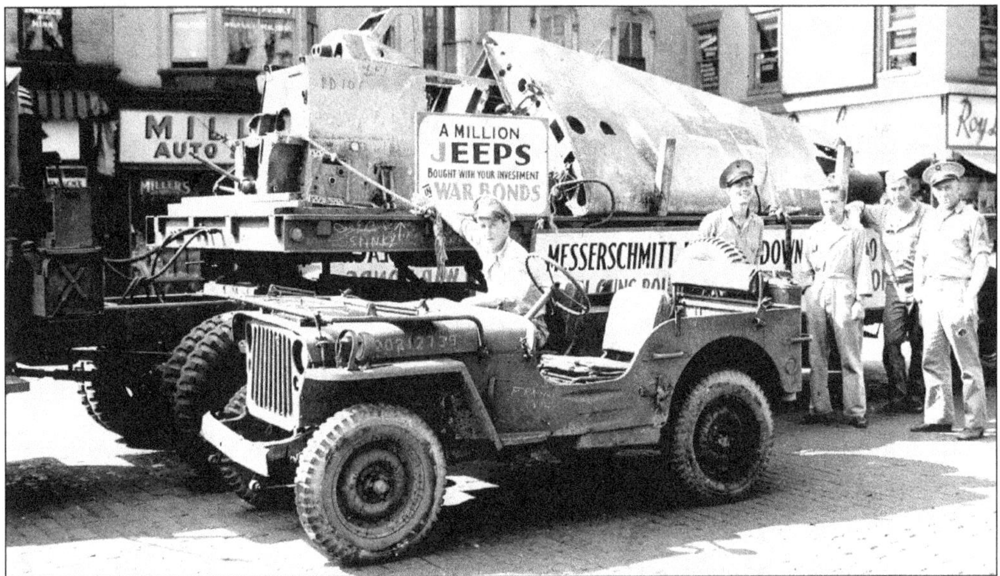

Part of a captured German Messerschmitt fighter plane and a U.S. Army jeep were put on display in downtown Williamsport in July 1944 for a war bond rally concluding the fifth war loan. The German Luftwaffe flew numerous models of the 109 from 1936 to 1945. More 109s were built (about 35,000) than any other single-engine fighter in history.

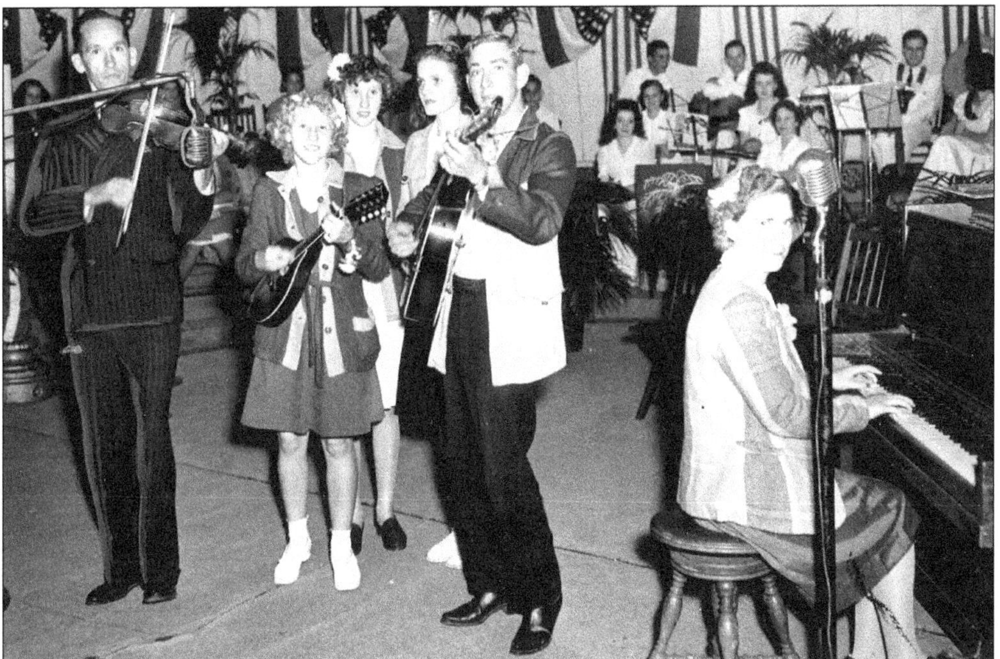

Pictured here is the Unityville Hillbilly Band while performing at the annual Kiddies Sing at the Brandon Park band shell on August 23, 1944. More than 2,000 people turned out for the event despite some chilly weather. Mayor Leo Williamson started the community sing as a way to highlight Williamsport's musical talent and to bring free, wholesome entertainment. The Kiddies Sing helped encourage a younger generation of singers and musicians. The sings were a popular fixture into the 1960s.

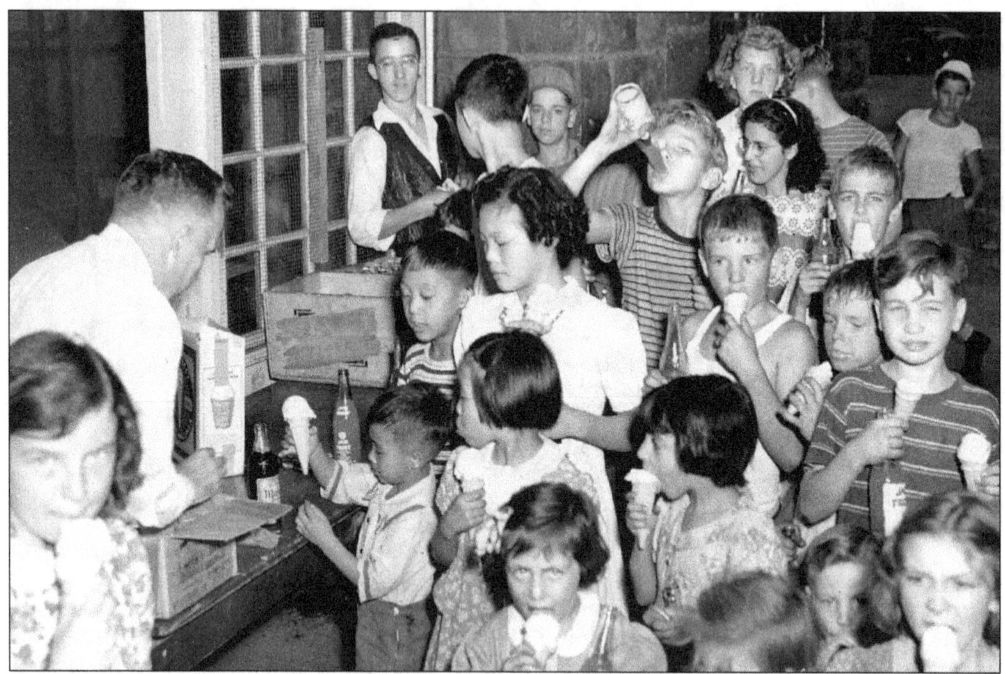

This photograph was taken as the 1944 summer program for boy and girl members of the Boys' Club ended with a party. Established in 1906 in Boston as the Federated Boys' Clubs to help young people, especially those who are disadvantaged, the club now has more than 1,006 organizations. Headquartered in Atlanta, Georgia, most clubs consist of a neighborhood building dedicated to children and young people and staffed by professionals and volunteers.

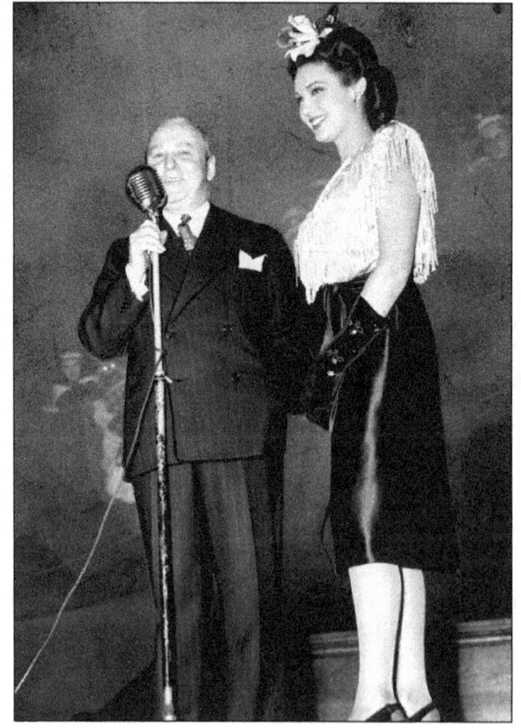

The highlight of the sixth war loan rally held at the Pine Street Methodist Church in December 1944 was the appearance of film star Linda Darnell, pictured here with Williamsport's most noted raconteur, Tommy Richardson. The rally drew an estimated 3,500 people. It raised more than $765,000 in war bond sales.

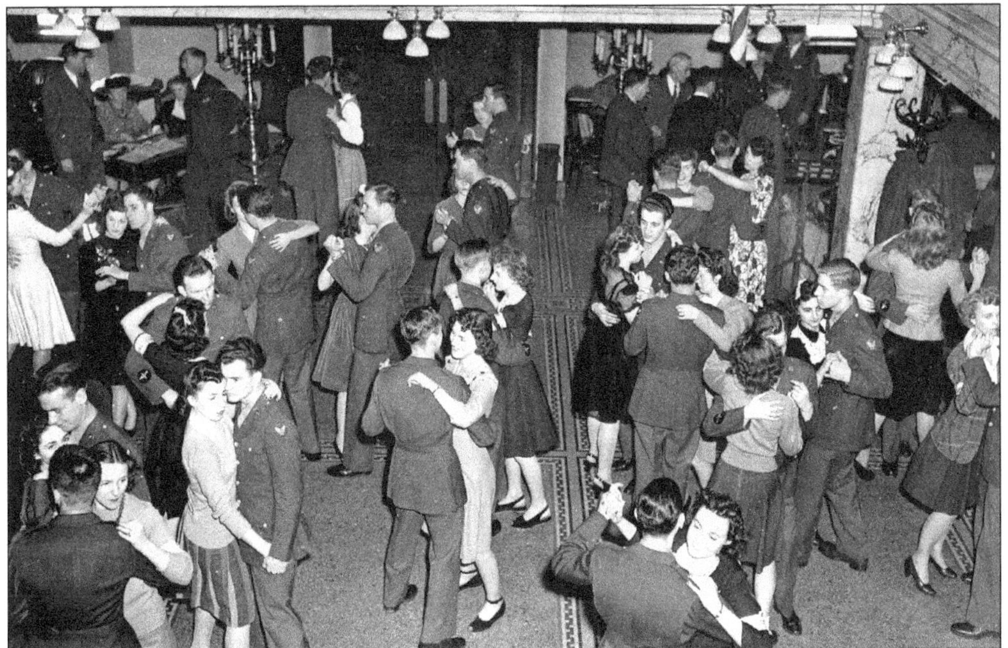

GIs dance with young ladies at the serviceman's canteen of the Acacia Club on Market Street in Williamsport during World War II. Canteens provided entertainment and a place to blow off steam for young soldiers and sailors. They also provided a safe alternative to the local bars and dance halls.

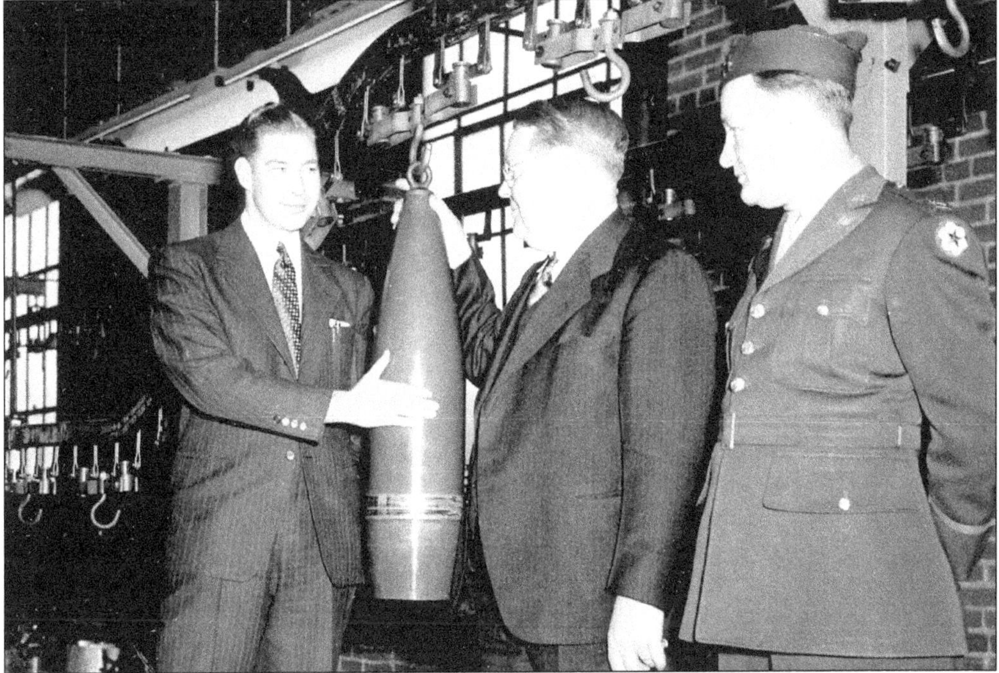

The Rheem Manufacturing Plant, a munition factory, opened its door on January 18, 1945, at the former Crooks Door Plant at the foot of Park Street. A company official is shown inspecting a shell made at the plant, along with military and war production officials.

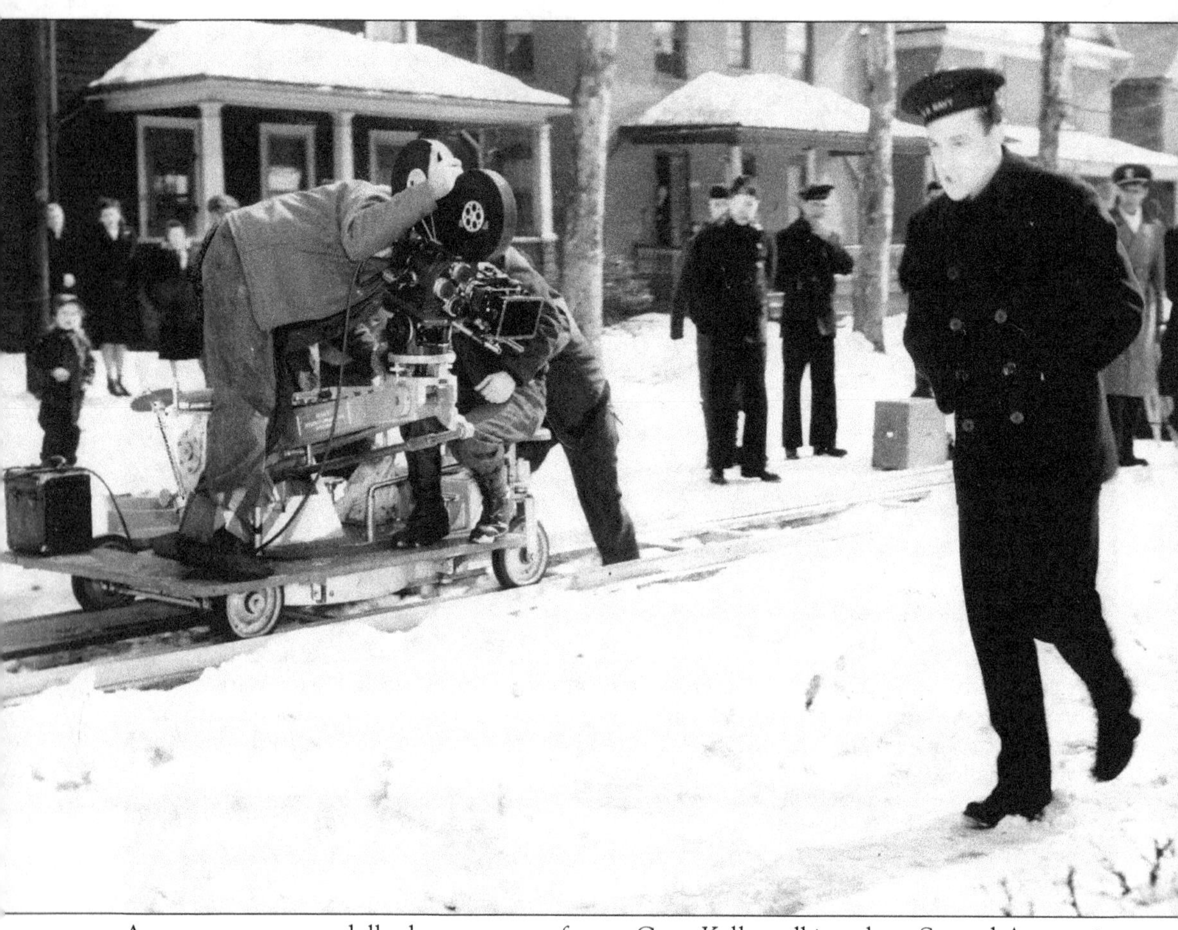

A camera crew on a dolly shoots scenes of actor Gene Kelly walking along Second Avenue in Williamsport in February 1945. Kelly was in town to make a U.S. Navy film intended to help returning war veterans adjust. Kelly, who died in February 1996 at the age of 83, was at the peak of stardom when he played a disturbed Guadalcanal veteran revisiting prewar haunts and his hometown. That same year, he was nominated for a Best Actor Oscar for his performance as a love-starved sailor on leave in *Anchors Aweigh* with Frank Sinatra. Local resident Abe Gordon, who had just returned from North Africa with a Silver Star, was cast as a veteran with only one arm. Williamsport native Hugh MacMullan, the dialogue coach for the U.S. Navy's photographic section, convinced the U.S. Navy to bring Kelly and the film crew to his hometown. MacMullan later was an English instructor at the former Williamsport Area Community College.

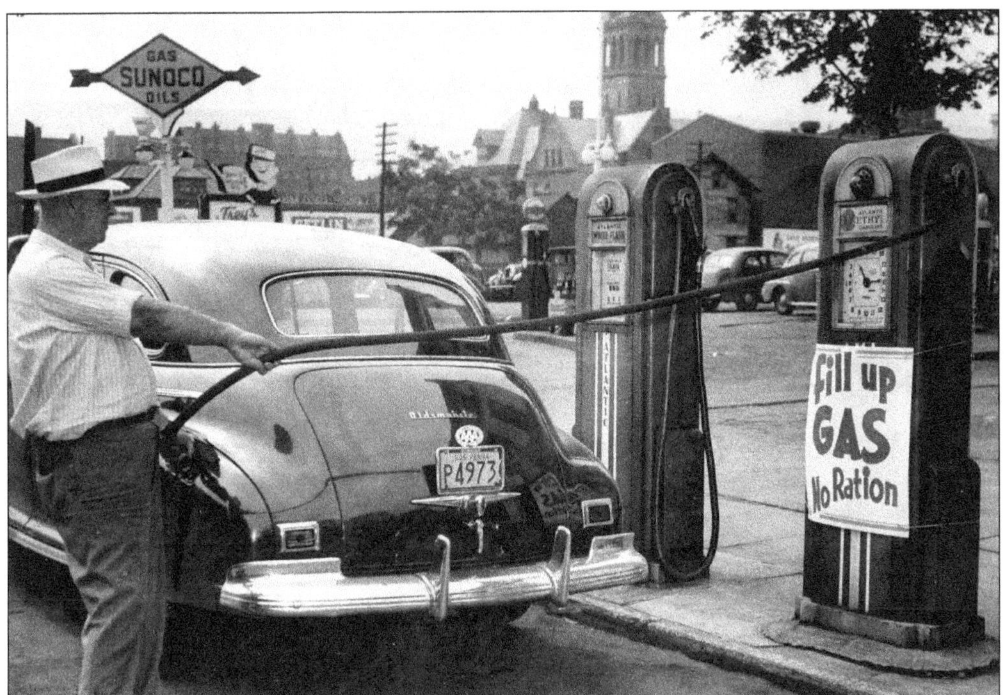

"Fill 'er up" is the plan as gas rationing ends. Wholesalers in the Williamsport area had tanks full enough to take care of demand. Pictured here is one of the filling stations in downtown Williamsport, near city hall on Pine Street, taking pains to point out to motorists that they can buy any amount of gas without ration stamps, shortly after war with Japan ended on August 14, 1945.

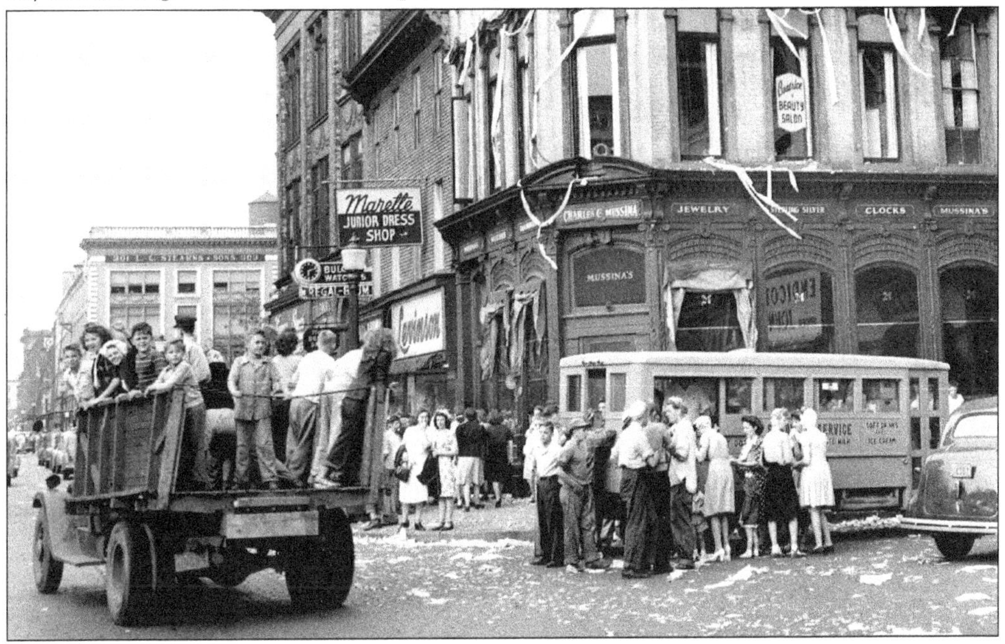

August 14, 1945, was a day of great celebration and joy in Williamsport as people of all ages crowded the streets for a parade. With the end of World War II, many Williamsport fathers and sons returned home to their families.

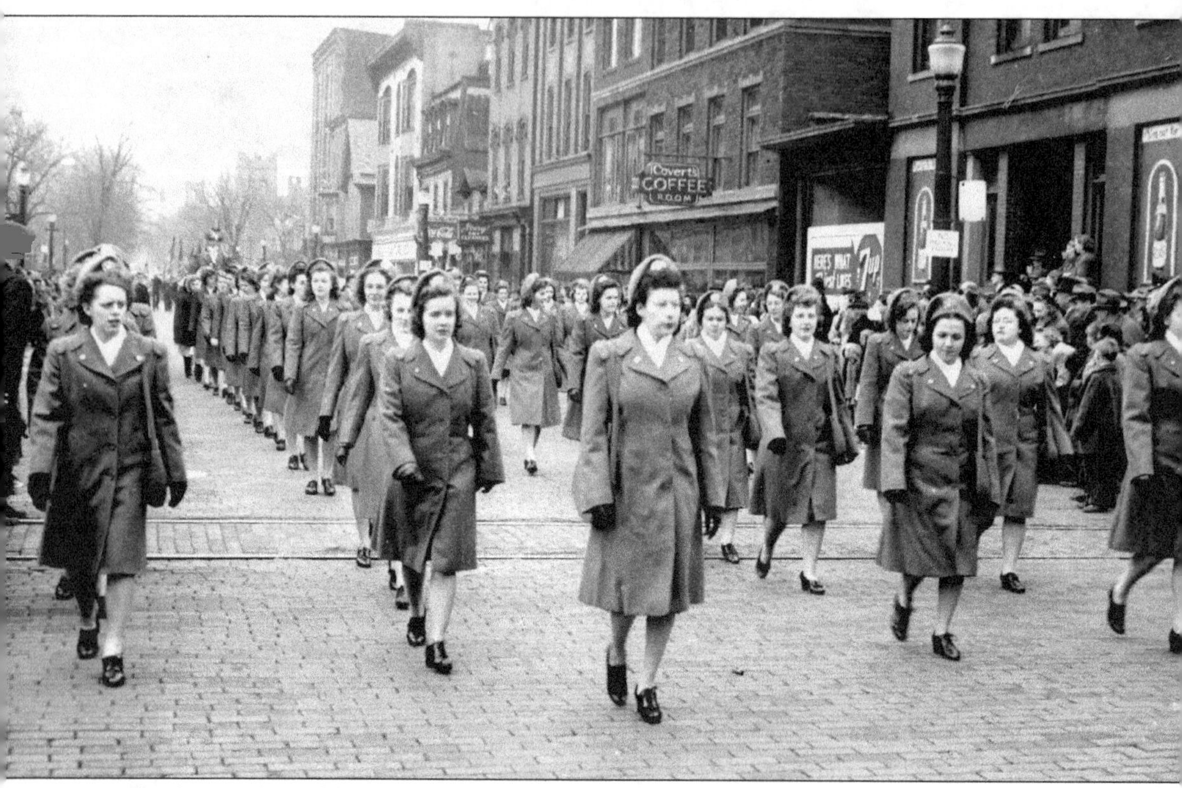

The first post–World War II Armistice Day parade is observed in downtown Williamsport on November 11, 1945. Pictured here are the cadet nurses of the Williamsport Hospital marching in the parade that commemorated the anniversary of the end of World War I, which occurred on the 11th hour of the 11th day in the 11th month of 1918. The war ended when the Allies and the Germans signed the armistice at Rethondes, France. It is a public holiday in several countries, and for years following World War I, the day was recognized as the day for parades, memorial services, and reunions of those veterans who did survive. World War II ended with the complete defeat of the Axis. Troops from all over the world began returning to their homes to once again take their proper places in their communities. It was then that Armistice Day became Veterans Day to recognize America's male and female veterans.

Five

THE BABY BOOM

Home again, Williamsport's men and women rejoiced, fell in love, and began families. The nationwide population boom was reflected in Lycoming County, and with it, a plethora of new businesses and forms of recreation began. Little League Baseball, in its infancy during World War II, enjoyed a boom also, as fathers found their favorite pastime had been modified for young boys. As families began to revolve around their children, groups such as the Boy Scouts, Girl Scouts, and YMCA and school athletics began to blossom. Williamsport expanded and new, sprawling schools replaced the aging, decrepit monoliths.

Even devastating childhood illnesses could be overcome, and new vaccines meant children were living longer and growing up healthy. A new Divine Providence Hospital was built to keep them that way. Aghast, perhaps, at the slaughter during the previous decade, Americans treasured their children.

Therein, however, may be the problem that the new generation faced. What are the traits that enabled the previous generation to accomplish great things? Much attention is now given to the World War II generation, and it springs from an unaffected feeling of respect. In contrast, many baby boomers sensed their inadequate legacy when compared to their indulgent, protective parents.

New products and parenting philosophies arose, and Dr. Benjamin Spock became a best-selling author for his books about child rearing. With the debut of television broadcasting and greater availability of television sets, baby boomers became the television generation. By the time the first boomers reached first grade, they had watched roughly 5,000 hours of children's programming.

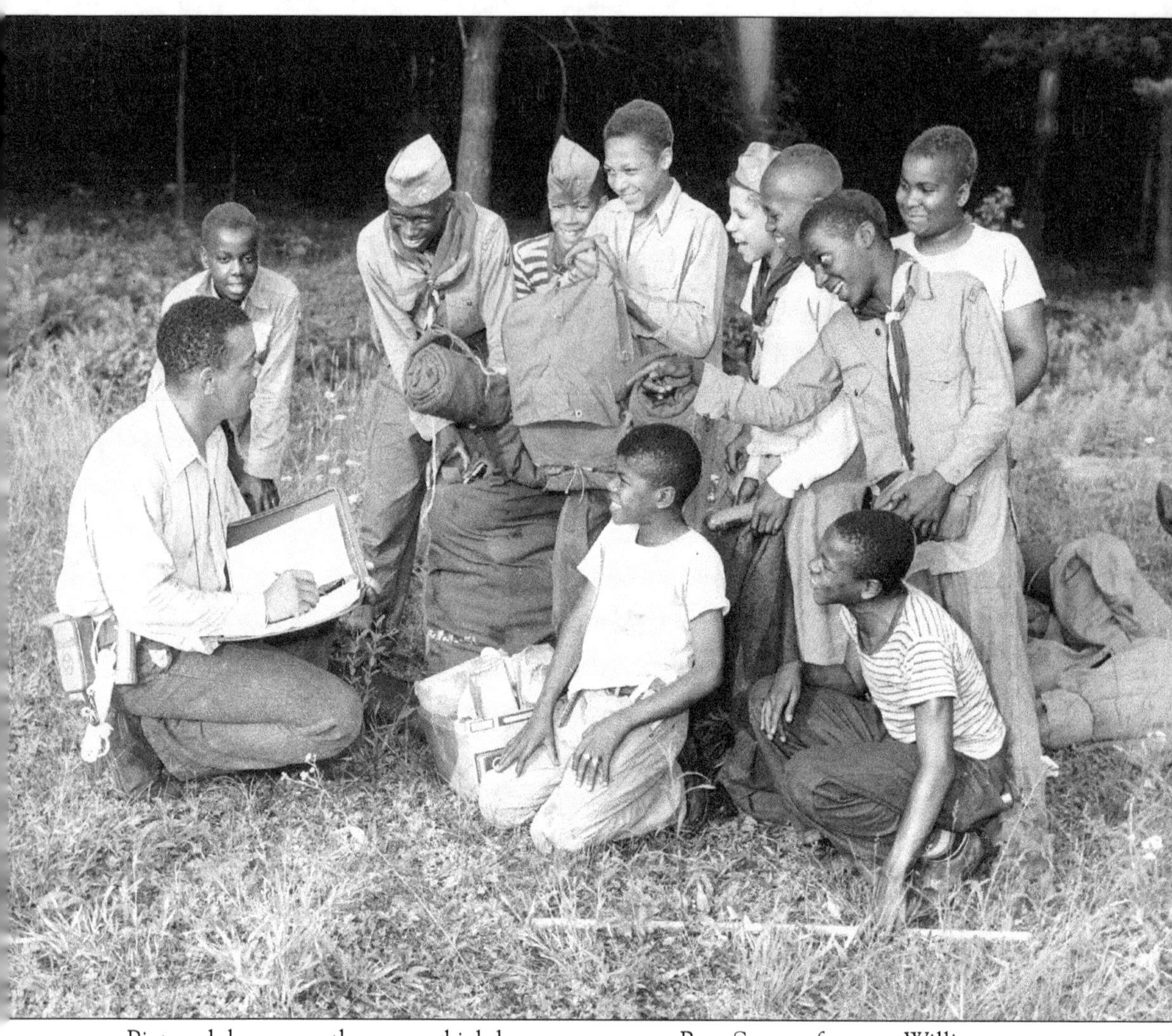

Pictured here are the proverbial happy campers. Boy Scouts from a Williamsport troop participated in a Scout Jamboree near Loyalsock Creek in June 1947. The camp provided scouts an opportunity to qualify for advances in rank and for merit badges to be earned under the leadership of various instructors. Chicago publisher William Boyce founded the Boy Scouts of America (which also uses the name Scouting USA) on February 8, 1910. At that time in the United States, there were several other loosely structured, outdoor-oriented youth organizations, some using the name "Boy Scout" and some using other names, and there were already a number of troops in existence using some variation of the British Boy Scout program. Two men who influenced the Boy Scouts of America's development more than any one else were Ernest Thompson Seton, a famous writer and artist, and James West, a Washington, D.C., attorney active in juvenile cases.

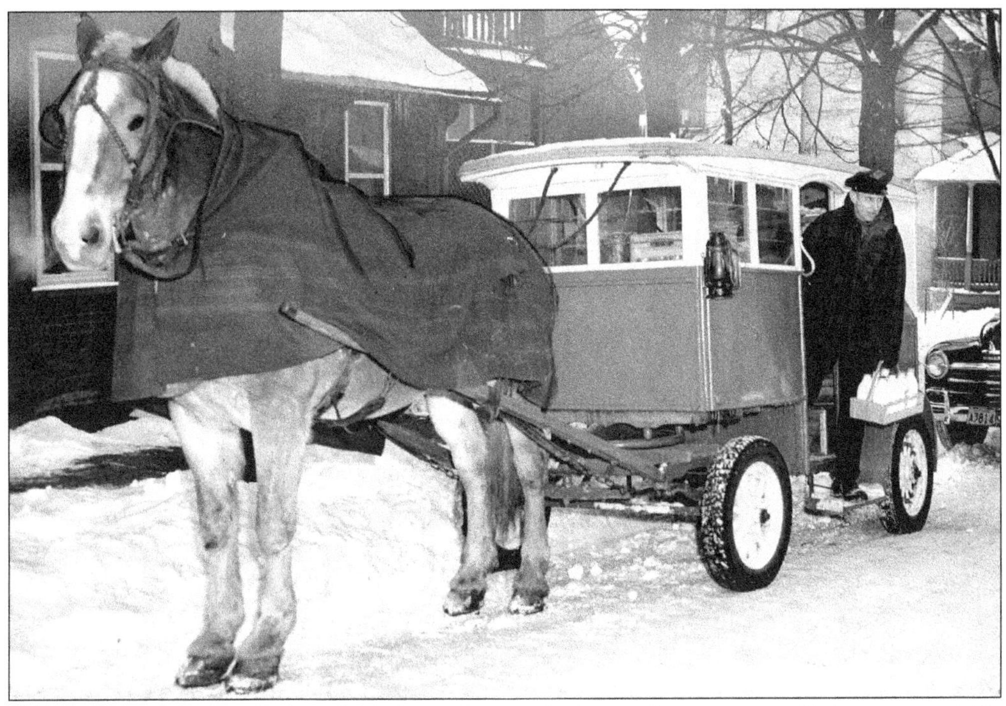

A milkman delivers milk the old-fashioned way—by horse-drawn wagon. This was especially useful in February 1948, when there was an abundance of snow on the ground. Home delivery of milk began in 1942 as a war conservation measure. Home milk delivery started to fade in the late 1960s, as large supermarkets sprang up. By 1973, only 10 percent of Americans used milkmen, and in 1995, less than one percent enjoyed home delivery.

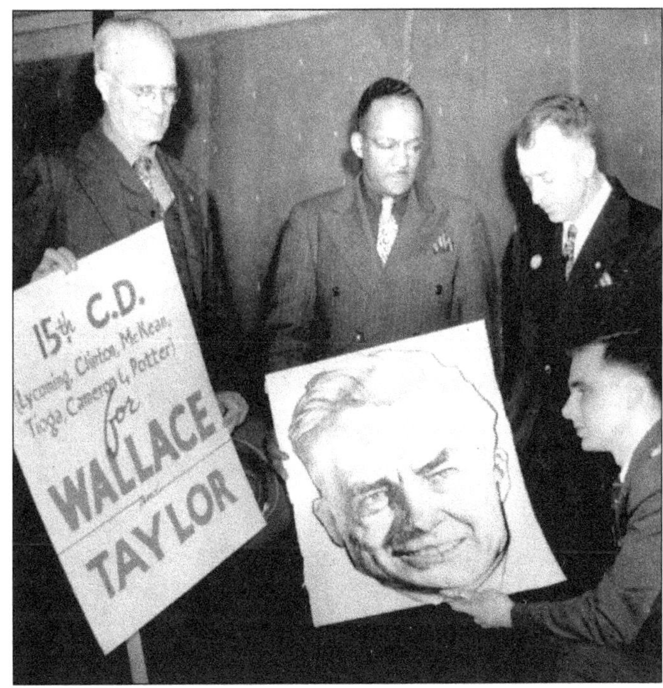

These four men from Lycoming County display banners at the Pennsylvania convention of the Progressive Party in which former Vice President Henry A. Wallace, the party's 1948 presidential nominee, spoke. Pictured from left to right are Ralph Kocher, Williamsport; Clarence Diggs, Cogan Station; and James Ault and William Kern, both of Williamsport. The Progressive Party, a newly organized third party with a pro-Soviet platform, attacked the Marshall Plan and called for disarmament. Although polling a popular vote of more than 1 million, Wallace failed to carry any state.

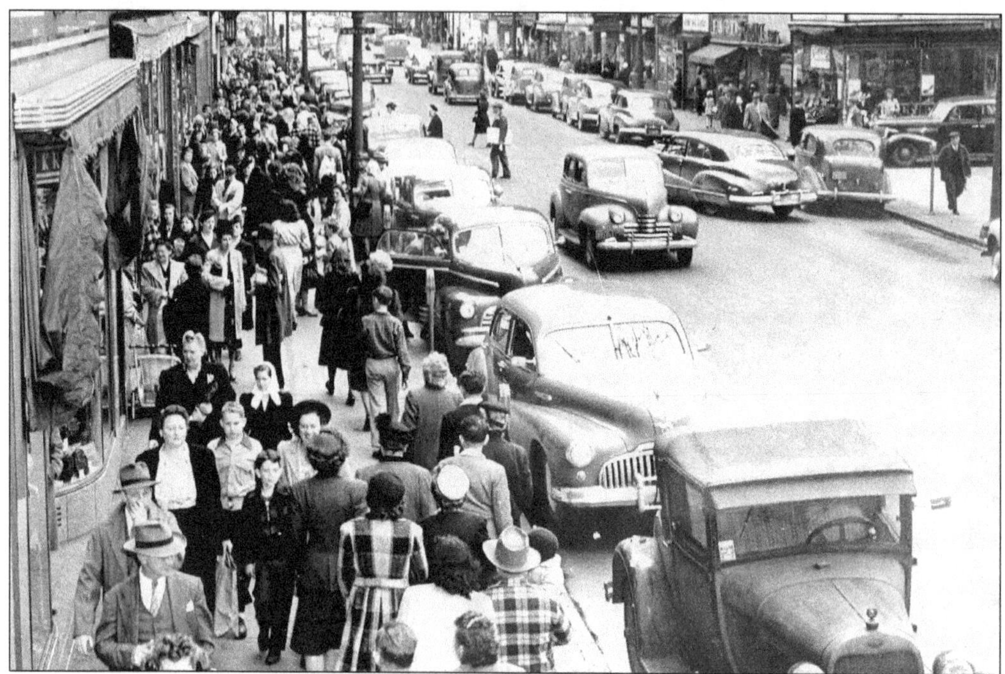

Easter shoppers are out in force in downtown Williamsport in March 1948. Ducking between raindrops, throngs of last-minute shoppers crowd the streets. Merchants reported one of their most successful sales seasons in years. This is a view of crowded Pine Street.

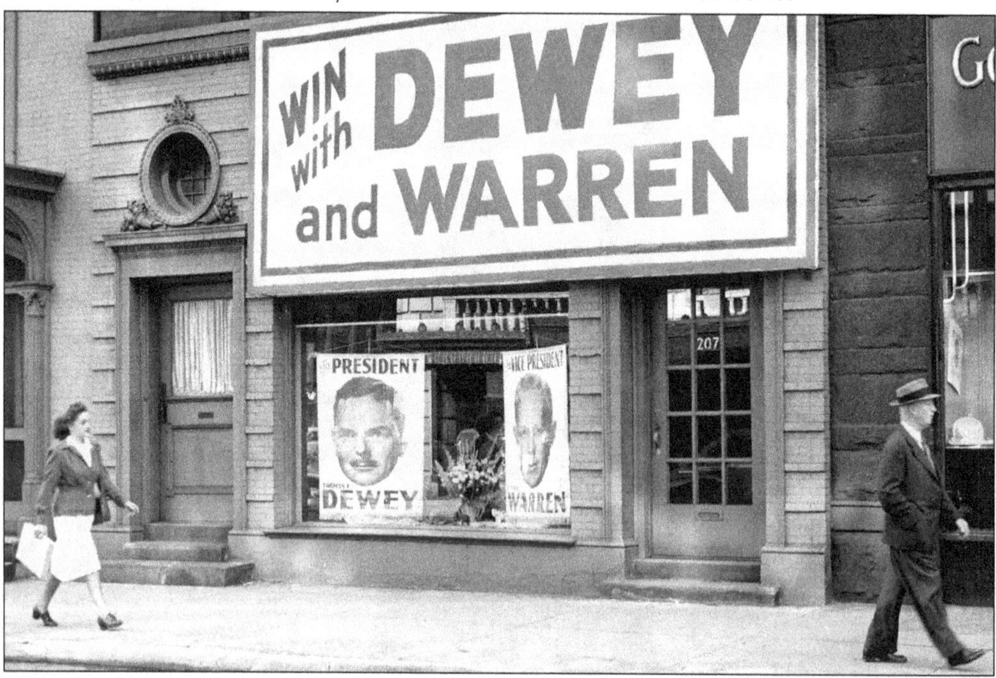

The second week of October 1948, special Dewey-Warren campaign headquarters were opened at 207 West Fourth Street by the Lycoming County Republican Committee. The Democratic Party had been in power for almost 16 years, and Alvin R. Bush Sr., the county chairman, and Frank R. Sharrar Jr., his assistant, were determined to turn the tide.

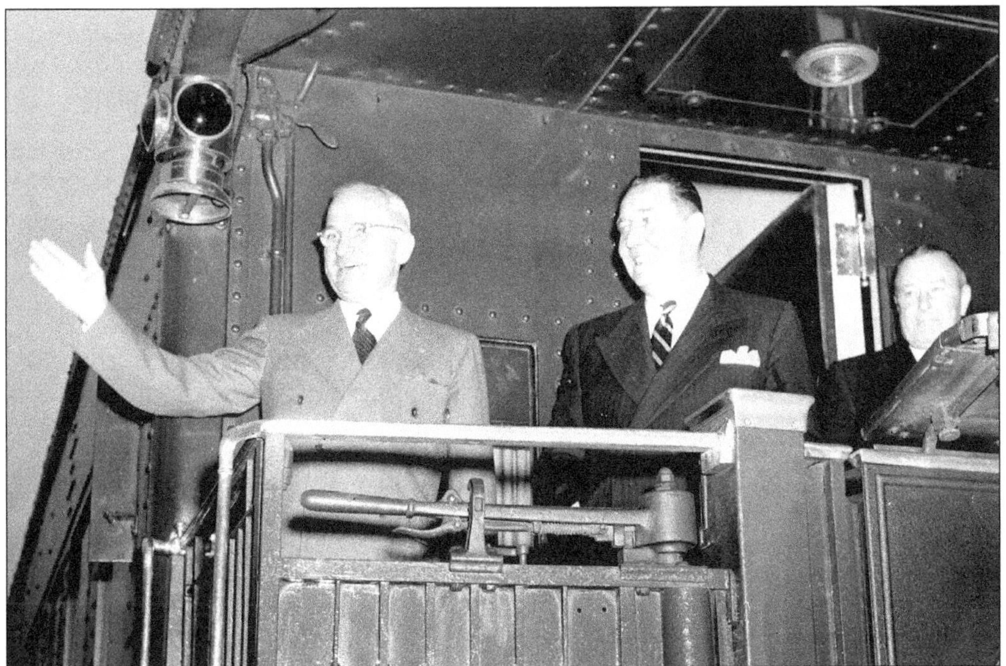

Pres. Harry S Truman waves to the throng of several hundred persons as his special train passes through Williamsport at noon on October 23, 1948, en route to Pittsburgh. With Truman was Sen. Francis J. Myers of Philadelphia. The train did not stop but passed slowly as it went through Williamsport.

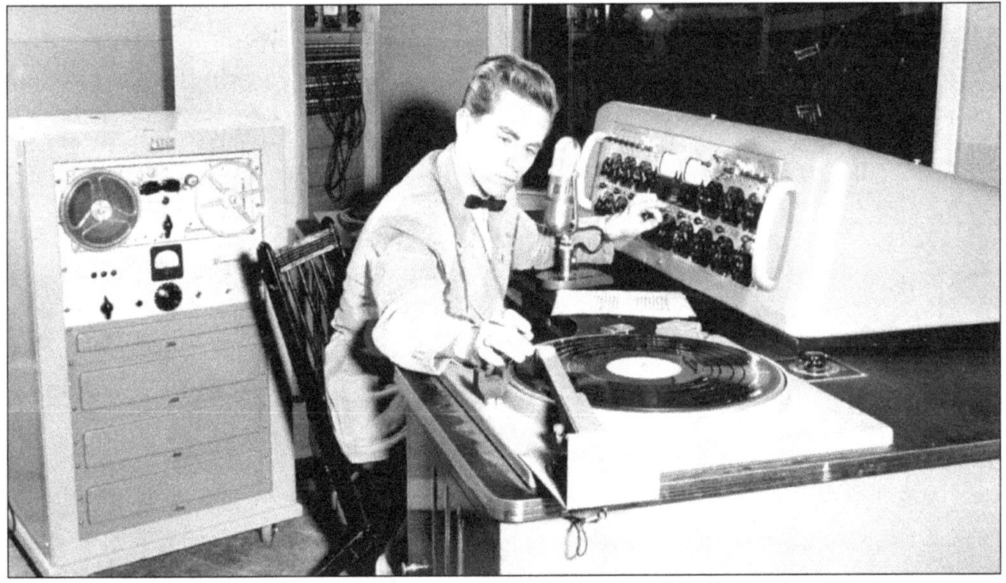

The radio station WWPA goes on the air in May 1949. It was then located at 330 Government Place. Tower facilities were in South Williamsport. Pictured here is announcer Michael Elsem operating a turntable. Radio was the lifeline for Americans in the 1940s, providing news, music, and entertainment much like television does today. Programming included soap operas, quiz shows, children's hours, mystery stories, fine drama, and sports. The U.S. government relied heavily on radio for propaganda.

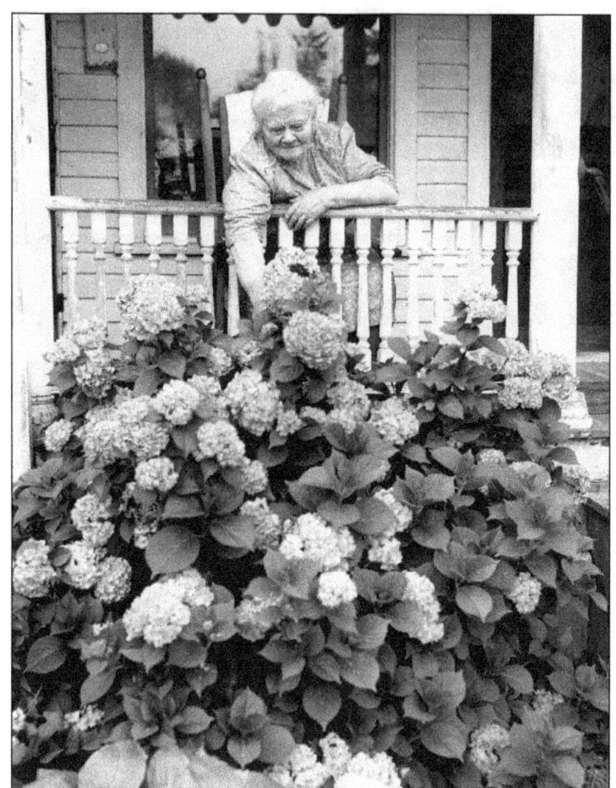

Life returned to normal after World War II, and the news of the day showcased people enjoying their lives. Here, Louise Keller of Williamsport counts 168 blooms on her giant hydrangea bush that she is mighty proud of. The bush was about 10 years old when this photograph was taken in July 1948.

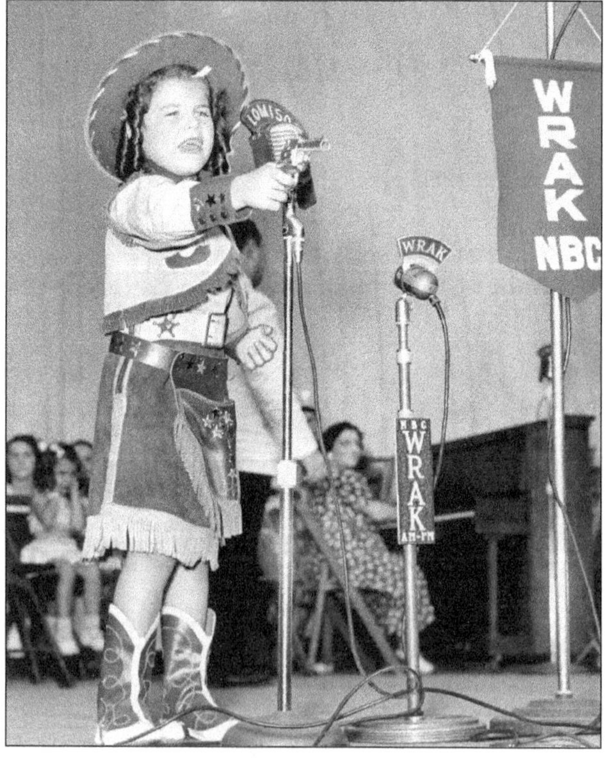

Diane Reifsnyder is seen here singing and illustrating her number "I Didn't Know the Gun Was Loaded" at the annual Kiddies Sing at the Brandon Park band shell in July 1949. Reifsnyder is now Diane Ellis and is city clerk for Williamsport.

Like conducting a great orchestra, directing city traffic involves alertness and ingrained training, and all Williamsport patrolmen took turns at intersections. Patrolman Sgt. Harold Hand halts traffic at William and West Fourth Streets in this October 16, 1949, photograph.

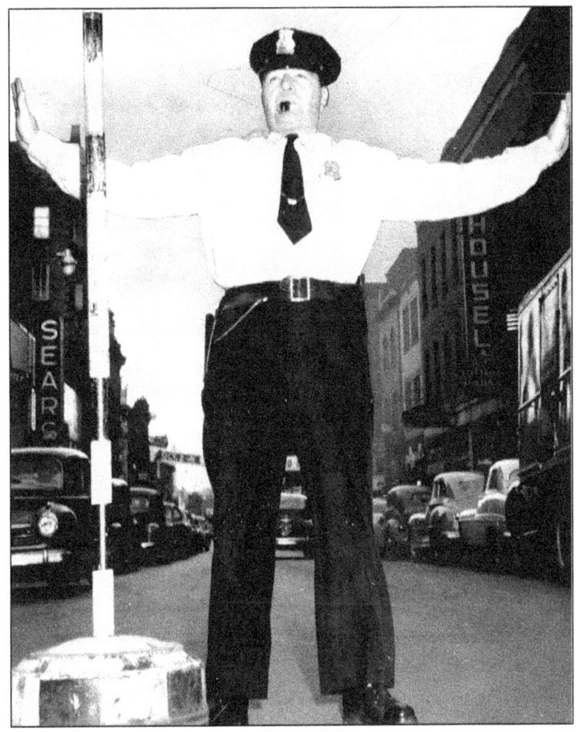

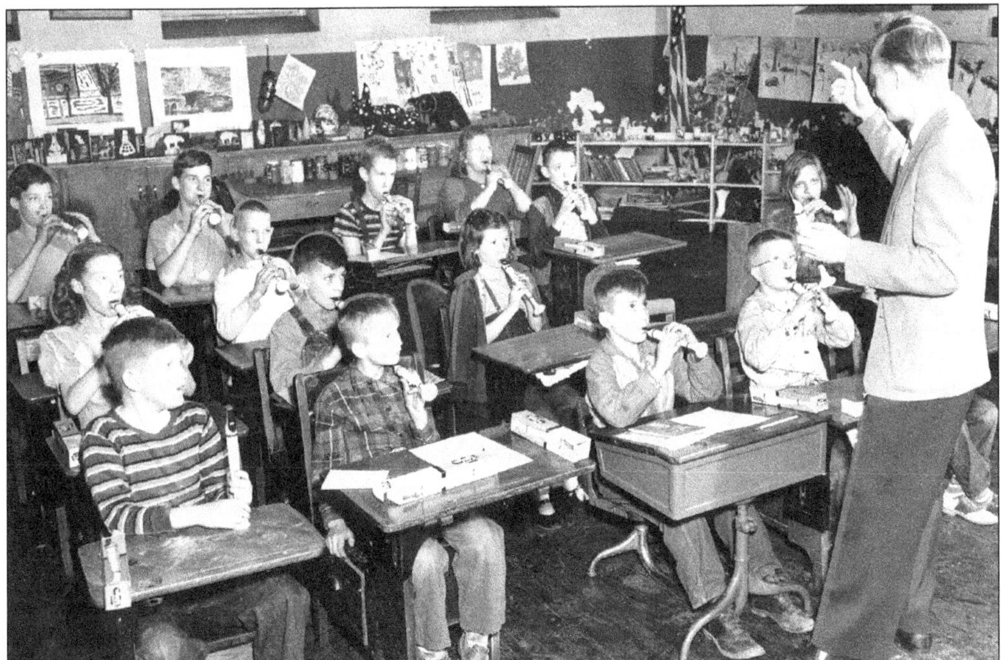

Music teacher Donald Freed supervises a class playing flutophones at the Jefferson Elementary School in April 1950. A flutophone looks much like a clarinet. The foot-long instrument has a small bell, a mouthpiece, and finger notes. Flutophones are still important in elementary schools today, where children are first introduced to music, learn first notes and playing techniques, and perform in assemblies.

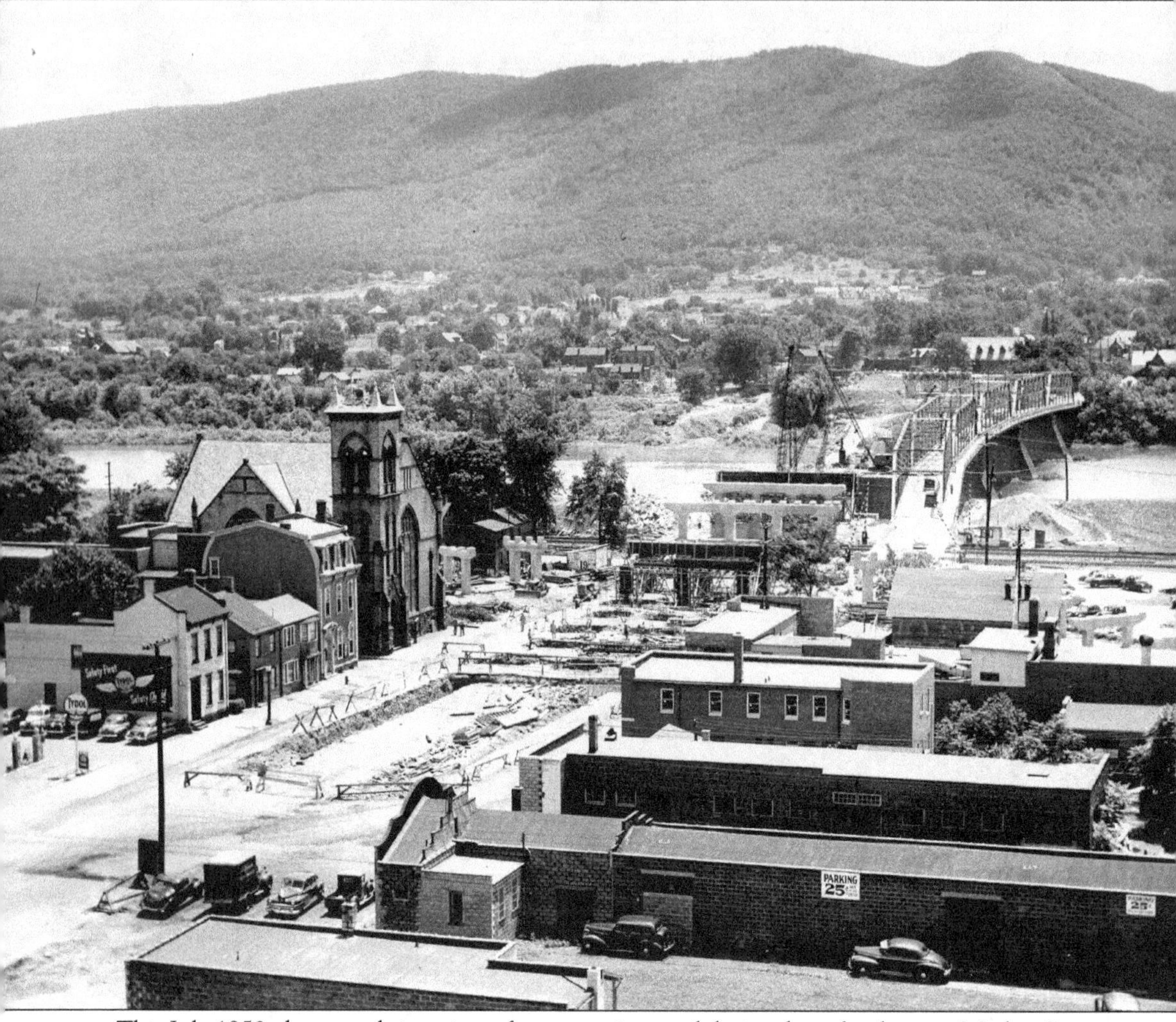

This July 1950 photograph is a view of construction work being done for the new Market Street Bridge, looking south from the former First National Bank on Third Street. The major route through Williamsport, the Market Street Bridge is slated for replacement beginning in 2004, with construction expected to last four years. The new bridge will include a direct connection to Interstate 180 on the Williamsport side of the Susquehanna River. Various strategies have been advanced to revitalize the downtown area; the most ambitious proposed a $72 million plan that would integrate a new Market Street Bridge with river front recreational facilities and possibly even a downtown civic arena. The proposal is still on the drawing board, so it remains to be seen if revitalization will work and if additional jobs and commerce will result.

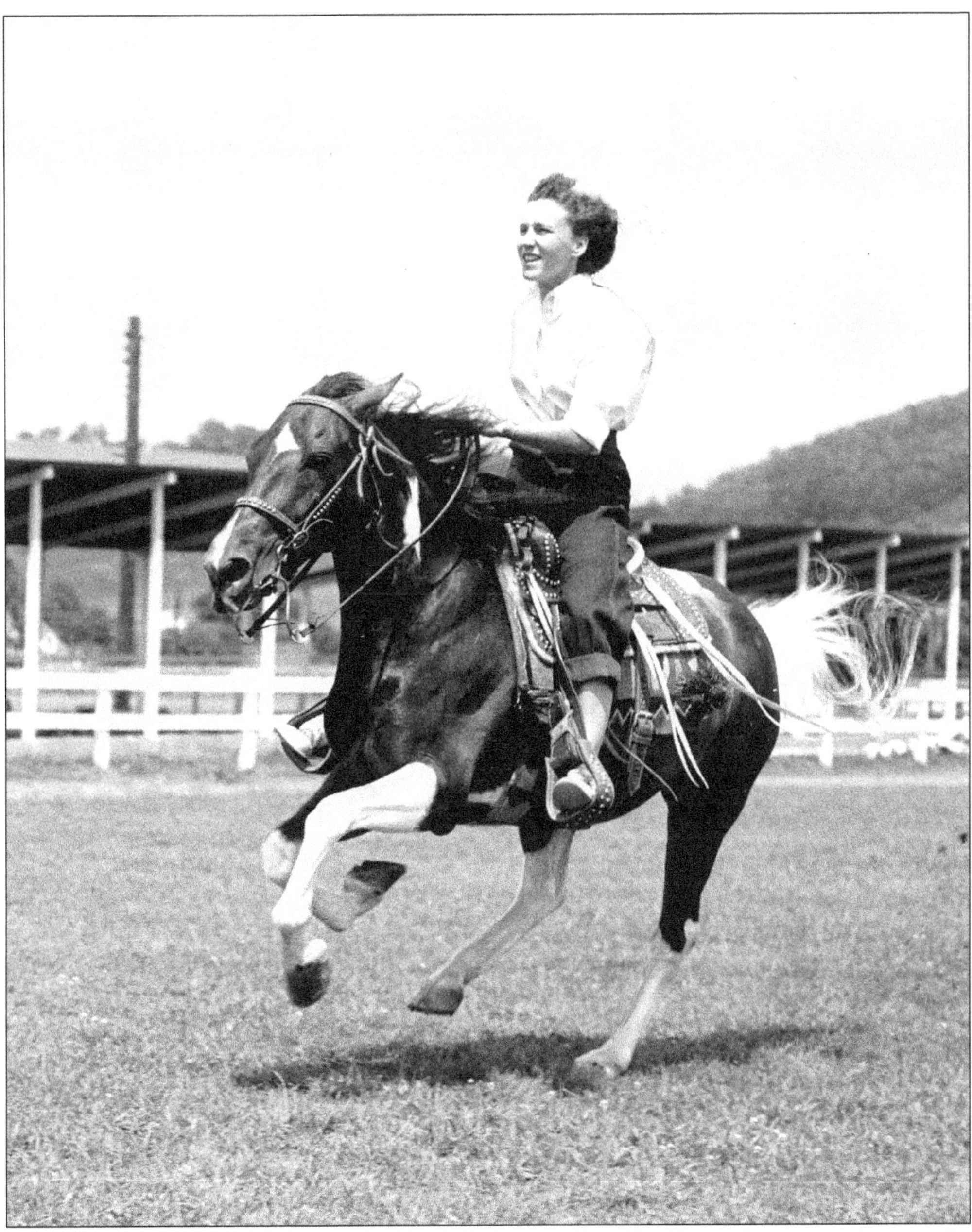

Rider Peggy Nittinger is seen here "opening the throttle" on her horse during preparations for the Susquehanna Riding Club's annual horse show to benefit Kiwanis Club charities in July 1950. Horseback riding still is a popular recreation in the Susquehanna Valley, and many events and shows are held at the Williamsport Riding Club on Poco Farm Road. Nittinger seems to be thrilled by the experience. She is riding Western, a style of riding born from the daily works of the cowboys chasing cattle. Today, the style is practiced not only in the United States but also has become a popular style worldwide. Western riding requires the smart movements necessary for chasing cattle, but because cowboys must also stay aboard their horse all day, it is a style that allows a person to ride for long periods of time, without tiring either the rider or the horse. It also is a style that allows the horse to move in its most natural form.

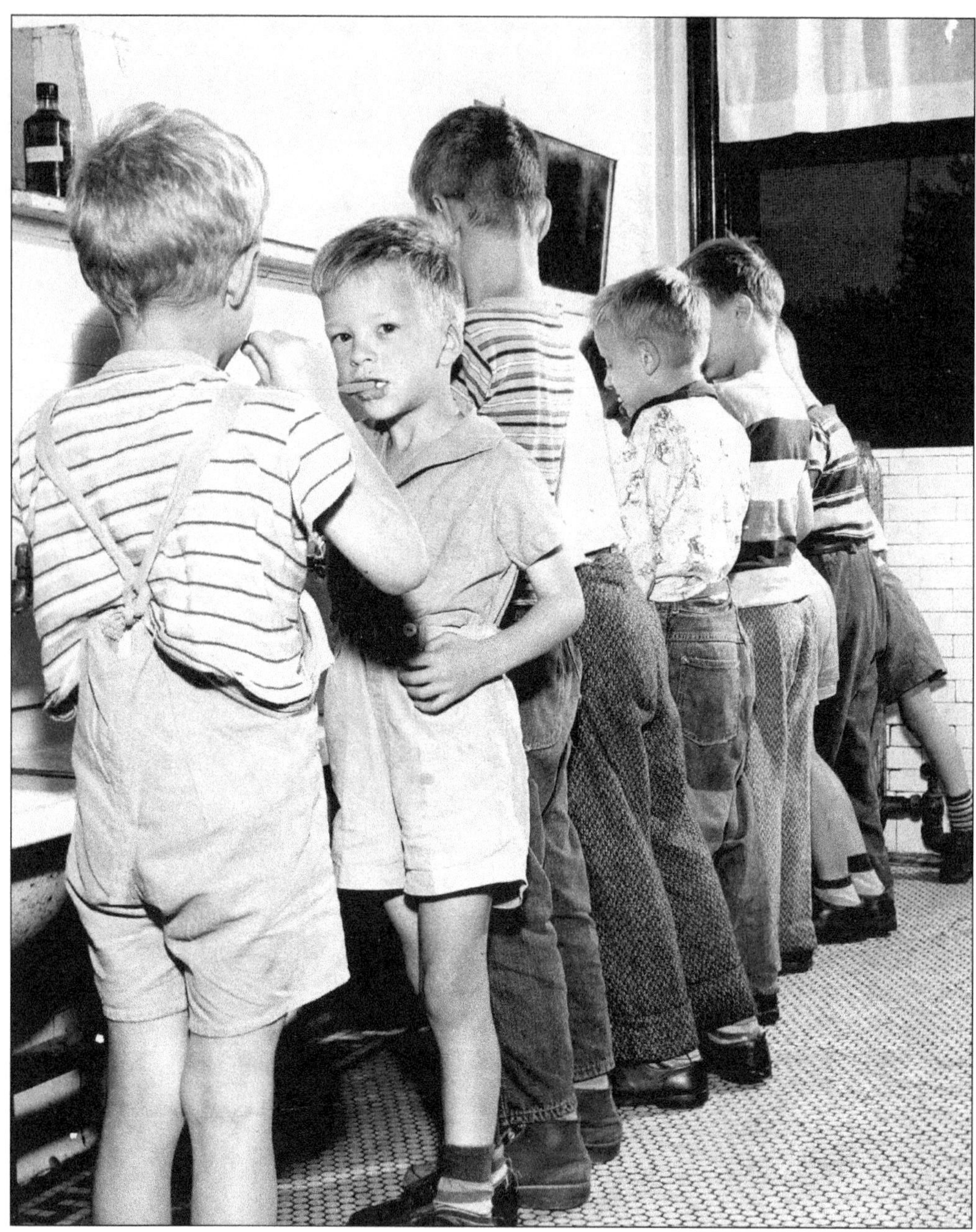

The morning routine included teeth-brushing sessions at the Williamsport Home for the Friendless in August 1950. The home later became the Williamsport Home and had both orphans and elderly women as residents. The home was funded through the Community Chest, the predecessor to the Lycoming United Way. The Williamsport Home first opened as the all-female Home for the Friendless in 1872. In the mid-1970s, the business, no longer an orphanage, moved to its current location at 1900 Ravine Road and began accepting male residents. It also features a new assisted-living wing that has given the retirement community a chance to further expand the level of care offered. The 1890s building that was the original home still sits on the northeast corner of Campbell Street and Rural Avenue and currently houses medical practices.

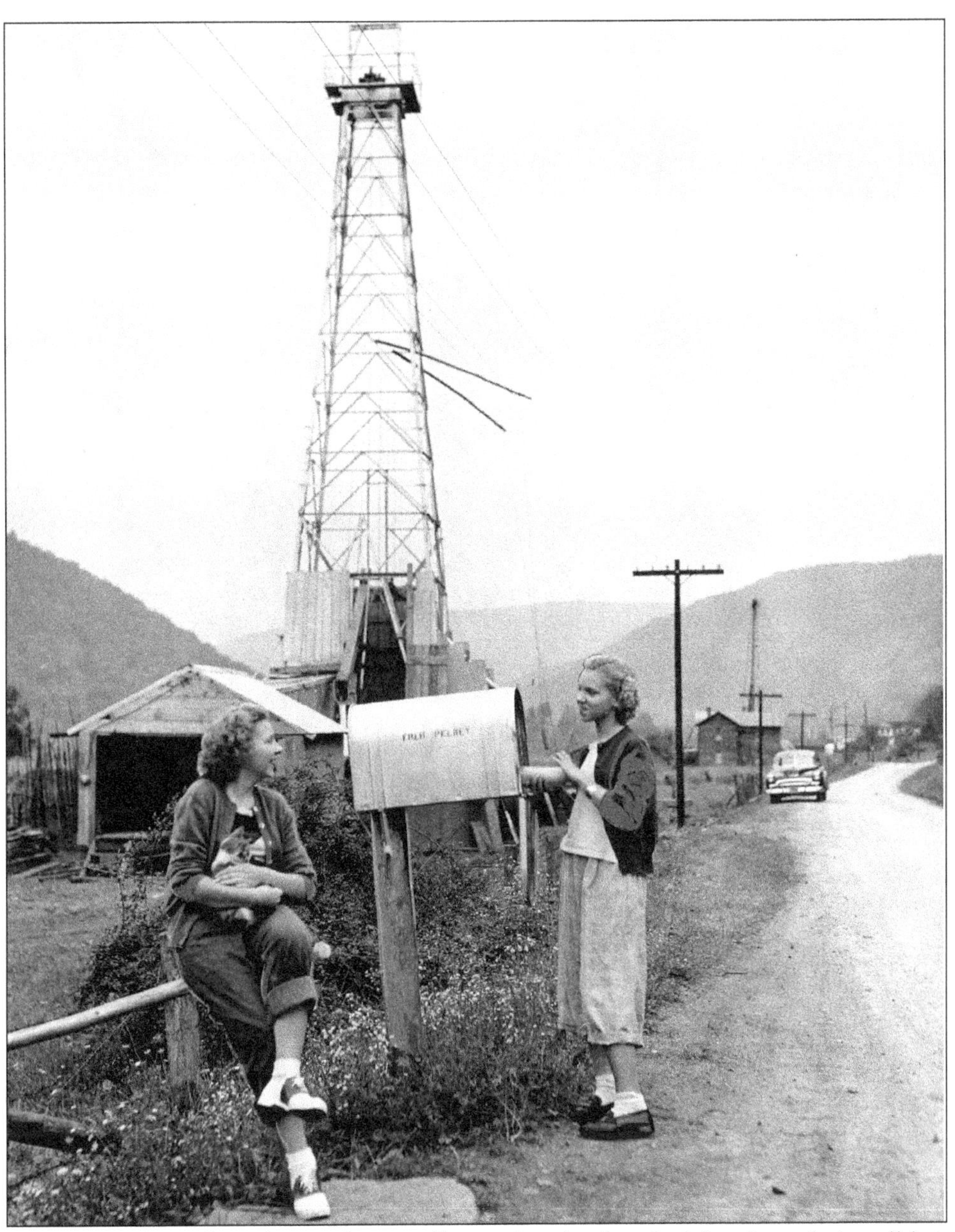

Lois and Dorothy Pelkey chat at their mailbox only a few hundred feet from their well being drilled by Noyley Development Company at the Leidy Natural Gas Field in October 1950. In 1920, the United Natural Gas Company developed Pennsylvania's first gas storage project. According to the Pennsylvania Department of Environmental Protection, gas was discovered at Leidy in 1950, which spurred new interest in drilling throughout the Appalachian basin. Set in 1951, the record for the largest gauged initial production of gas for both Pennsylvania and the Appalachian basin is held by the Finnefrock No. 1 well in the Leidy field. The well flowed from the Lower Devonian Ridgeley or Oriskany Sandstone at 6,339 feet. Actually, another well, Natural Gas No. 1 PA Tract 45 might have flowed more, but it caught fire and burned before it could be gauged. Famous well control expert Red Adair celebrated his 40th birthday snuffing that well fire.

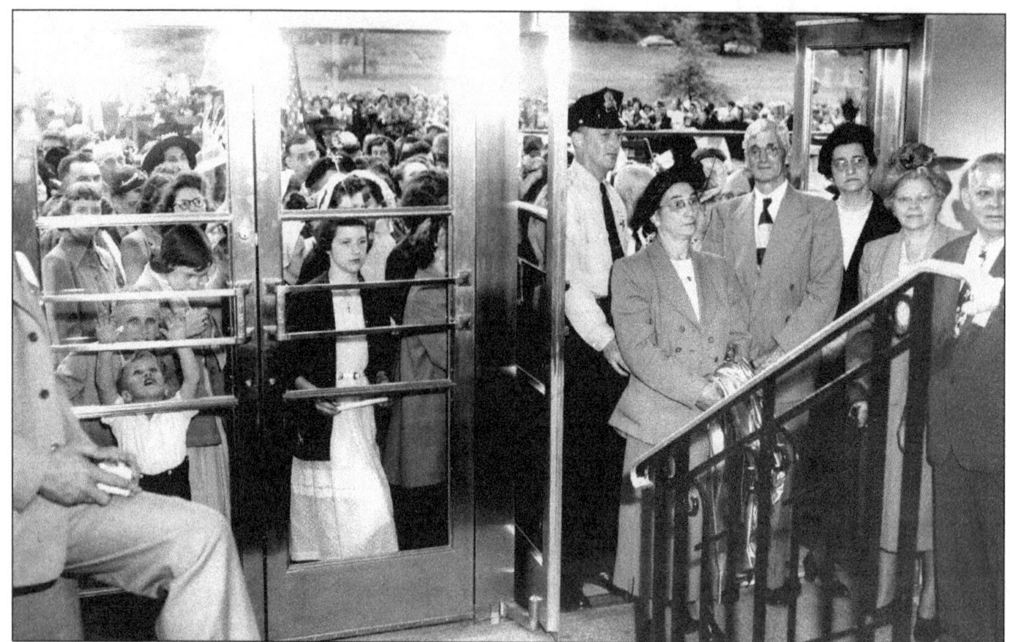

A baby boom in the region, as well as the nation, meant a demand for more health care services. A new hospital, Divine Providence Hospital, was viewed by more than 10,000 visitors during its open house on May 20 and 21, 1951. Divine Providence Hospital and Williamsport Hospital merged in 1994 to form the Susquehanna Health System.

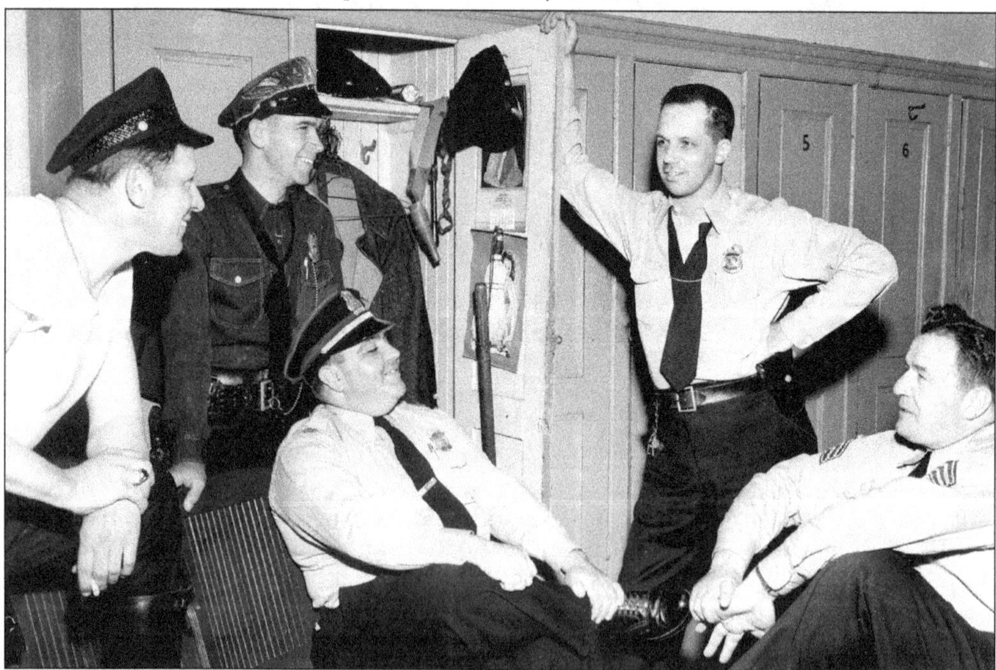

During a gab session in June 1951 in their locker room, Williamsport city policemen recall some of their irregular duties in service to the public. Pictured from left to right are Sgt. Harry Garman, Patrolman Leonard Ulmer, Capt. William Kinley, Patrolman William Polcyn, and Sgt. Harold Hand.

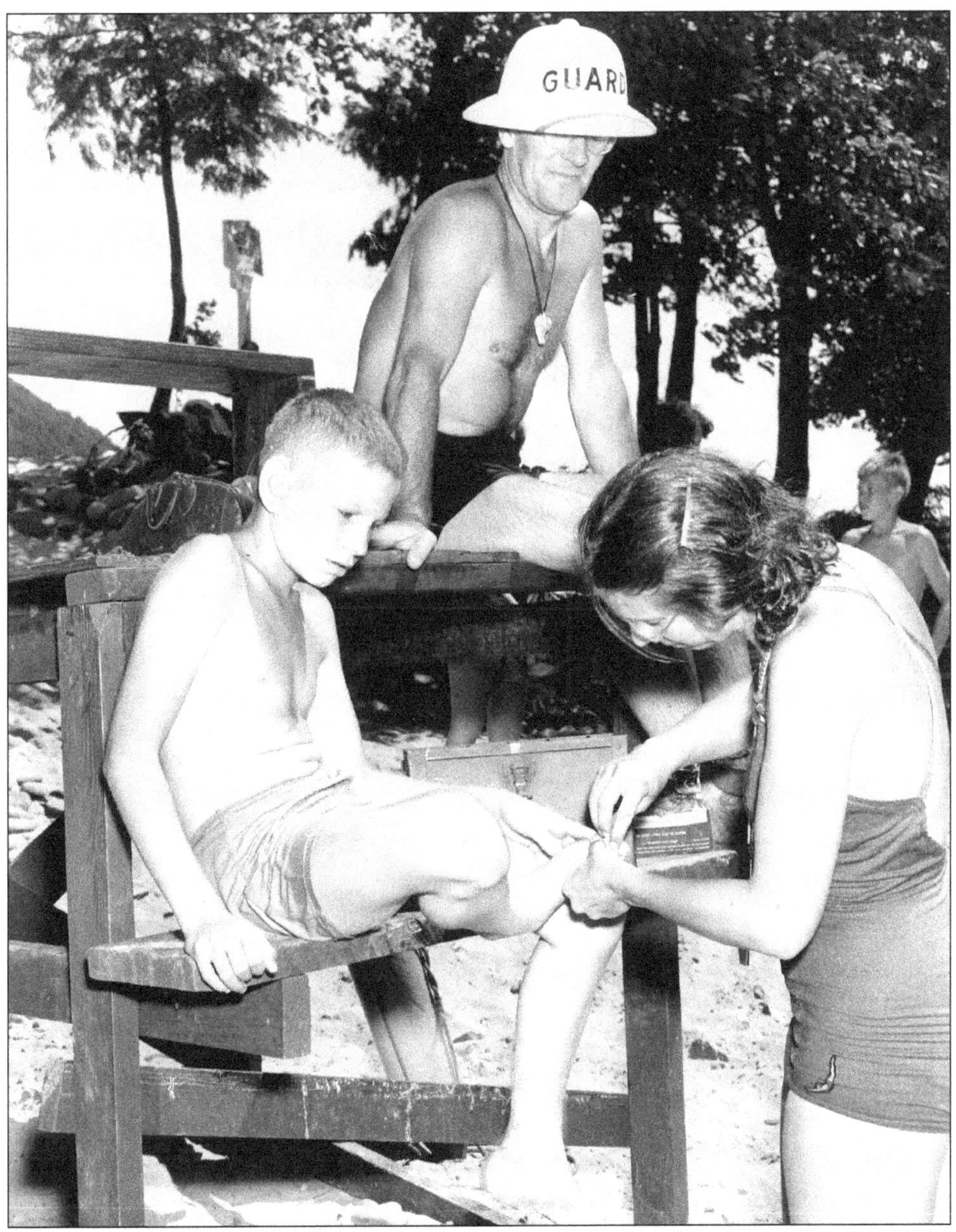

A woman gives first aid to a young boy under the watchful eye of a lifeguard at the Consolidated Sportsmen of Lycoming County's swimming beach along Loyalsock Creek. The club offered the use of its beach during the summer of 1951 after state and county health officials closed municipal beaches along Lycoming Creek. The Williamsport school board provided buses to transport children to the beach. It was part of the Williamsport Recreation Commission's A Day in the Country program. The "Club," as it often is called, is actually a nonprofit organization incorporated in the state of Pennsylvania and open to the public on a fee basis. The facilities are located along scenic Pennsylvania Route 87 North and the Loyalsock Creek about six miles north of Montoursville. It includes areas for archery, various shooting disciplines, camping, hiking, and swimming and is used by the local Little League for baseball along with other groups.

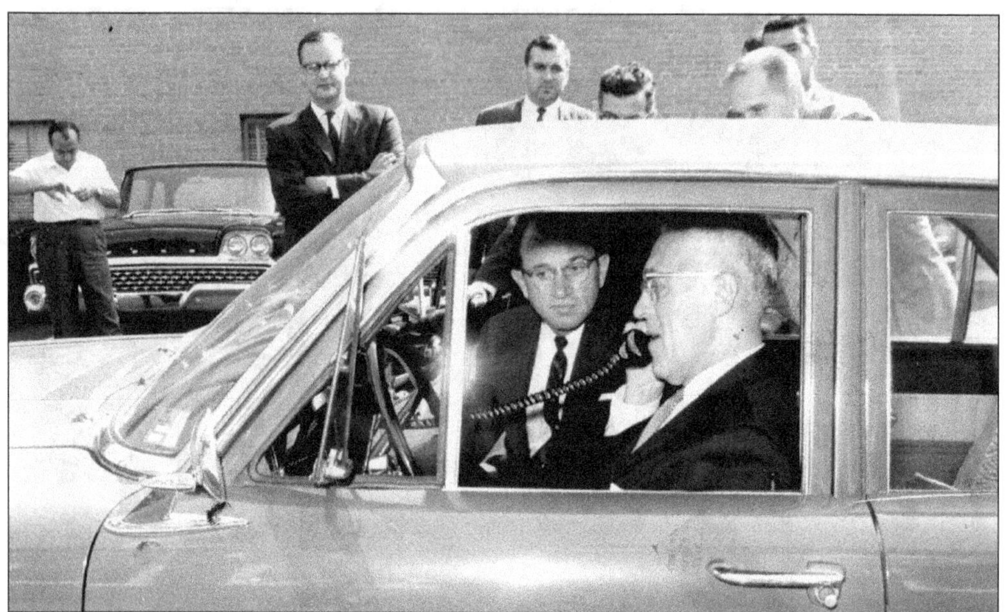

To introduce urban radiotelephone service in Williamsport, Curtis D. Thomas, city banker and president of the Greater Williamsport Chamber of Commerce, places a telephone call on September 9, 1951, from an automobile at the corner of West Fourth and Elmira Streets. The calling equipment was mounted on the car's dashboard, and the transmitter was in the trunk. All a caller had to do was depress a button on the receiver and tell the operator the number of his car telephone and the number he wanted to call. Looking on is C. A. Welliver, local manager of the Bell Telephone Company.

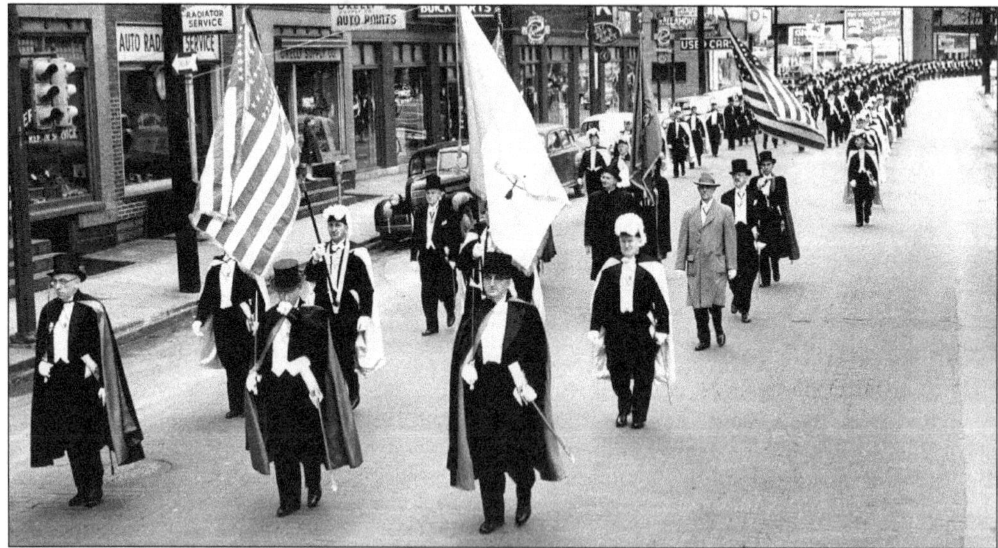

Members of the Williamsport Knights of Columbus Fourth Degree Team march east on West Third Street on April 19, 1953, after attending benediction services at the Church of the Annunciation. More than 200 Williamsport area men took the top degree of the Knights of Columbus. The local council has a long and enduring history of serving the Catholic community. It was first chartered in September 1898, 16 years after the Reverend Michael J. McGivney founded the order in New Haven, Connecticut.

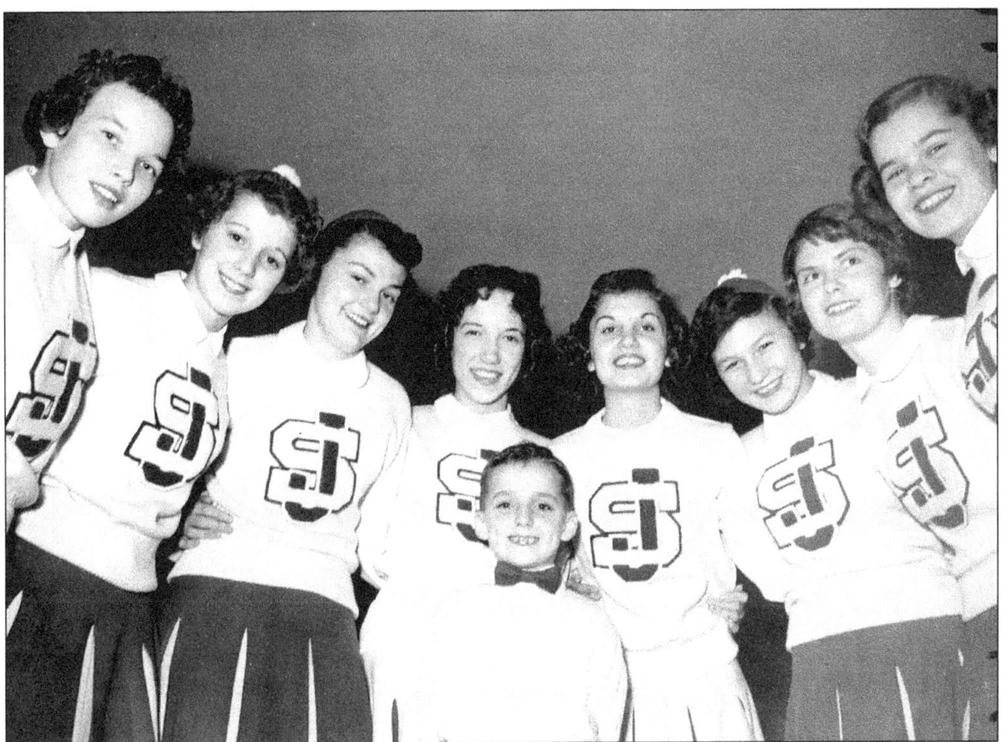

Cheerleaders of St. Joseph High School prepare for a full house at the Williamsport High gym for a basketball game between St. Joe's and St. Mary's in January 1954. Cheerleaders, from left to right, are Susan Beck, Andrea Hugar, Yovanne Smith, Pat Heindl, Helen Eveleth, Mary Guthrie, Rosemary Gallagher, and Silvia Williams. In front is Tommie O'Connor.

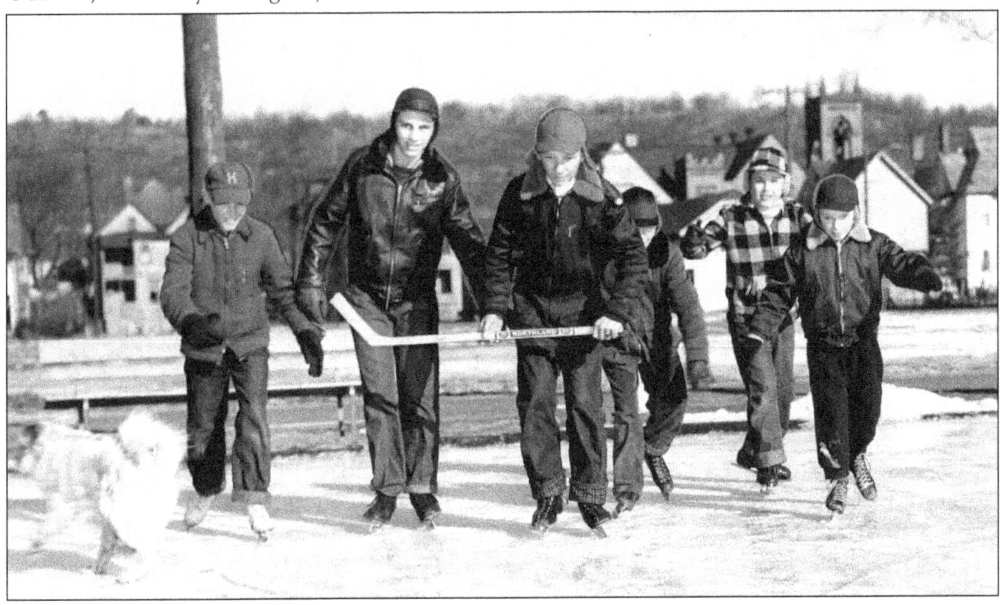

These boys take to the ice at the old Jackson Playground in the west end of Williamsport in January 1954. They took advantage of a cold spell to play ice hockey on the ice rink. Ice-skaters also enthusiastically utilized rinks at the Penn Street armory and other locations in the area.

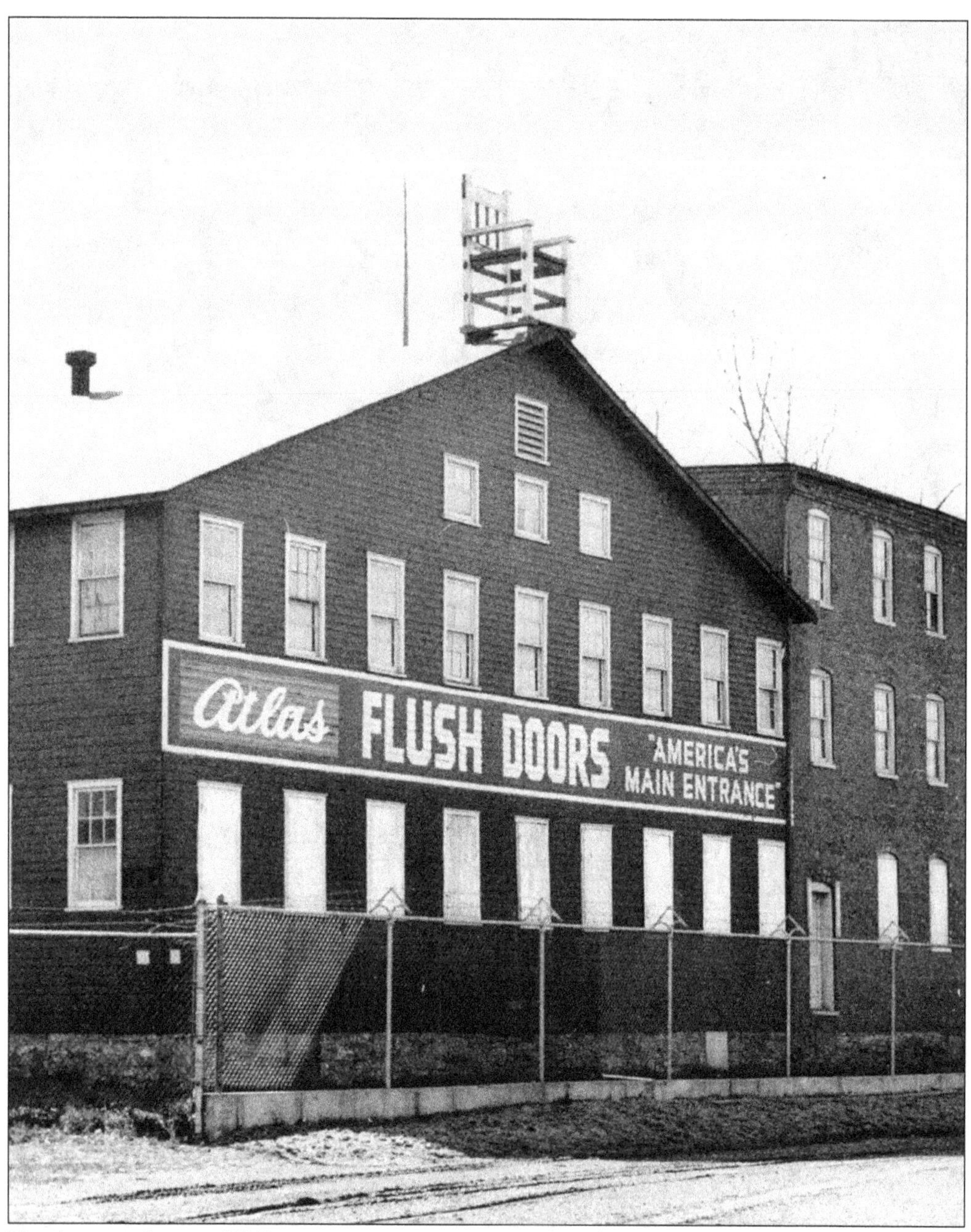

The biggest chair in Williamsport sat at one time atop the Atlas Plywood Company at 200 Susquehanna Street. The former Culler Furniture Company, which occupied the building located just south of the Williamsport High School athletic field, built the chair. The Culler Furniture Company was formed in 1892, and the chair was built shortly before that time. Sports fans vividly recall when the immortal Babe Ruth hit a home run over the chair during an exhibition game in Williamsport on October 31, 1923. Babe Ruth was once again associated with Williamsport when the Babe Ruth Birthplace and Museum's traveling exhibit visited major- and minor-league cities during the 2003 baseball season. In addition to stops at the Field of Dreams in Dyersville, Iowa, the exhibit was featured at the Peter J. McGovern Little League Baseball Museum during the 2003 Little League Baseball World Series in Williamsport.

Five-year-old Glen Rafe watches the South Williamsport Mummer's parade from inside his father's coat in October 1954. More than 10,000 spectators jammed the streets to view the parade. It took five hours to complete the parade that featured floats, high school bands, trick-or-treaters, and vendors.

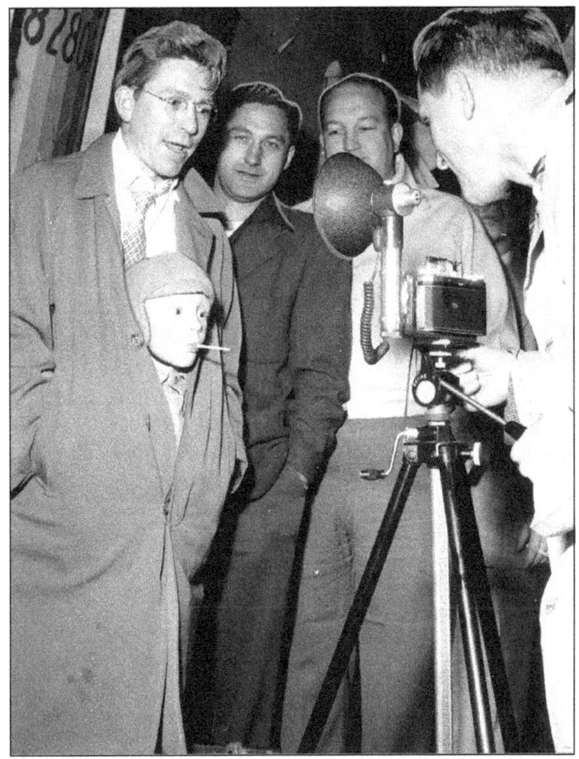

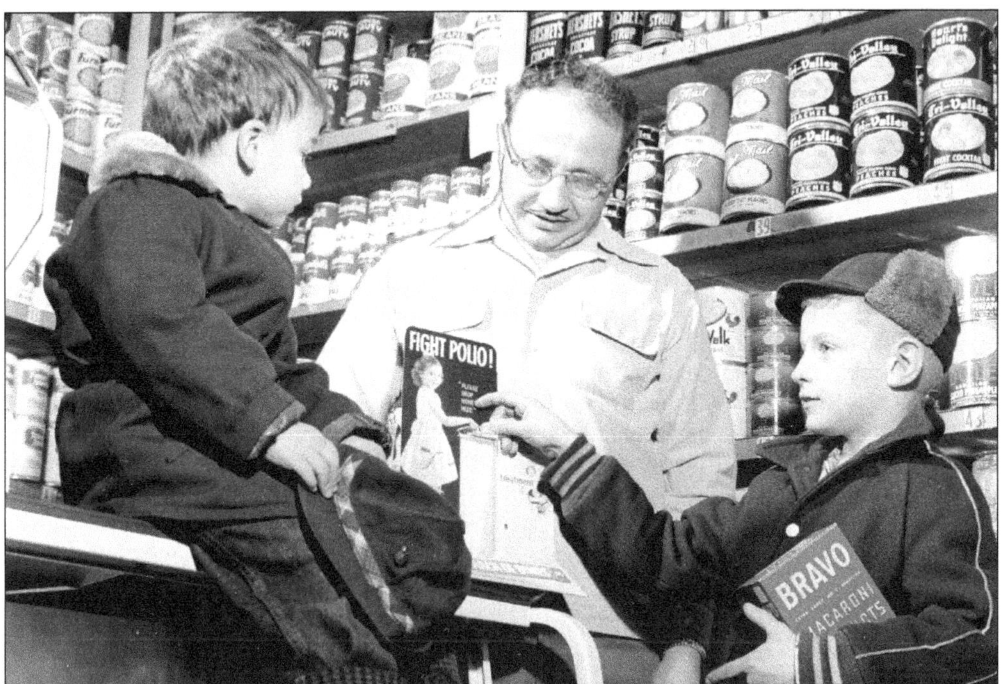

Grocer Albert Rosata of 628 East Third Street watches two youngsters who never forget the March of Dimes polio drive on their visits to his store. Ricky Lee, left, watches Charles Lynch make a contribution on January 16, 1955. Charles always put his change in the container.

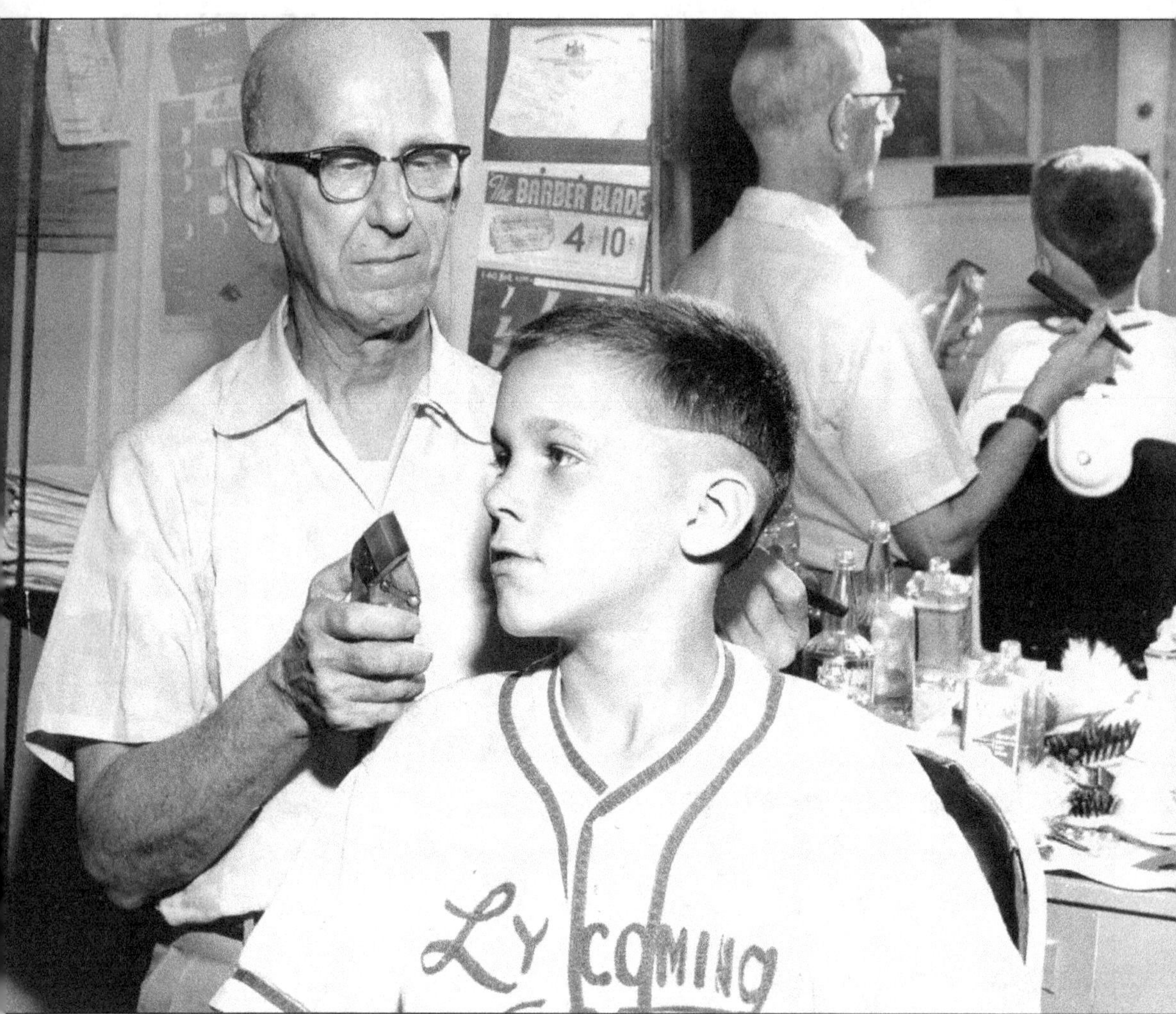

As part of the short-lived Davy Crockett craze of 1955, 10-year-old Harold Mauer Jr. of the Lycoming Dairy Little League Baseball team got a Davy Crockett haircut from barber John Kinn of 679 Wildwood Boulevard, Williamsport, but not until the boy had an OK note from Mauer's father. The hair style emphasized the Davy Crockett coonskin hat style with a tail down the back. The nation's excitement over Crockett began in December 1954, just days after ABC broadcast *Davy Crockett, Indian Fighter*, starring Fess Parker. After the Walt Disney movie was released, the coonskin cap headgear worn by Parker became the most popular item among the Davy Crockett product line, which netted $100 million. The caps were very popular with young boys, but many adults, including presidential candidate Sen. Estes Kefauver, joined in the craze, wearing them at numerous public appearances. After a shortage in raccoon tails caused people to turn to using muskrat, rabbit, and fox tails, the fad died out by December 1955.

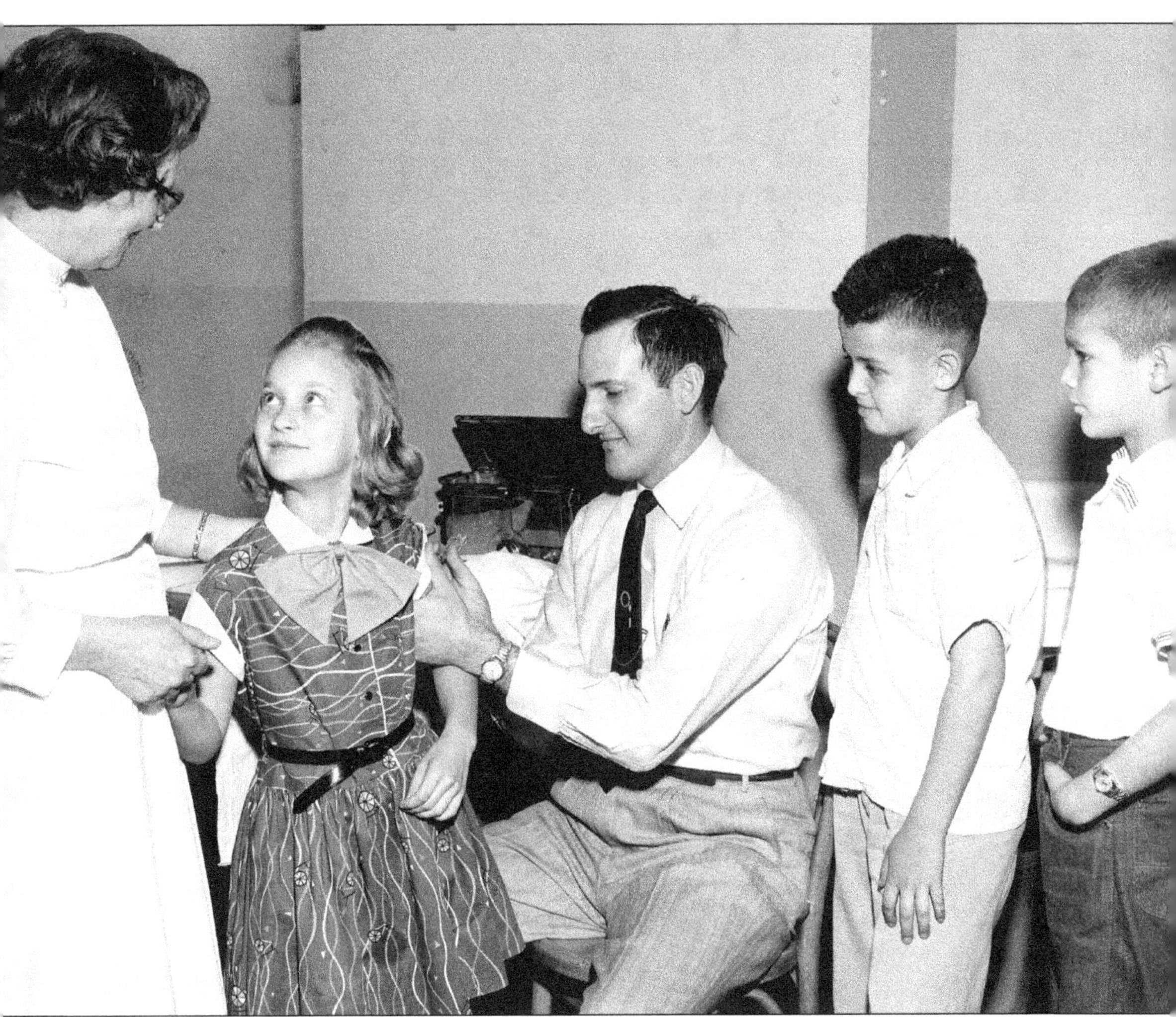

City schoolchildren receive Salk antipolio inoculations, the wonder-drug treatment supplied free to all schoolchildren by the National Foundation for Infantile Paralysis. Given in a series of two free shots (spring and fall), the first shots were given between April and June 1955 to 4,083 first and second graders. At the Jackson School, from left to right, are nurse Dorothy Ray Singley, Kay Jones, Dr. Warren Hayes, Adam Campone, and Ray McKee. It was at the University of Pittsburgh's Virus Research Lab that the bulk of the work in research was carried out and the vaccine initially was produced. Dr. Jonas Salk had 81 million dimes contributed by the National Foundation for Infantile Paralysis to spend on the vaccine. This was part of the three billion dimes subscribed by the public to the national foundation. In order to vaccinate the million children as proposed in the 1954 tests, it was necessary to hand over the manufacture of the Salk vaccine to five pharmaceutical firms: Parke Davis & Company in Detroit, Pitman-Moore and Eli Lilly & Company in Indianapolis, Wyeth in Philadelphia, and the Cutter Laboratories in Berkeley, California.

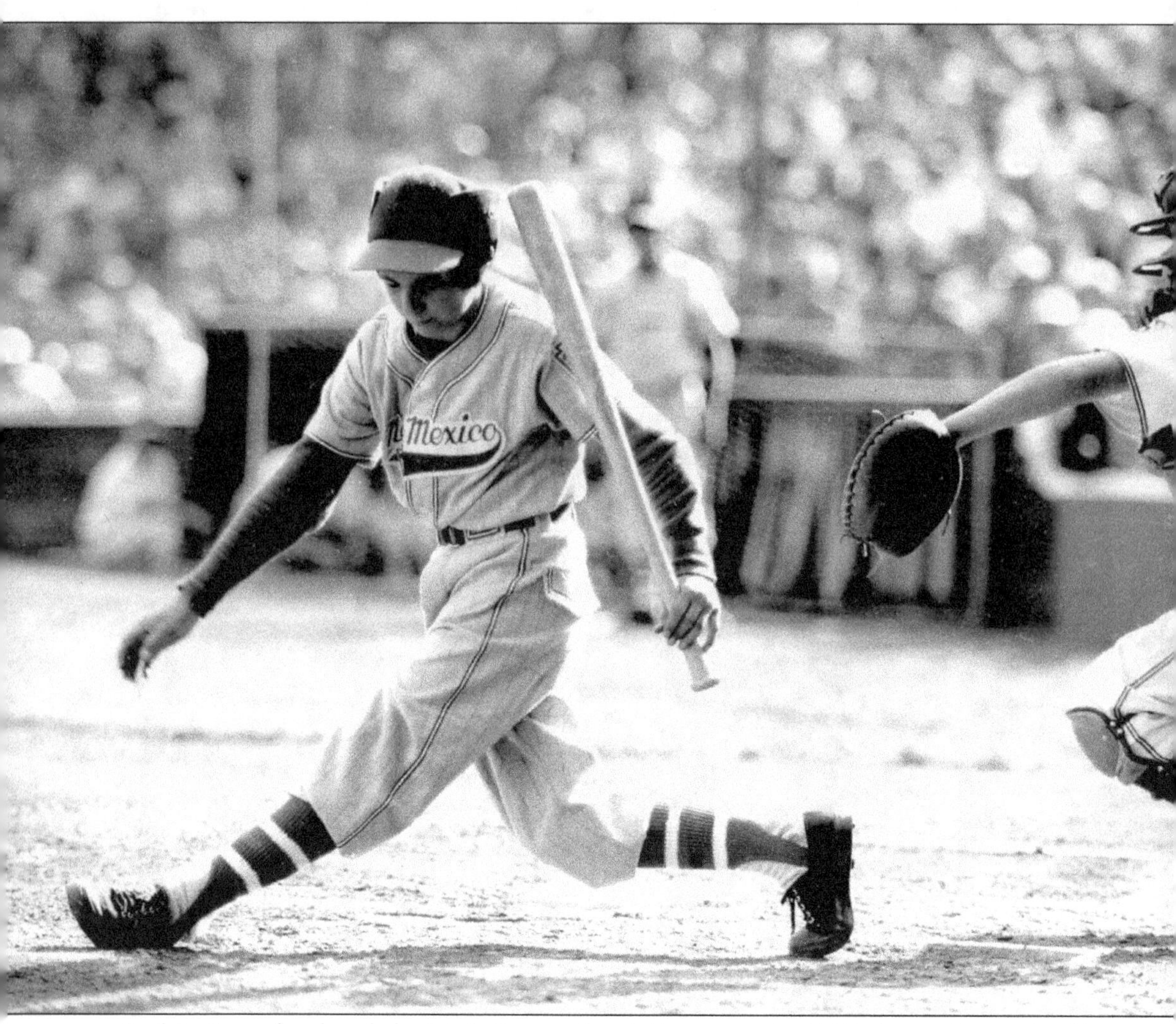

Carl E. Stotz developed the Little League Baseball program in 1939. Stotz, George Bebble, and Bert Bebble were the first three managers after a $30 donation sufficient to purchase uniforms for each of the first three teams was made. The teams were named after their sponsors: Lycoming Dairy, Lundy Lumber, and Jumbo Pretzel. The first season was played in a vacant lot near the outfield fence of Bowman Field. Soon, the program became a popular form of recreation, and each year, beginning in 1947, thousands of people began making pilgrimages to the small mountainous region of Williamsport to watch young children play baseball during the Little League Baseball World Series. Millions more people watched the games on television. An international pastime, Little League is found in places such as Bosnia and Herzegovina, South Africa, Taiwan, Australia, Venezuela, Israel, and all 50 U.S. states. Here, a member of the New Mexico team swings at a pitch in the 1956 Little League Baseball World Series.

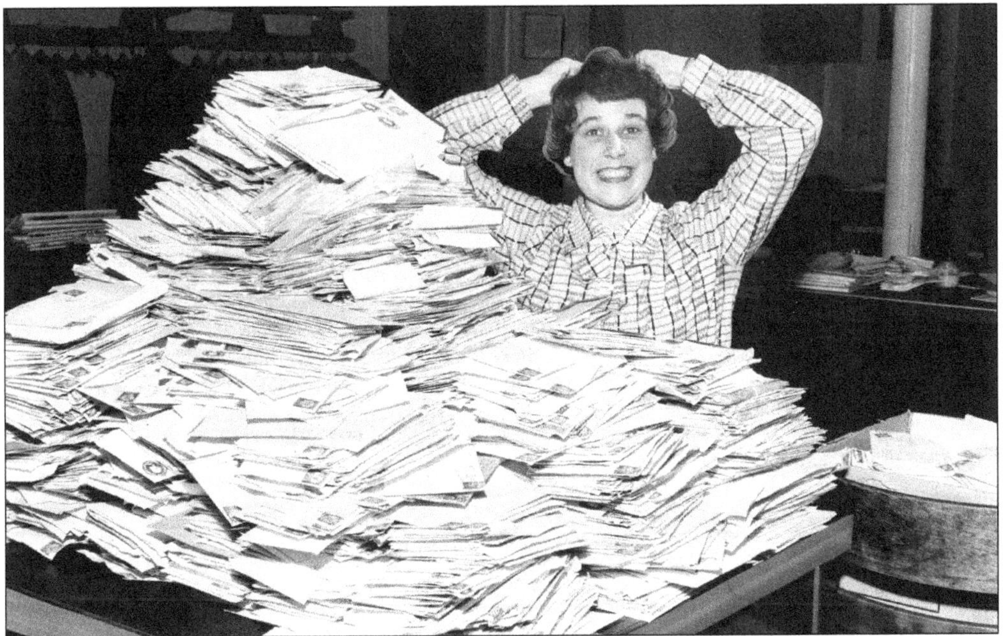

Ready to tear out her hair, Norma Bower, a *Grit* editorial department secretary, is swamped by mail from readers in answer to one of the *Grit*'s popular contests. An avalanche of letters in response to a valentine coloring contest in 1956 yielded more than 13,000 entries.

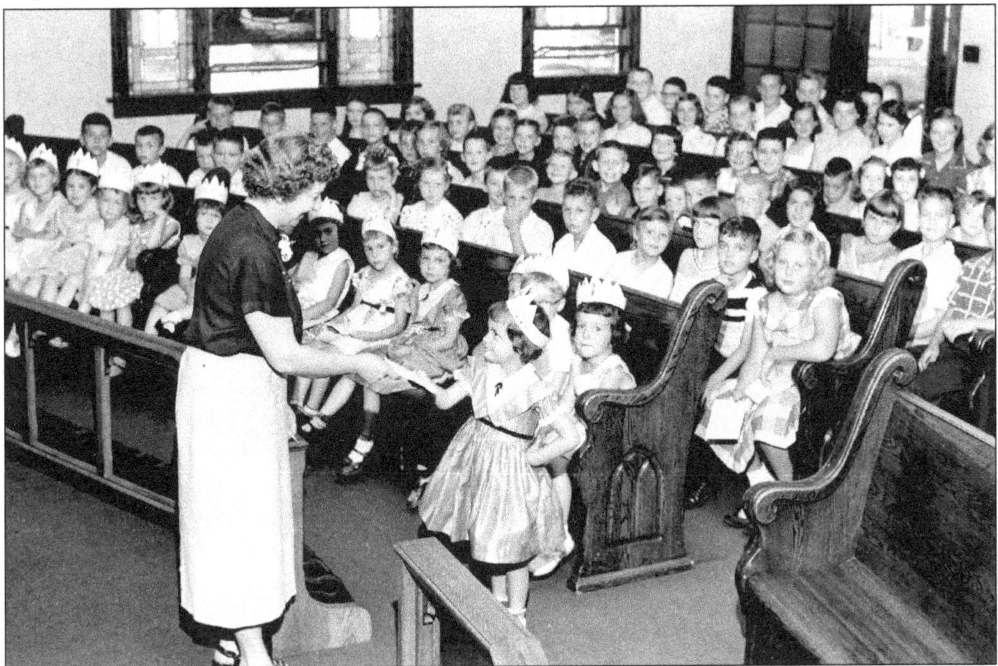

Youngsters receive attendance certificates at the final Bible school exercises at Grace Evangelical United Brethren Church in South Williamsport in July 1956. In an intensive week of summer Bible school, children receive more biblical teaching than they would in months of Sunday school. The theme is universal; Bible schools often use crafts and music as well as athletics to teach children moral lessons.

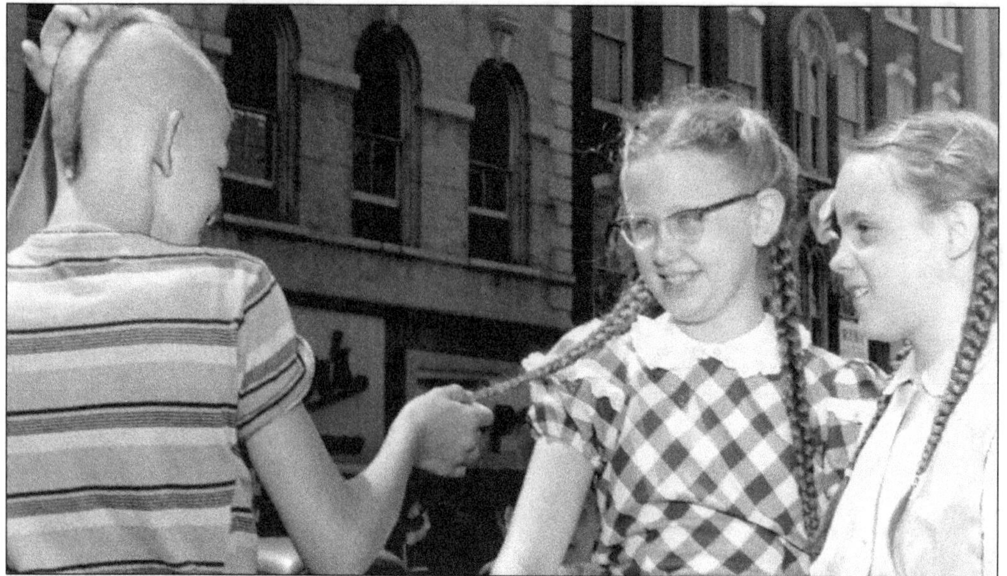

Who could resist snapping a photograph when this young man with a Mohawk haircut mingled with two contestants in a ponytail contest held in conjunction with Williamsport's sesquicentennial celebration in July 1956. Pictured here are Raymond Nittinger, Hope Webster, and Judy Stewart.

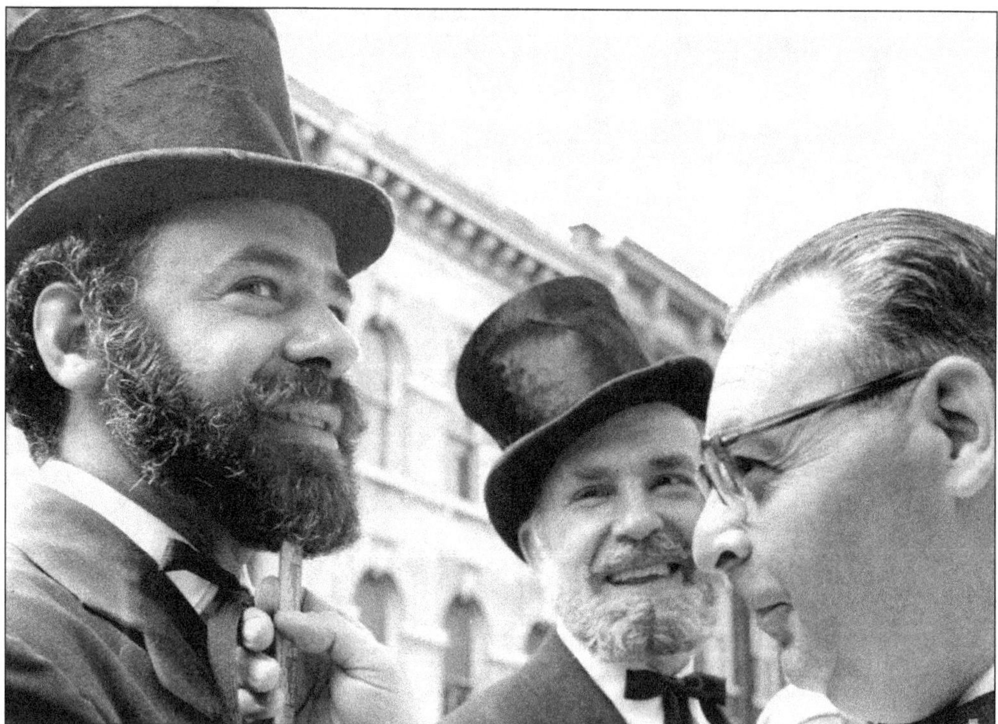

A laughing Sammy Ray has his beard measured by barber John Rhea during Williamsport's sesquicentennial celebration in July 1956. The sesquicentennial featured a beard contest, Lycorama, a pageant celebrating Williamsport's historic past, and a mammoth parade through the downtown that drew more than 80,000 spectators.

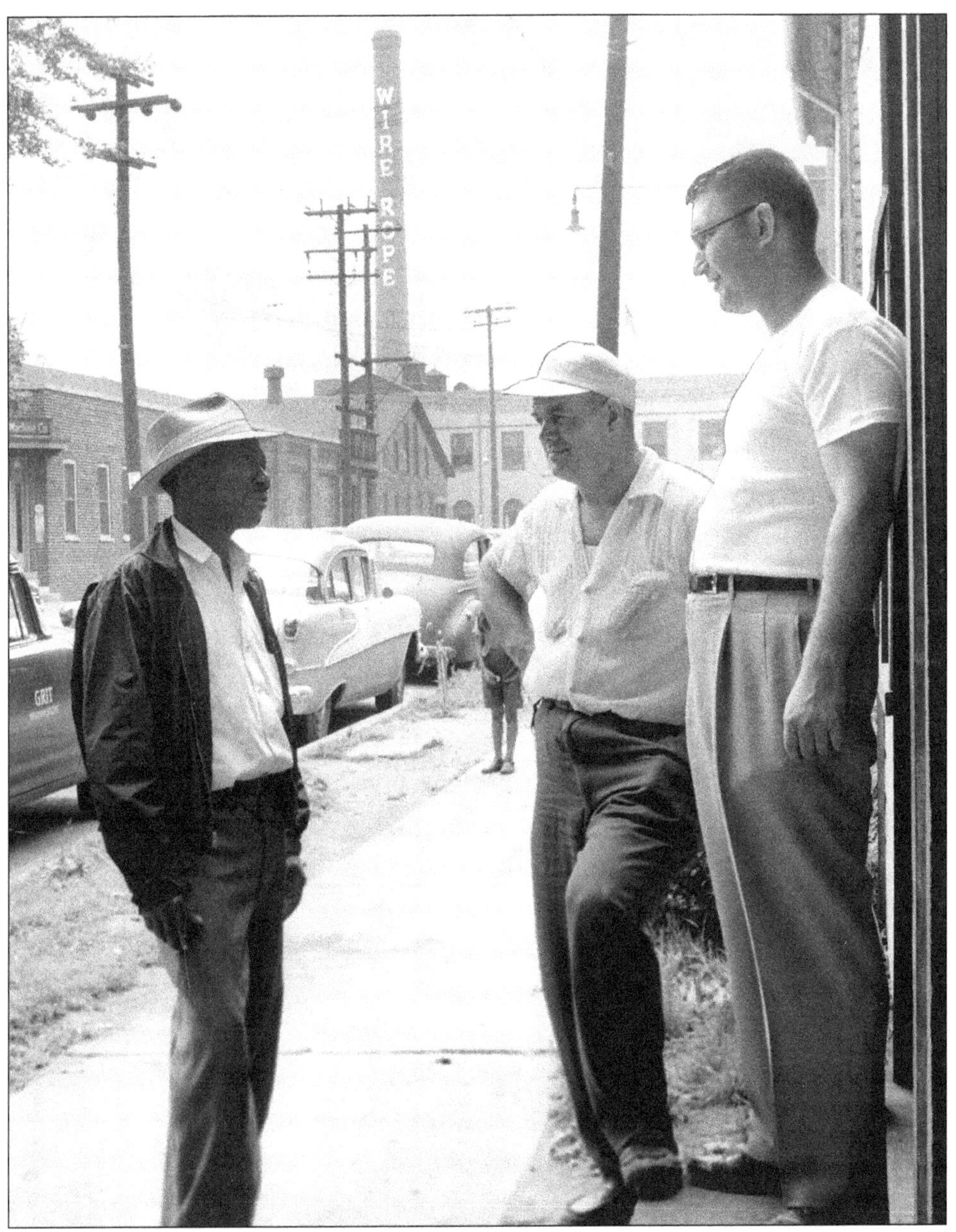

These Bethlehem Steel workers are shown outside their plant waiting for a contract to be ratified in July 1956, before returning to work. About 900 Bethlehem Steel and 300 Jones and Laughlin steelworkers were idled by a three-week strike. After the acknowledgment of the United Steelworkers Union in 1941, there was a pattern of a labor strikes after the expiration of each three-year contract. Each time, the company granted substantial wage increases, and substantial steel price increases followed. Employment costs increased at a rate of 8 percent per year until American steelworkers were the highest paid industrial workers worldwide (America: $3.03 hourly, Europe: $0.95 hourly, and Japan: $0.40 hourly) in 1958. The contract agreed upon in 1956 contained a new element, Clause 2B, which stated that "established labor practices cannot be changed unless there is a change in underlying conditions." This addition haunted the company in future years.

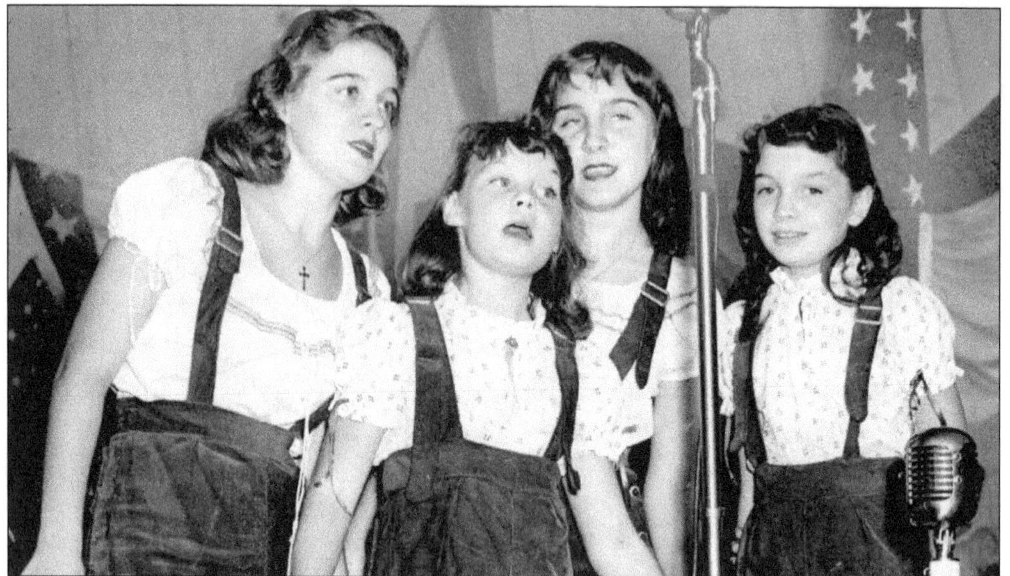

The 1940s were a golden time for vocal groups who served as backup voices for the era's various big bands. There were the Modernaires, the Pied Pipers, and the Andrews Sisters, who were an attraction on their own. Williamsport's counterparts to these vocalists were the Brownlee Sisters. Here, the group performs in August 1946 at the annual Kiddies Sing. The sisters later went on stage with Tommy Dorsey's big band.

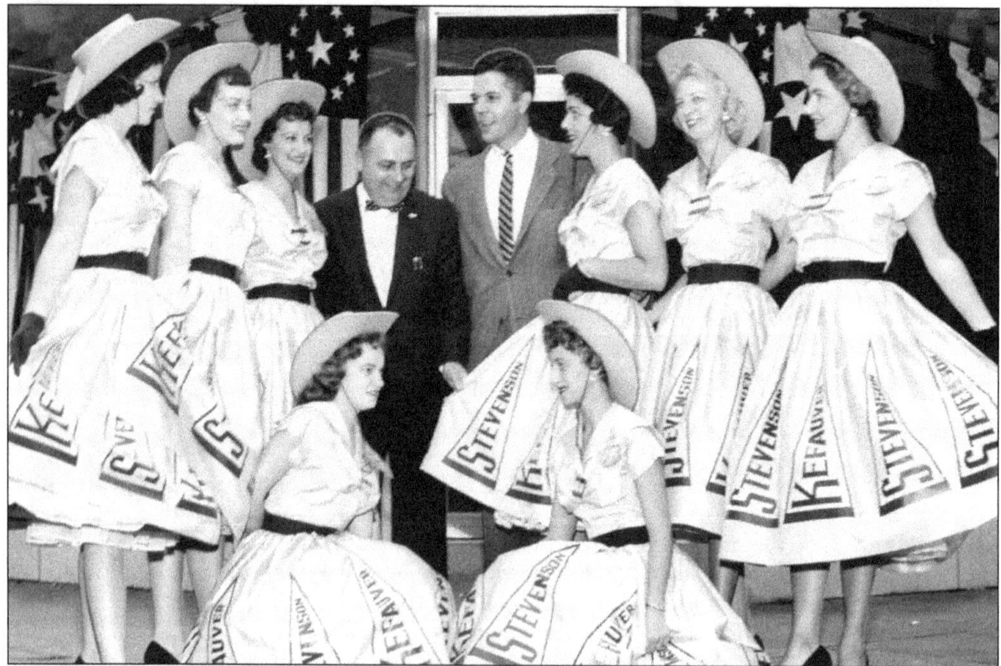

These Stevenson Girls wearing colorful skirts and hats are promoting the presidential campaign of Illinois governor Adlai E. Stevenson, who was running for the second time against the popular Dwight D. Eisenhower in September 1956. The girls are flanked by Lycoming County Democratic chairman Charles C. Hallow and local candidate Dean Fisher at the opening of Democratic headquarters in downtown Williamsport.

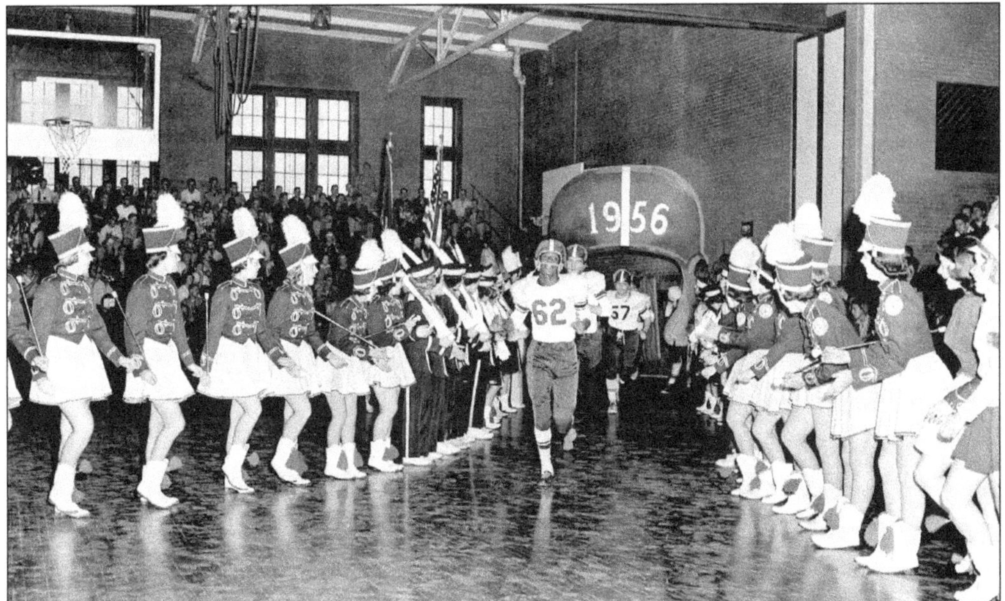

One of the most stimulating pep rallies held at Williamsport High School occurred in November 1956, when the band, the cheerleaders, and the students perked up the football team for its game against longtime rival Steelton. The Millionaires won, 26-6, to claim another Central Penn Conference championship. Following the weekend victory, there was no school on Monday.

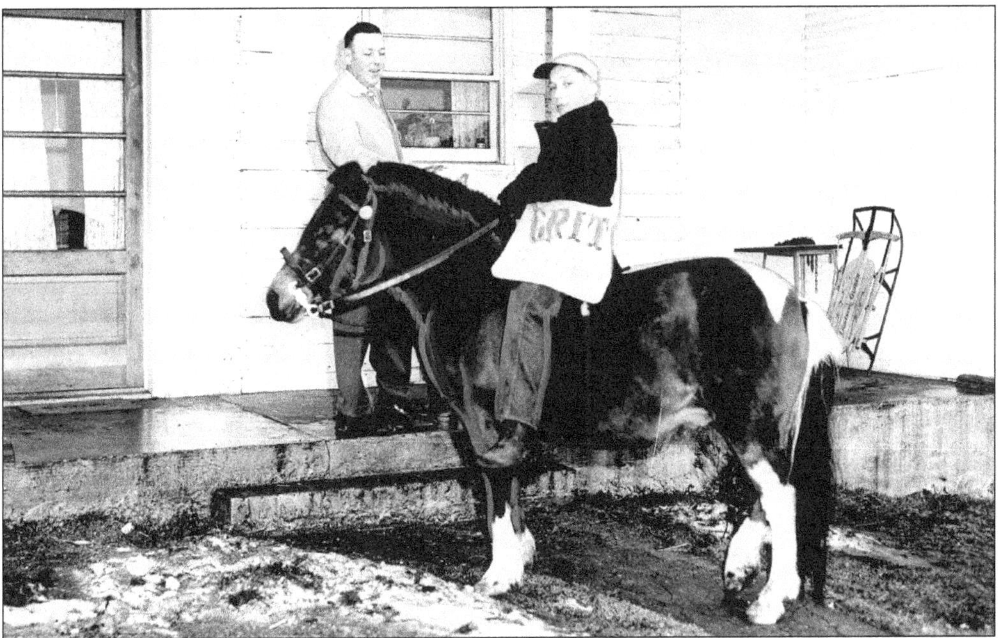

Living in rural Pennsylvania is not a deterrent for this *Grit* newsboy. James L. Harteis uses his pony for selling the newspaper as well as deliveries. An early advertisement for newsboys read, "Join the thousands of others who earn free prizes and make cash profits every week introducing *Grit* to friends, relatives, neighbors and others." Boy Scouts who took a route would earn a salesmanship merit badge.

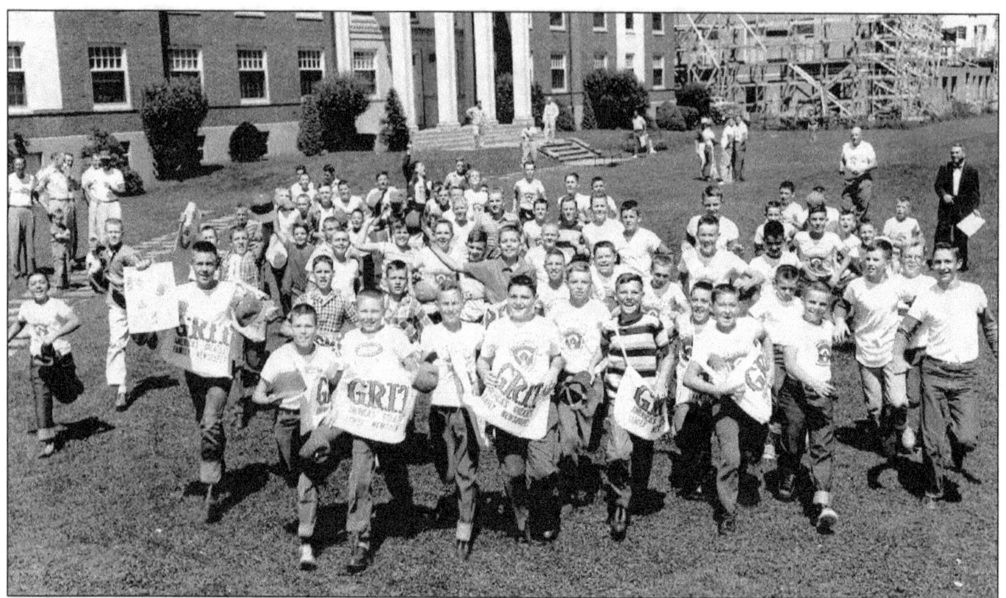

Players from the 1958 Little League World Series on the quad at Lycoming College proudly display *Grit* newspaper bags. Players stayed at the dormitories at Lycoming College before the construction of dormitories in 1961 at International Grove on the Little League complex in South Williamsport.

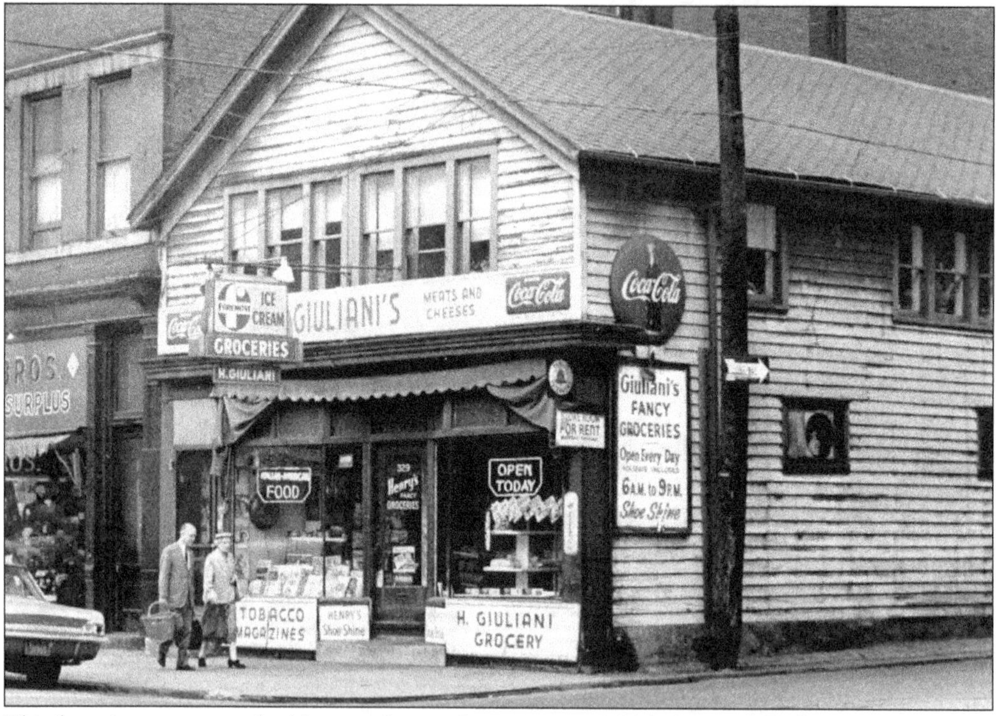

This longtime two-story building at the southwest corner of Market and Willow Streets, which housed the Giuliani grocery store, was purchased by Williamsport attorneys Michael Casale Sr. and George Hess Jr., who built a two-story colonial brick building on the site to house their law offices. The community grocery store existed from 1940 to 1961 and is a landmark that is sorely missed.

Six

The Cold War to the Present

By 1950, the Red Scare was sweeping the world. In the United States, anticommunism became strident and those who refused to renounce communism and its supporters were considered suspect. This was underscored by the actions of the Federal Bureau of Investigation, under its leader J. Edgar Hoover, and Sen. Joseph McCarthy. During Senate hearings, McCarthy claimed to have lists of communists in the U.S. military, State Department, and other government agencies. For months, McCarthy attacked reputations at will.

In 1949, U.S. Air Force planes flying over Russia detected radiation and soon revealed that the Union of Soviet Socialist Republics (USSR) had detonated its first atomic weapon. America was not alone in the atomic age. C. Urey, a Nobel Prize–winning scientist, said, "There is only one thing worse than one nation having an atomic bomb, and that's two nations having it." Americans at first were excited about the atomic bomb, but anxiety began to fester. Williamsport was not immune, and fallout shelters and duck and cover exercises were well known to all, including children.

America soon found itself in the midst of the Civil Rights movement and a conflict in Vietnam. In addition to national crises, Williamsport contended with its own problems, including the building of dikes along the West Branch of the Susquehanna River. Completed in 1955, the dikes kept the flood waters at bay, however the city needed a financial shot in the arm. In 1956, industry and residents subscribed $650,000 for the Lycoming Industrial Fund, to be used to procure new industries and expand employment.

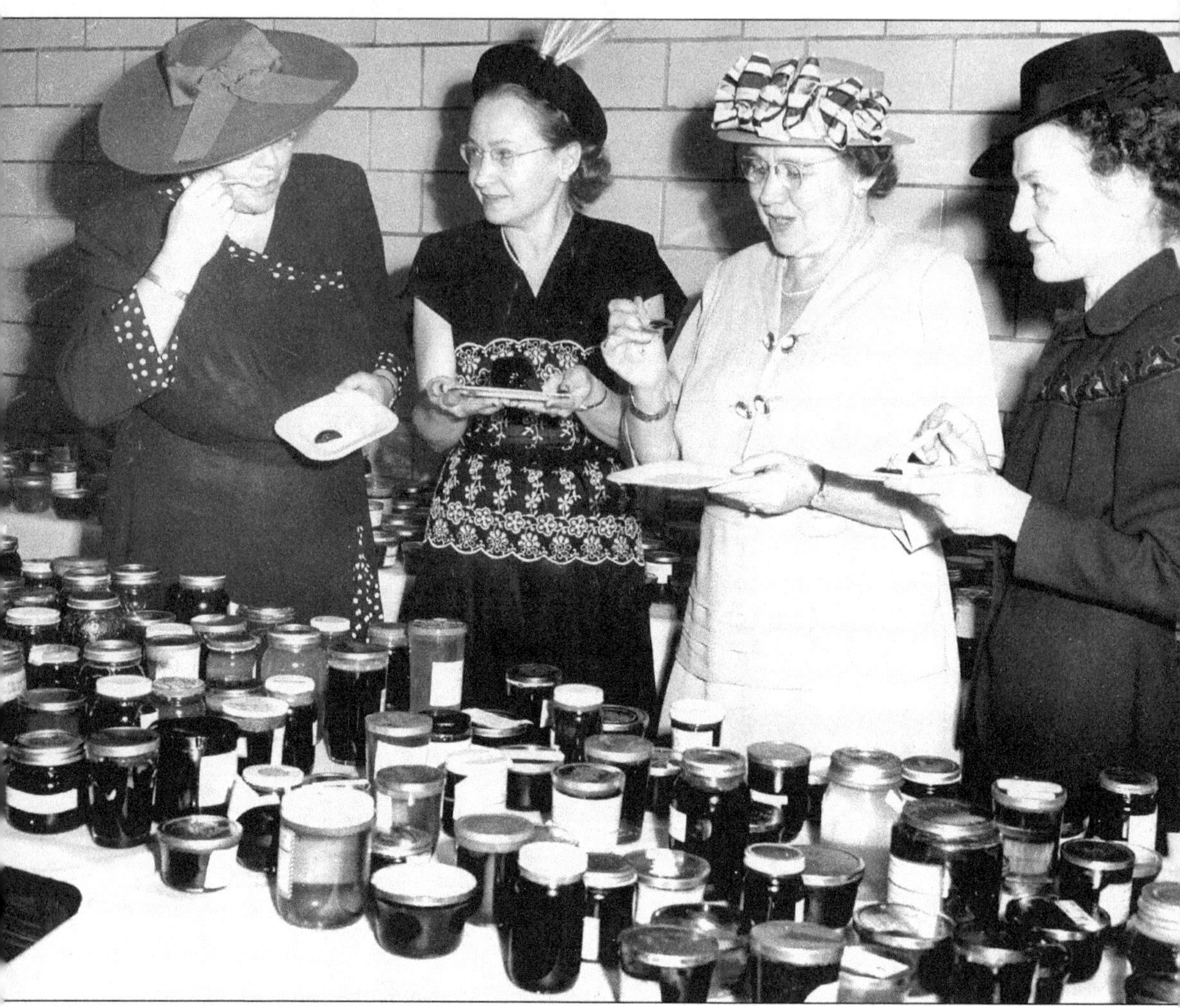

Emma M. Winner, *Grit* women's editor, second from the left, joins three judges of the *Grit*'s homemade jelly contest. From left to right, the judges are Doris Eames, Fanny Woodside, and Gilma M. Olson. The *Grit* sponsored contests that garnered thousands of responses and helped increase and maintain its circulation. The jelly contest not only resulted in thousands of letters but also jelly samples were sent to the newspaper. Often, the results of contests were used to create new publications that were inserted into the newspaper, a service for *Grit* readers. Some of the titles of the pamphlets and publications include *Favorite Recipes of Governor's Wives*, *Those Hated Hickeys*, *Games for Good Parties*, *Tips for the Too-Thin Teen*, *Hair Care and Styling*, *So You're Getting Married*, *New Ideas for Handmade Rugs*, and *Slim Ankles and How to Have Them*.

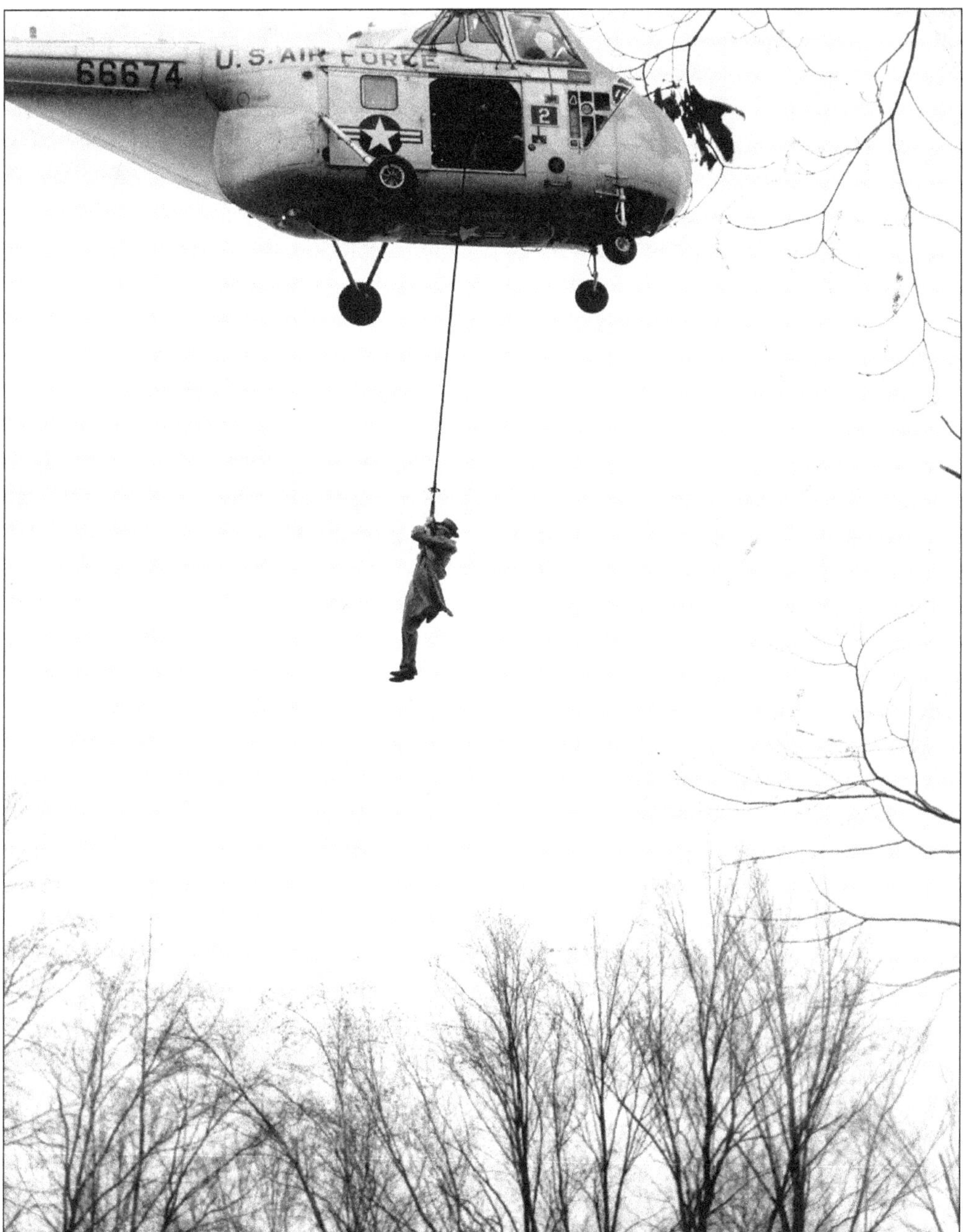

Dr. W. W. Wilcox, a physician from Montoursville, was lowered to the crash scene of Allegheny Airlines Flight 371 by a U.S. Air Force helicopter on December 1, 1959. Wilcox was lowered by means of a winch while the helicopter hovered overhead. He administered emergency first aid to three survivors of the crash, two of whom later died. A total of 25 persons died and one man survived the aircraft crash into Bald Eagle Mountain, south of the Lycoming Airport. According to the Aviation Safety Network, the Martin 2-0-2 was cleared for an approach to Williamsport runway 27. The approach was too high. After a series of turns, the plane disappeared into snow showers and clouds. The aircraft crashed into the mountain.

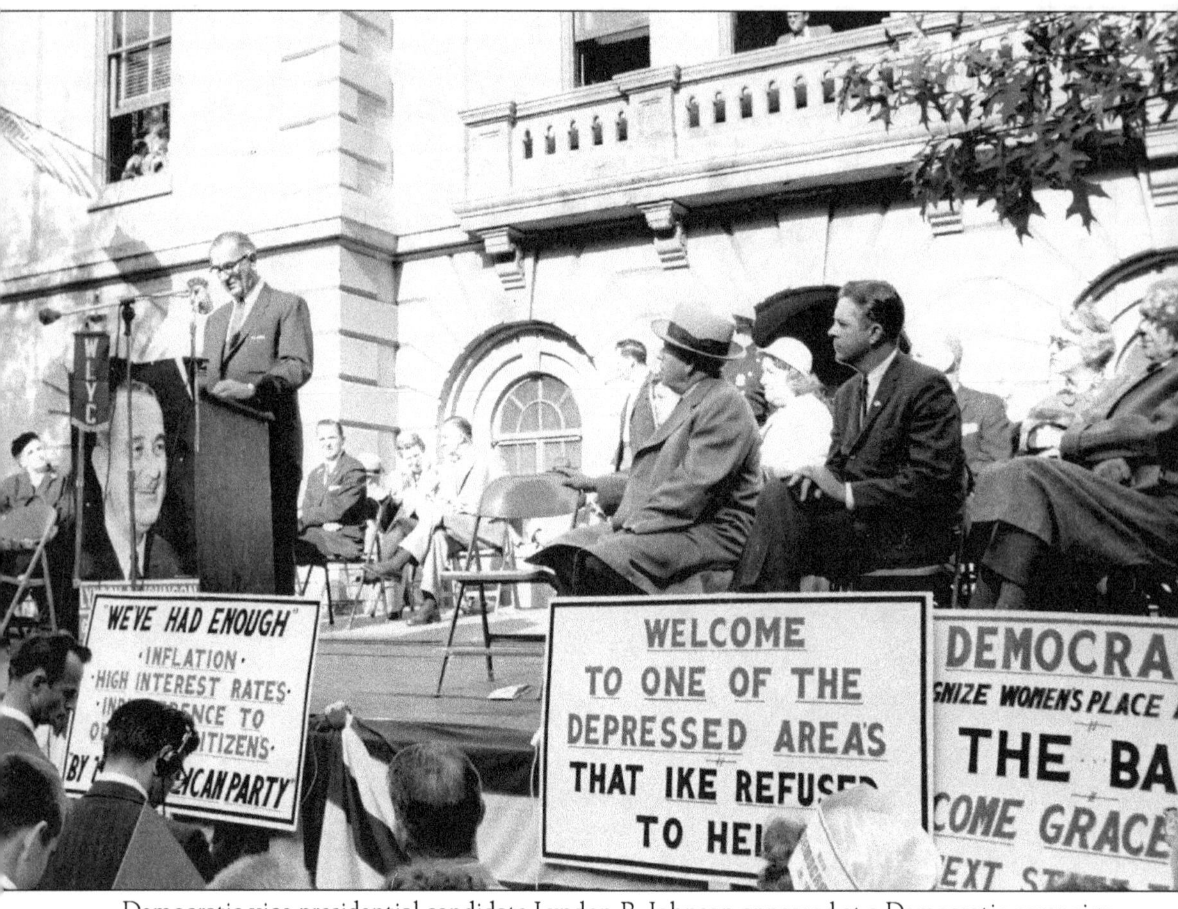

Democratic vice presidential candidate Lyndon B. Johnson appeared at a Democratic campaign rally on the grounds of the Lycoming County Courthouse in October 1960. With Johnson on the speaker's stand were Pennsylvania governor David Lawrence and various Democratic office seekers from the Williamsport area. The presidential nomination of 1960 went to Sen. John F. Kennedy of Massachusetts. Kennedy, a northern Roman Catholic, then selected Johnson as his running mate to balance the Democratic ticket. Johnson later became the nation's 36th president, serving from 1963 to 1969 after Kennedy's assassination. A skilled promoter of liberal domestic legislation, Johnson also was a staunch believer in the use of military force to help achieve the country's foreign policy objectives. His escalation of the American involvement in the Vietnam War eroded his popular standing and led to his decision not to run for reelection to the presidency in 1968.

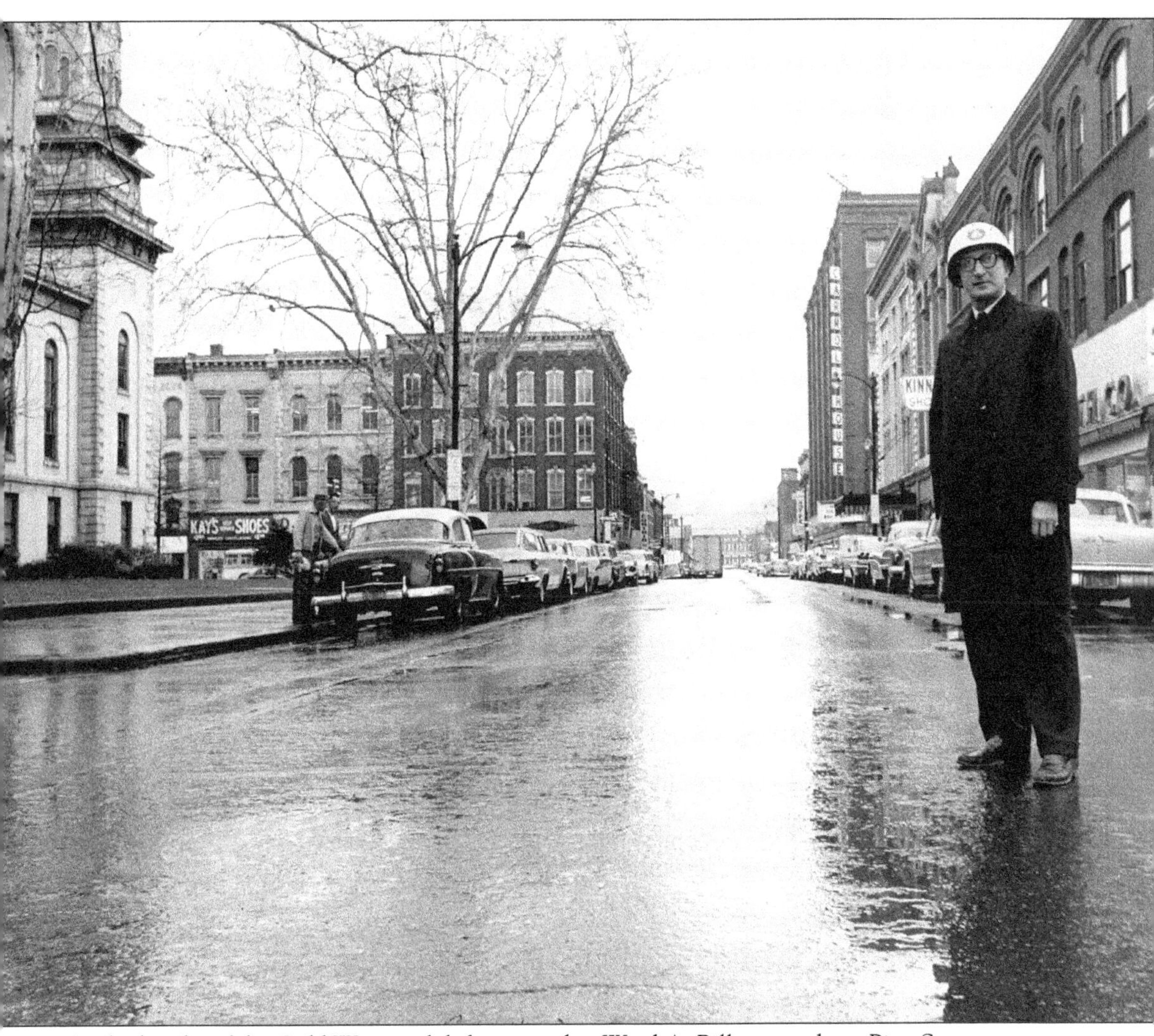

At the height of the Cold War, civil defense warden Ward A. Billett stands on Pine Street, near the Lycoming County Courthouse, after halting traffic during Operation Alert 1961 in April 1961. A number of theoretical problems were dealt with by civil defense officials in connection with the exercise to help determine their efficiency. Between World Wars I and II, civil defense initiatives produced a scattering of air-raid shelters, most improvised in basements and subways. The federal government established the Office of Civil Defense, which trained citizens to fight fires, rescue people, and administer first aid, and the Civil Air Patrol, which taught them to keep their "eyes on the sky."

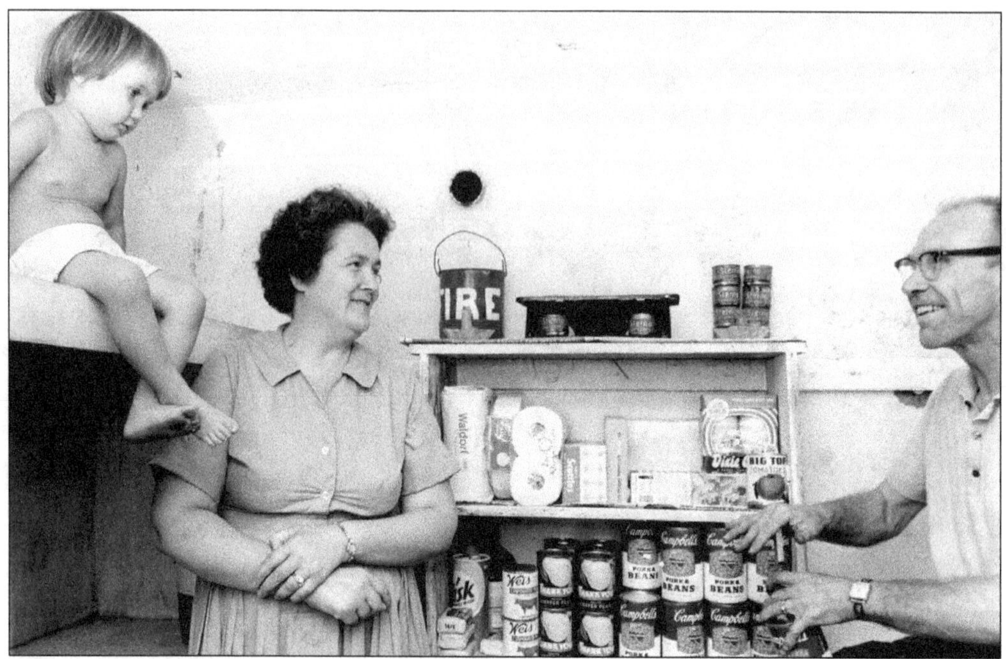

Well prepared inside their underground fallout shelter, Mr. and Mrs. Ben Burgoyne of Montoursville have stored a two-week supply of food and water. The small stove atop the cabinet is for cooking. Tracey, age two, has plenty of room in this six-person shelter that was built to civil defense standards. Standards for a family fallout shelter, according to a 1957 Office of Civil Defense release, were a 14-day shelter food supply that could be stored indefinitely, a battery-operated radio, auxiliary light sources, a two-week supply of water, first aid, sanitary items, and other miscellaneous supplies and equipment.

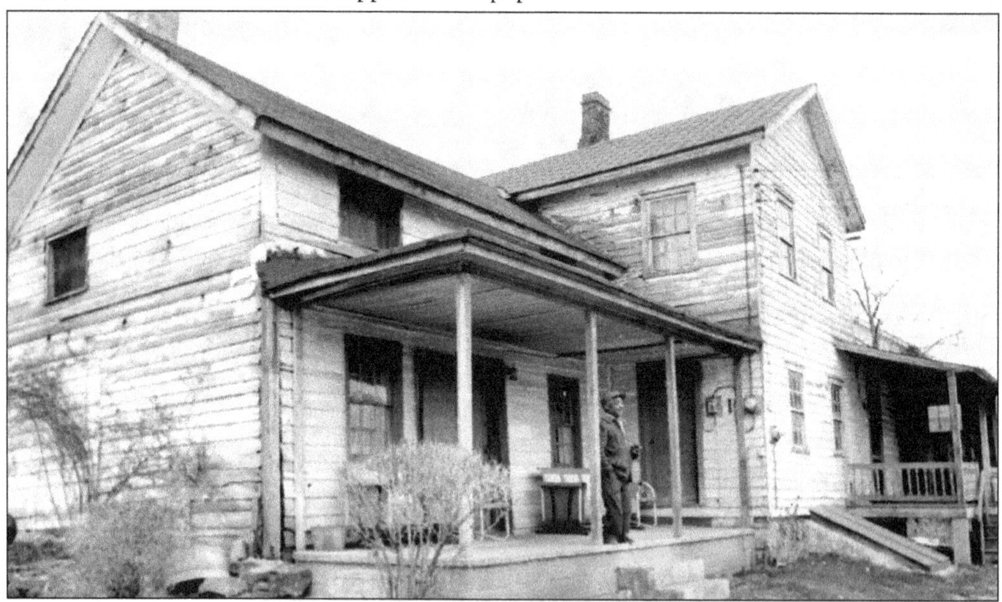

This photograph shows the home of Daniel Hughes, one of Lycoming County's most famous conductors along the Underground Railroad. Standing on the porch in April 1961 is one of his descendants. The house once stood on Freedom Road. It burned in 1976.

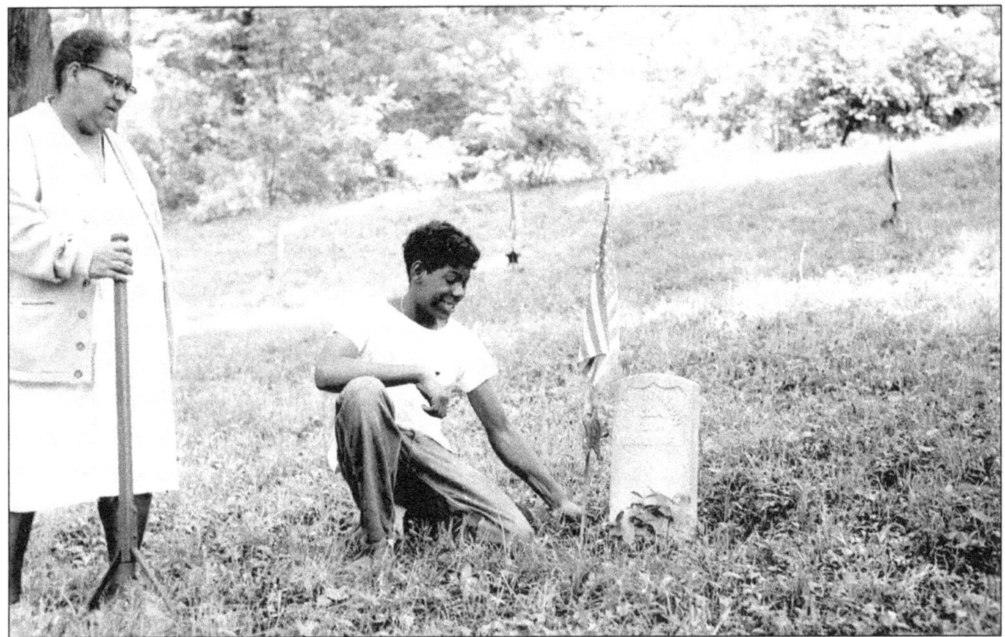

Descendants of Daniel Hughes, a former Underground Railroad conductor, tend to graves of African American Civil War veterans at the Freedom Hill Cemetery on land that was owned by Hughes. The Underground Railroad was an important component of Lycoming County history, and many residents either supported it or were conductors, helping runaway slaves bound for freedom. The family of Daniel Hughes not only helped runaway slaves but sheltered them along Freedom Road.

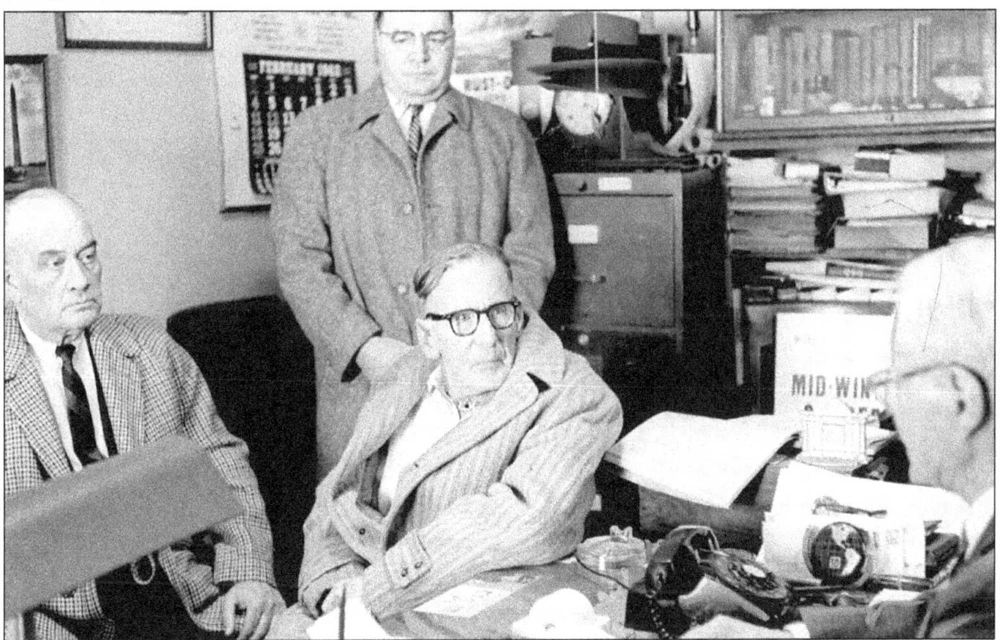

At his arraignment before police magistrate Hugh MacArthur (far right), Edward R. Robbins, (seated on the left) pleads not guilty as Detective Lt. Harold Hand looks on. Robbins was accused of murdering two elderly women at a boardinghouse on March 9, 1962.

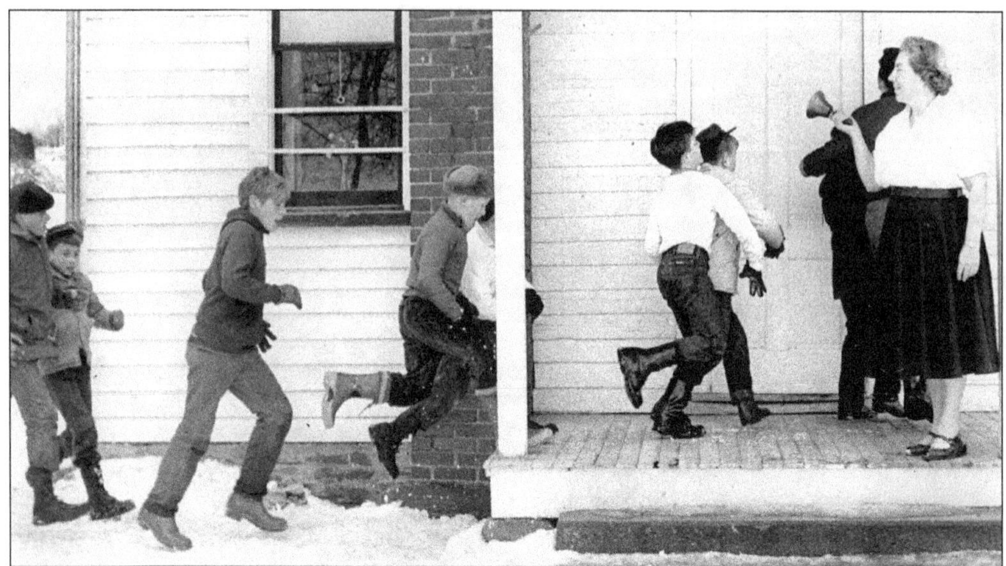

The one-room schoolhouse was not phased out quickly in the outlying areas of Williamsport. Here, schoolteacher Esther S. Grimes rings a short-handled bell to summon youngsters to classes at the one-room Beech Valley School in Gamble Township in January 1963. After its closing, the students attended Williamsport schools.

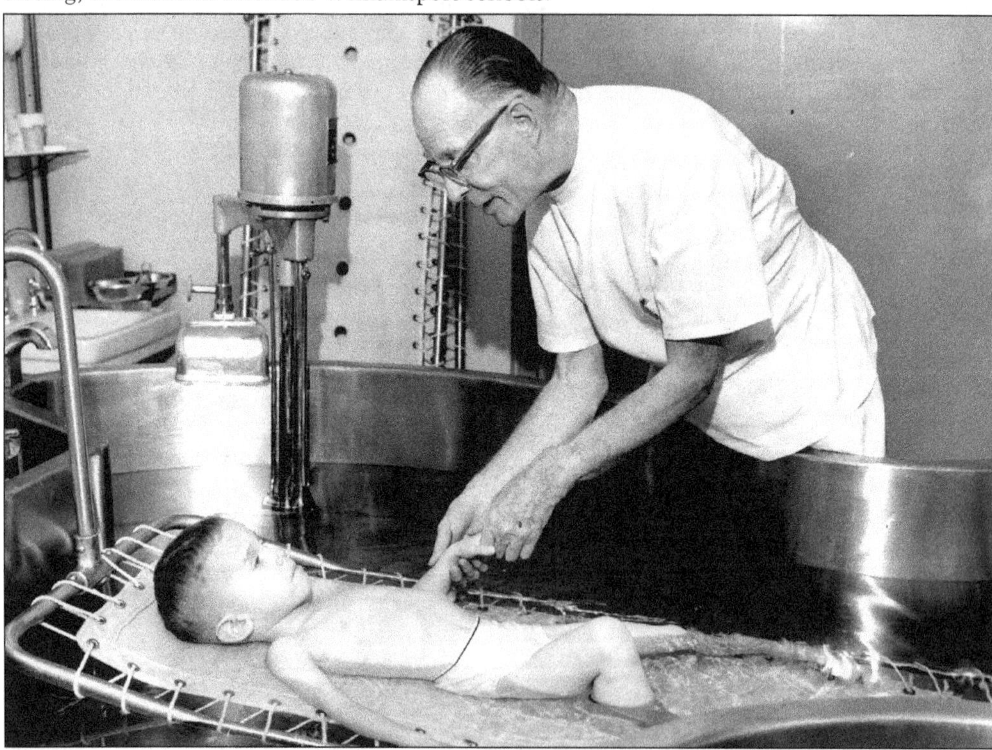

Four-year old Randy Houseknecht, shown here, was the youngest patient receiving treatment from the Lycoming County chapter of the Muscular Dystrophy Association of America. He is shown here with Harold Lyons, a physical therapist at the Muncy Valley Hospital, in November 1963.

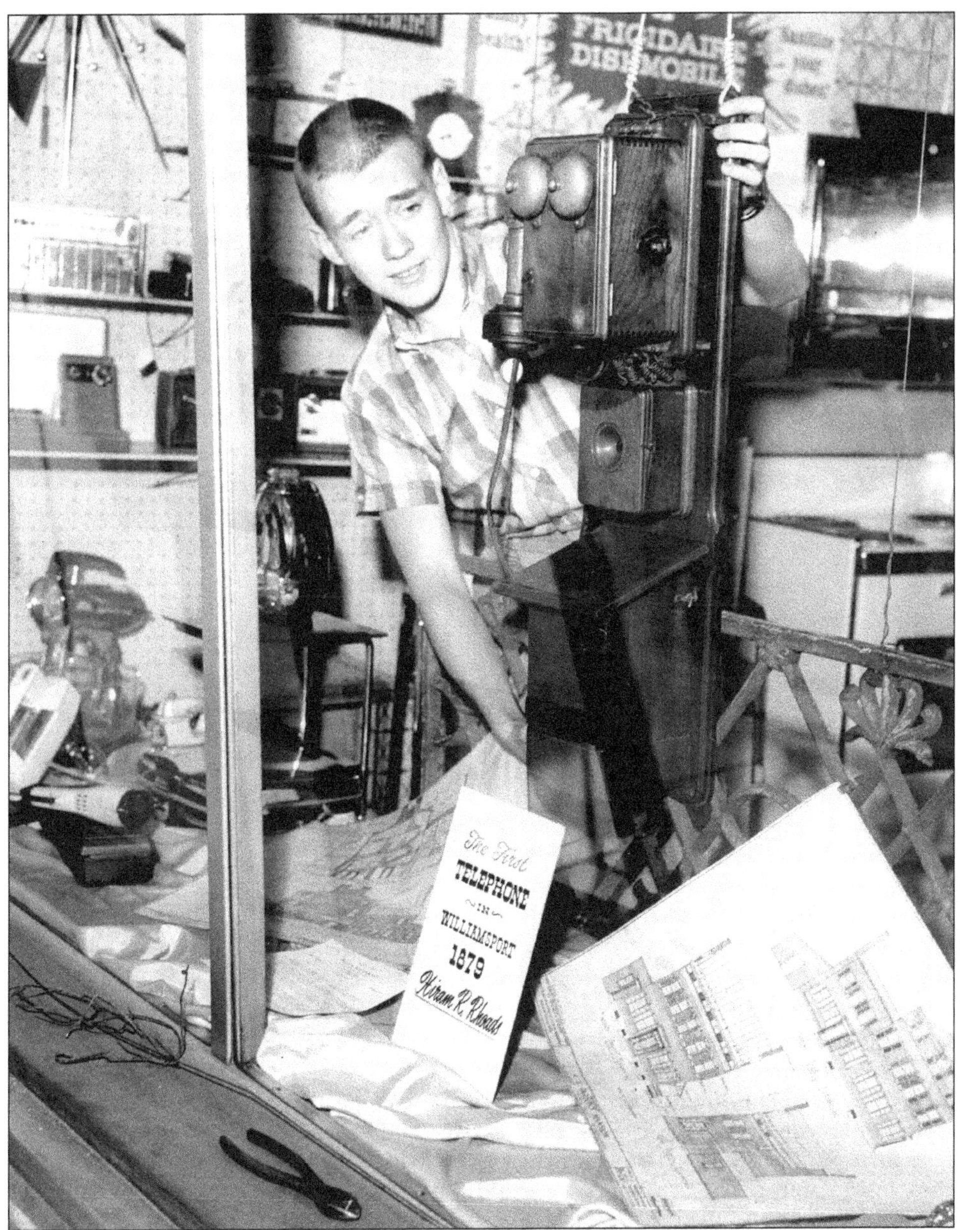

William Atkinson erects a historic display of the first telephone in Williamsport (1879) at the M. H. Housel Company. The Lycoming County Historical Society displayed some of its artifacts at various downtown businesses in the spring of 1964. Member supported, the historical society was founded in 1907 by Col. Herbert R. Laird and is a not-for-profit educational organization with a museum, library, and archives. In 1940, he helped launch a drive to give the organization and its holdings a permanent home, raising $6,000 by personal subscription toward the purchase of the Maynard mansion at 858 West Fourth Street. After the historical society burned in 1960, many of its artifacts were displayed throughout the city for safekeeping. Rebuilt at the same location, the Lycoming County Historical Society has been improved thanks to a recent capital campaign, and a $1 million donation by local philanthropist and historian Thomas Taber has resulted in the addition of the Taber Museum.

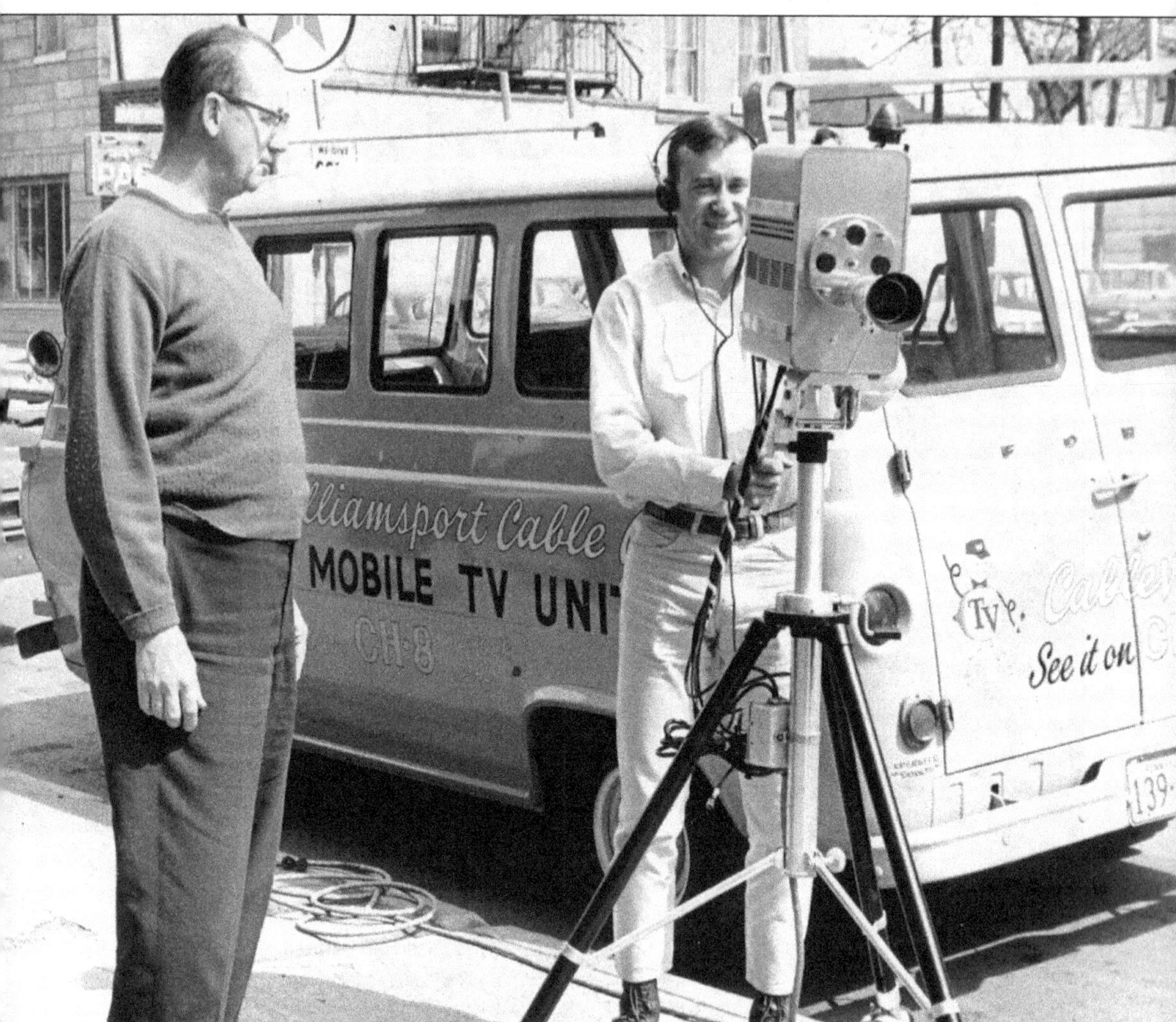

The Williamsport Cable Company conducted experimental tests of on-the-spot television coverage with its new mobile television unit in April 1965. Warren P. Lomison, left, and his son, Warren E., try out the new equipment. The cable company's officials said the unit would be used to provide coverage for civic, news, sports, and other events of community interest. At the time, Williamsport had probably the biggest community antenna system in the country with approximately 10,000 customers, according to Ben Conroy, a cable television pioneer. Williamsport is now served by Susquehanna Communications, a company that traces its roots to 1965, when the company received a franchise to build the cable television system in York, Pennsylvania.

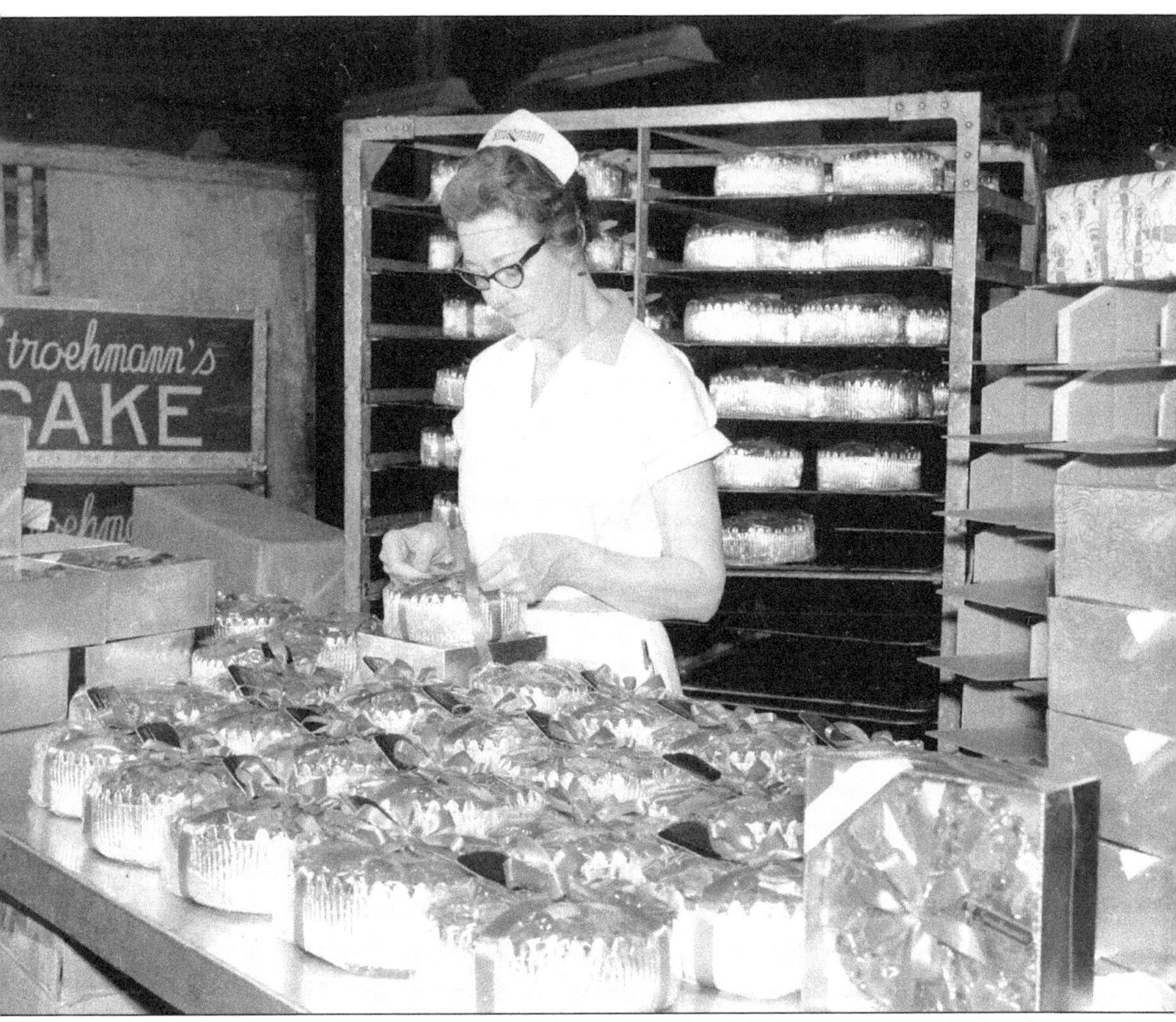

Helen Mausteller is pictured wrapping the last of the fruitcakes that were made by the Stroehmann's bakery from Labor Day to December 6, 1965. More than 100,000 of them were made that year. One of the most notable and enduring businesses associated with Williamsport, Stroehmann Brothers Bakery furnished thousands of residents with bread and bakery products, and hundreds of residents made a living working at one of the Stroehmann plants. Carl F. Stroehmann and his brother, Harold, founded Stroehmann Brothers Bakery. To deliver their products, the Stroehmanns purchased a new fleet of delivery vehicles, including seven wagons and three trucks. Another promotional innovation was to have a three-day open house at the bakery to display the bakery in operation. Few people had ever seen the inside of a bakery before, and this did a great deal to publicize the operation. In less than a year, Stroehmann's output increased from 5,000 loaves to 25,000.

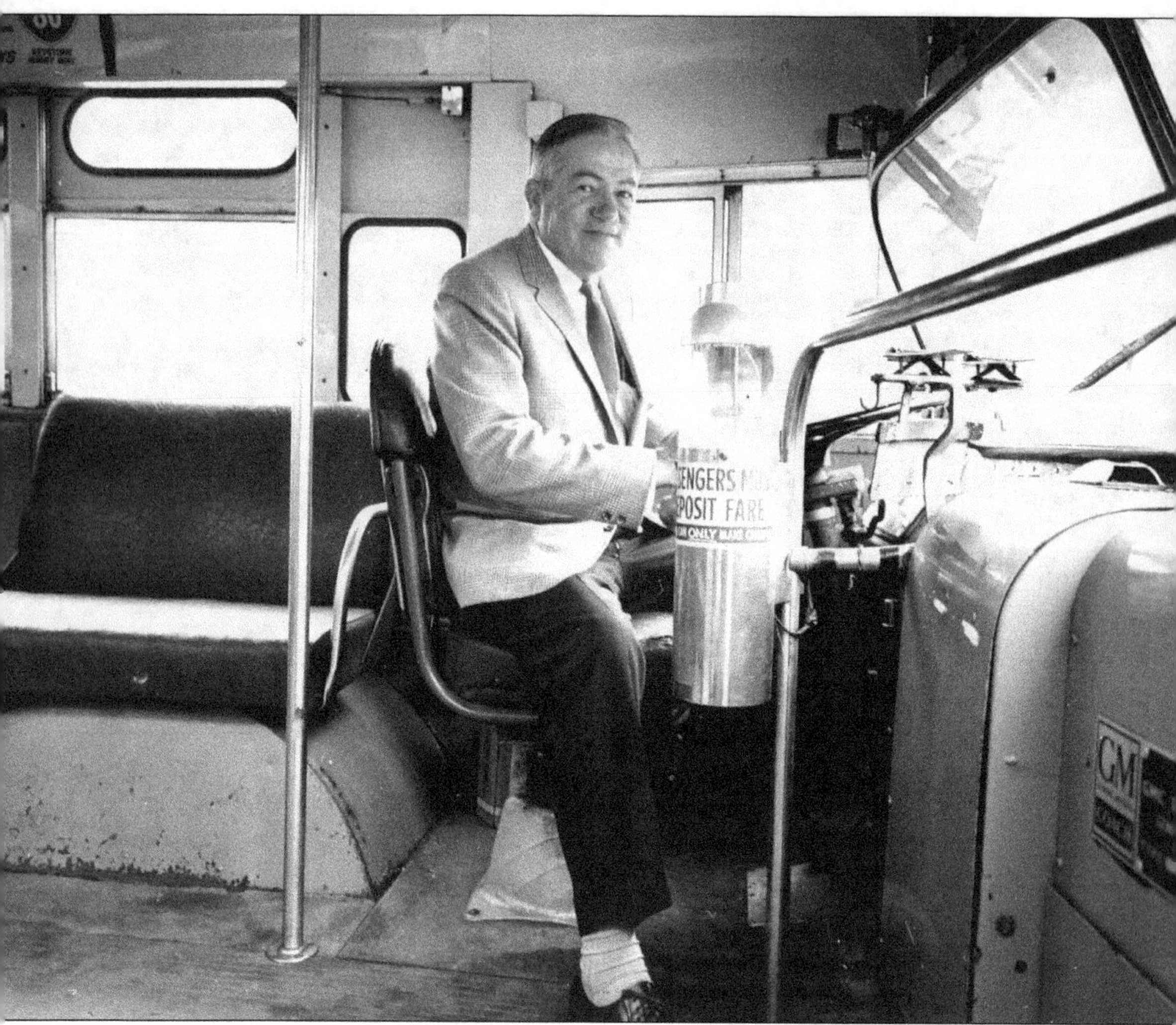

The city of Williamsport acquired the Williamsport Bus Company in August 1968. This transportation entity is still operated by the city and is known as City Bus. Pictured here is Williamsport mayor Richard J. Carey sitting in the driver's seat. During World War I, rising costs and increasing competition from jitney buses and automobiles cut into the profits of streetcar companies. The owners of the Lycoming Improvement Company sold their interests in 1923 to the Lehigh Power Securities Corporation, a holding company of the Pennsylvania Power and Light Company. In 1924, the Montoursville Railway Company, locally owned since 1909, also was sold to the Pennsylvania Power and Light Company. The railway company, $80,000 in debt, had not shown a profit for 10 years. Pennsylvania Power and Light was interested in acquiring the railway because of the railway's ownership of a power company. The streetcar interests were sold to the Lycoming Auto Transit Company, which brought in three new buses to replace the streetcars. The streetcars ran for the last time on August 7, 1924. In 1925, buses made their first appearance as part of the Williamsport system with a bus line to DuBoistown.

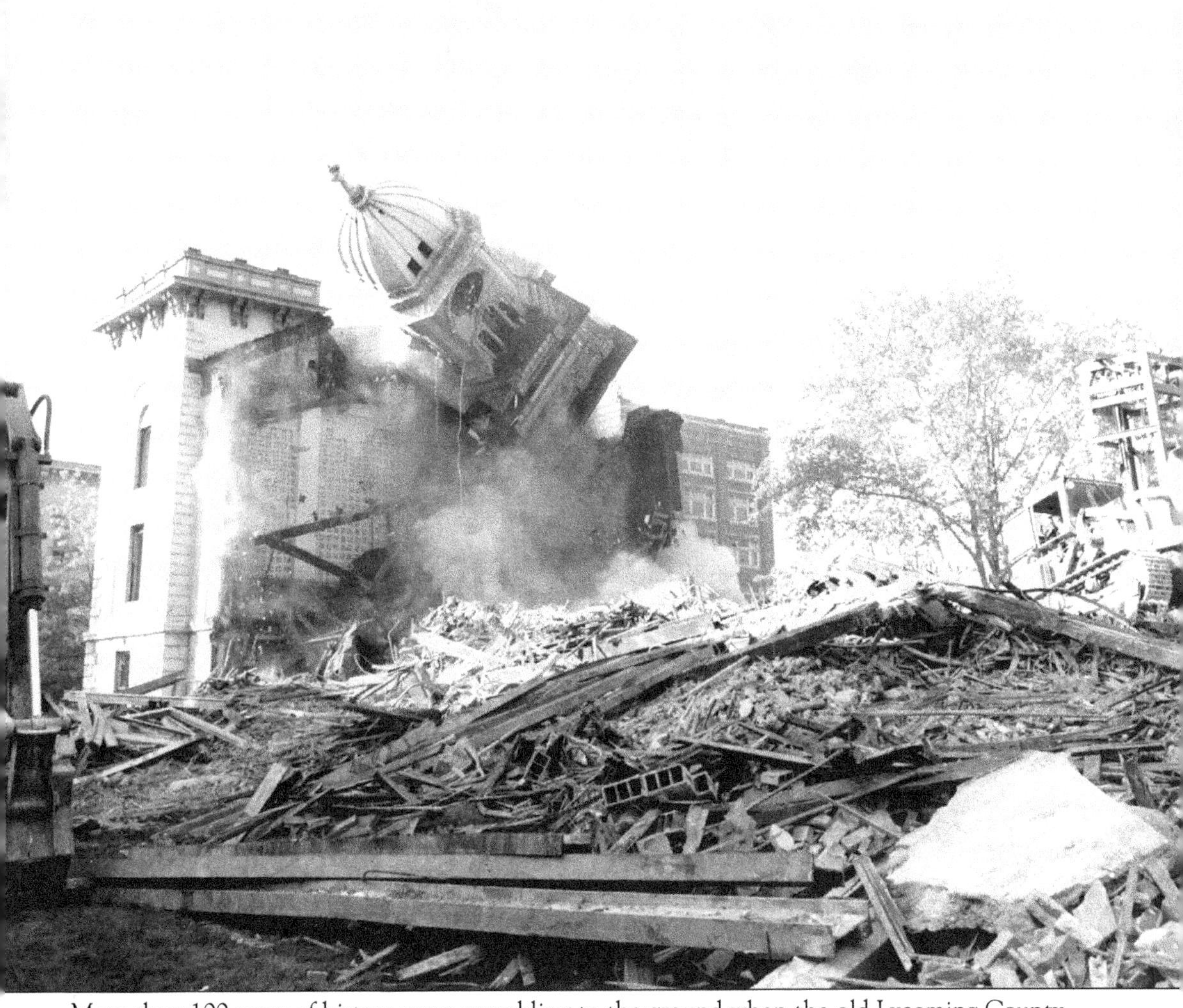

More than 100 years of history came crumbling to the ground when the old Lycoming County Courthouse was demolished during a five-day period in May 1969. It was a sad day for many Williamsport preservationists as this magnificent old building succumbed to the relentless blows of the wrecker's ball. Many preservationists believe that if the demolition of the old courthouse were to come into question today, a greater effort would be made to preserve the fine old courthouse. The original Lycoming County Courthouse was built on lots owned by city founder Michael Ross and was completed in 1802 for $20,417 by contractors John Turk and Edward Gobinn. The first payment for material for the courthouse's construction was $16 to Thomas Harris on February 6, 1801, along with $6 to Jacob Grafius for the purchase of nine gallons of whiskey. It may be that men working on the courthouse were paid with whiskey and perhaps drank some of their pay while on the job. The original courthouse only lasted 60 years. A new courthouse, shown above being demolished, was built in 1860 and served the county well for more than 100 years.

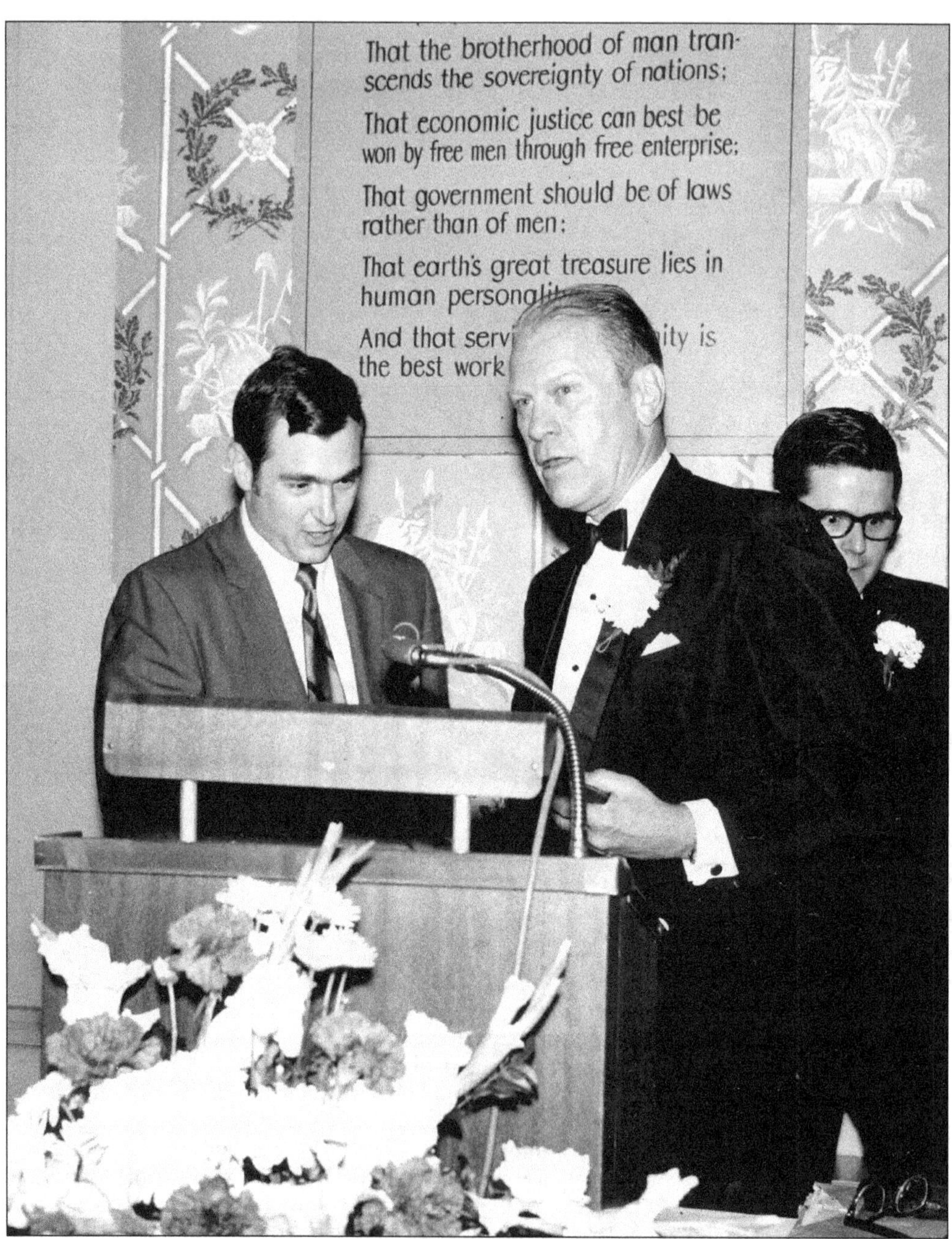

Fred M. Plankenhorn, left, is presented the Greater Williamsport Jaycees Outstanding Young Man of the Year Award in May 1970 by Republican congressman Gerald R. Ford of Michigan, the featured speaker at the annual awards dinner. Ford went on to become the 38th president of the United States, serving from 1974 to 1977. Ford was selected by Republican president Richard M. Nixon to take over as vice president in 1973 after Nixon's original vice president, Spiro T. Agnew, pled no contest to a tax evasion charge and resigned from office. Ford was then thrust into the presidency following Nixon's own resignation in the wake of the Watergate scandal in 1974. Ford, the only unelected president in U.S. history, lost to Democrat Jimmy Carter in the 1976 presidential election.

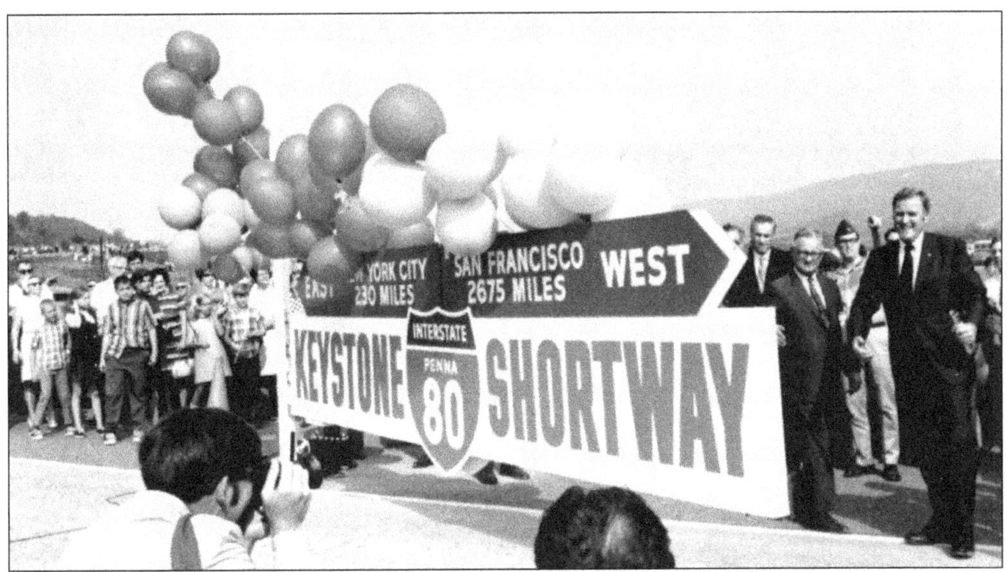

Pennsylvania governor Raymond P. Shafer releases balloons at the formal opening of the Keystone Shortway, Interstate 80, in September 1970. The moving force behind the building of the road was Zehnder H. "Dick" Confair, who envisioned a four-lane interstate highway that would link the markets and people of north-central Pennsylvania with larger markets in New York, Philadelphia, and Pittsburgh. His interest in a Keystone Shortway coincided with Pres. Dwight Eisenhower's drive to create a modern interstate highway system.

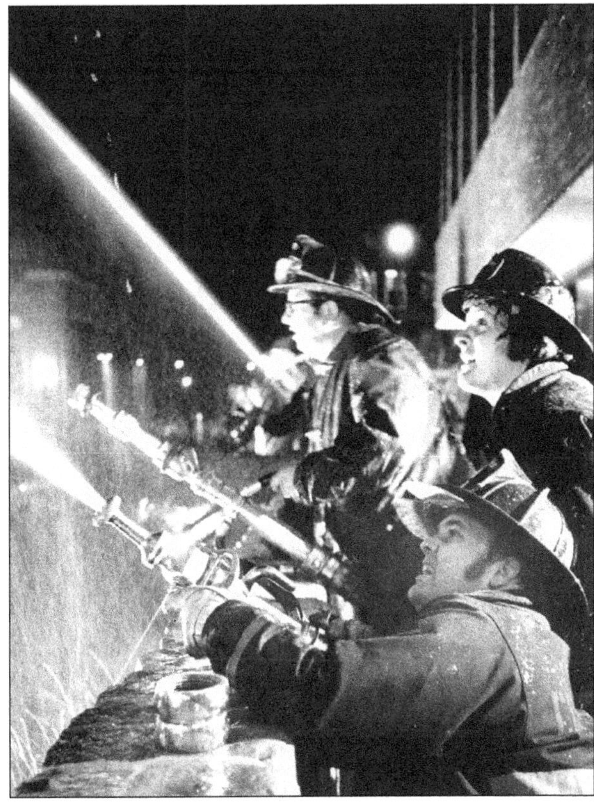

From the Lycoming County courthouse elevated walkway, Williamsport city firefighters direct a stream of water on a blaze at the Paolo Hotel on April 14, 1972, that claimed two lives.

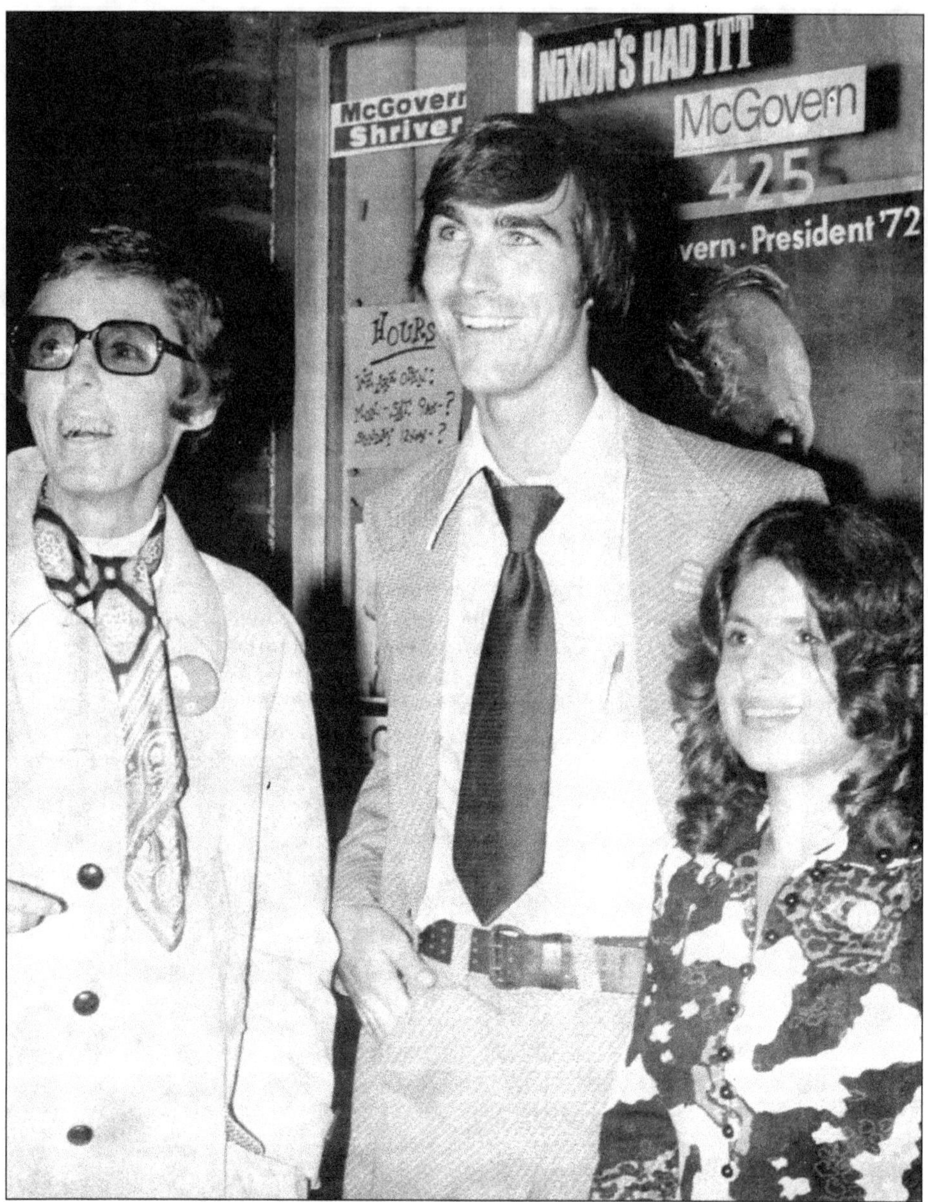

"Miss Jane" opens the Lycoming County Democratic Headquarters on September 29, 1972. Pictured here is Nancy Kulp (left), who played Jane Hathaway on the television classic *The Beverly Hillbillies*. She is accompanied by Michael Rosencrans, McGovern coordinator for Lycoming County, and Judy Blumenthal, assistant coordinator. More than 500 persons attended the opening of the headquarters. This also is the year of the Nixon-ordered June 17, 1972, burglary at the Democratic Party's National Committee offices in Washington, D.C. Five burglars were arrested at 2:30 a.m. during a break-in at the Watergate Hotel. Despite an October 10, 1972, report by FBI agents that established that the Watergate break-in stemmed from a massive campaign of political spying and sabotage conducted on behalf of the Nixon reelection effort, Nixon is reelected in one of the largest landslides in American political history, taking more than 60 percent of the vote and crushing the Democratic nominee, Sen. George McGovern of South Dakota.

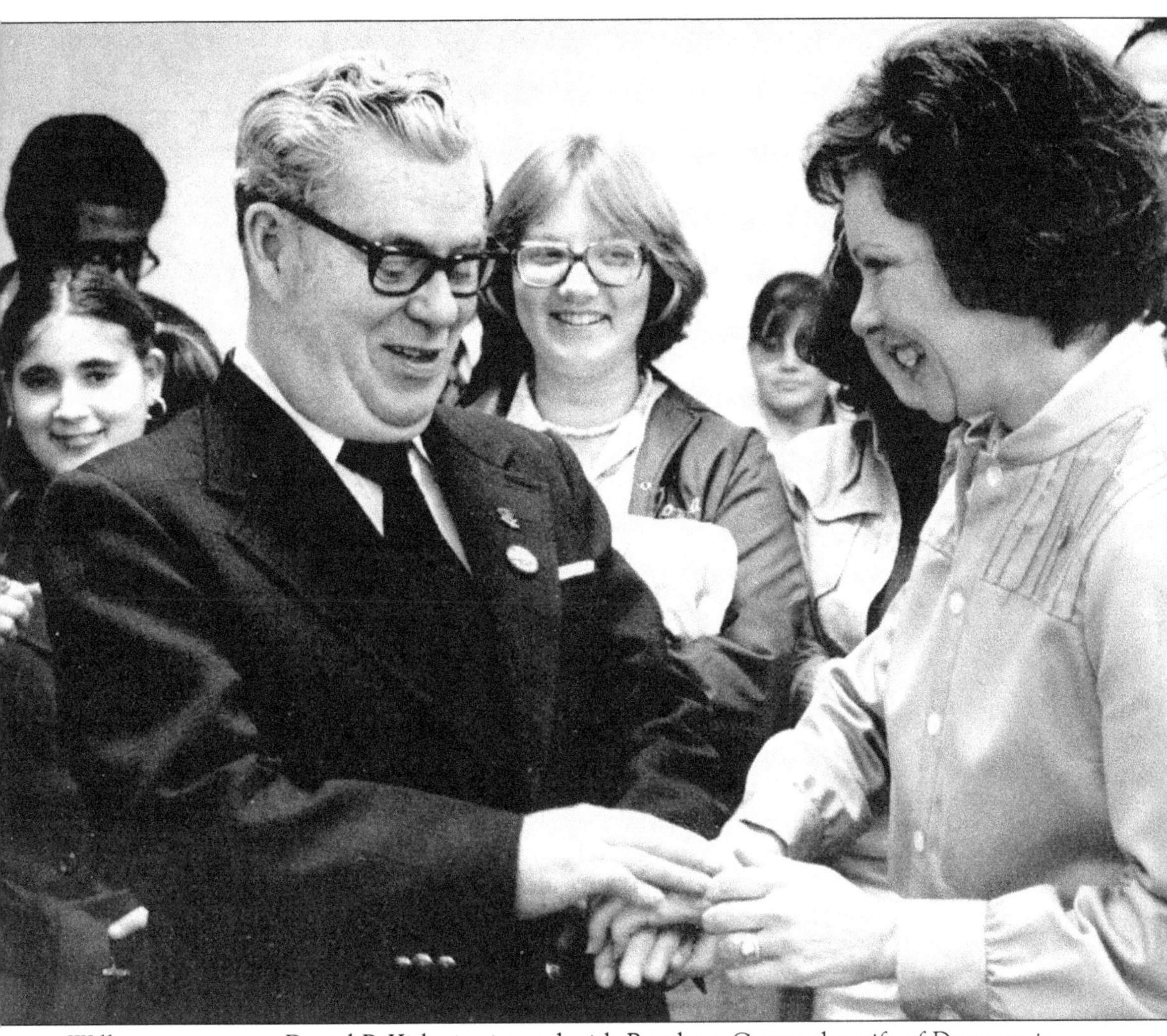

Williamsport mayor Daniel P. Kirby is pictured with Rosalynn Carter, the wife of Democratic hopeful and former Georgia governor Jimmy Carter, on April 17, 1976. During Jimmy Carter's presidential campaigns, Rosalynn traveled independently throughout the United States. Her belief in her husband's ability to lead the nation was communicated in a quiet, friendly manner that made her an effective campaigner. Carter was elected the 39th president of the United States on November 2, 1976. Jimmy Carter was inaugurated on January 20, 1977, and immediately began to take symbolic actions to demonstrate his disdain for what he considered to be "the imperial presidency." After taking the oath of office, he and members of his family walked to the White House. He sold the presidential yacht and eliminated some of the ceremonial trappings of the presidency. Rosalynn Carter brought a southern charm to the White House but also served as a strong advocate for mental health. The Carter presidency, however, was marred with a hostage crisis in Iran, and Carter served only one term.

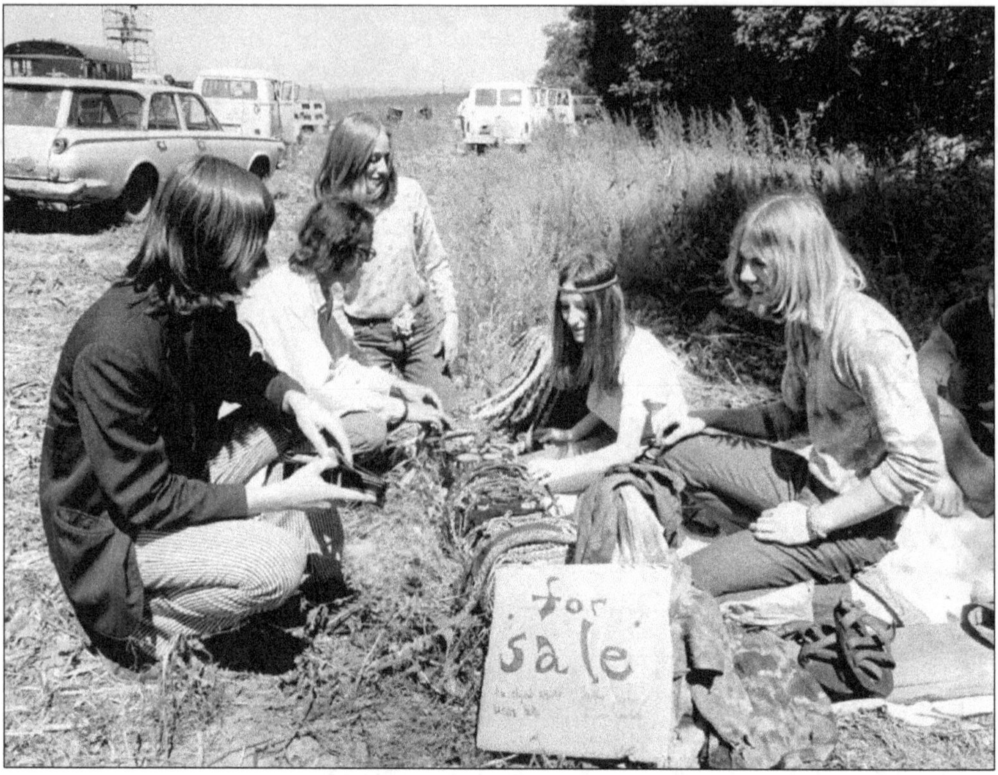

Young people attending a rock concert near Allenwood in May 1970 are seen here selling tie-dyed clothing and other knickknacks of the youth culture of the time. The rock concert originally called the Balls Mills Peace Festival and Rock Concert had to be relocated from the Balls Mills area, north of Williamsport, because of the legal opposition of residents of that area. More than 1,500 people heard five rock bands and several folk singers perform at the concert.

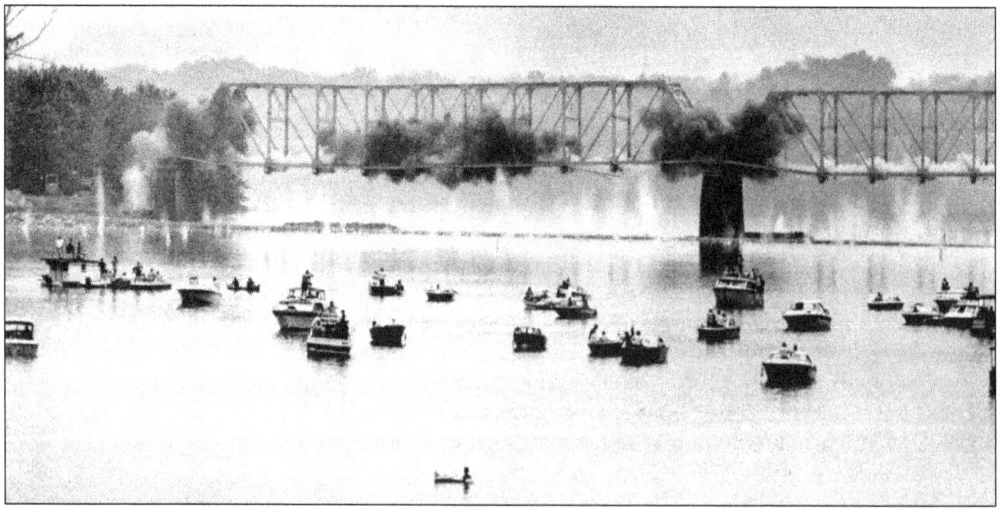

The old Maynard Street Bridge was destroyed with dynamite in June 1986, while hundreds of onlookers moored their boats on the West Branch of the Susquehanna River. A primarily concrete bridge replaced the classic steel structure. Hundreds gathered to see the destruction of this transportation landmark.

Seven

THE *GRIT*, THEN AND NOW

The little newspaper that could, *Grit* gained its popularity by appealing to small-town Americans. It offered three sections each week: a news section, a women's section, and a family section.

Established by Dietrick Lamade in the Williamsport area, the weekly newspaper grew from a circulation of 1,500 to more than 1.2 million. It remained under the management of the Lamade family for most of its run. After Dietrick Lamade's death in 1938, his son George R. Lamade, then general manager of *Grit*, became its president. Another son, Howard J. Lamade, served as vice president and secretary. Four grandsons also were in the business. It became a tabloid on January 2, 1944. Color made its first appearance in the family section on July 21, 1963.

When *Grit* left Williamsport it became a monthly magazine. Stauffer Communications of Kansas purchased *Grit* and then sold it to Morris Publishing in 1994. It became a holding of Odgen Publications Incorporated in 1996.

Grit now has a national, paid subscription of 290,056 with an estimated readership of nearly 1 million. *Grit* still tries to appeal to its largely small-town readers with positive human-interest stories. According to its current literature, *Grit* promotes the qualities of courage, dedication, and determination by profiling people and interesting places. Features are submitted by its readers and include articles about gardening, hobbies and crafts, inspirations, unsung heroes, unique retirement pastimes, travel, and pets. Its publisher is Bryan Welch.

Present-day *Grit* demographics report that the average reader is a woman (67 percent) over the age of 55 (94 percent) with a high school diploma (51 percent) and who owns her own home (80 percent).

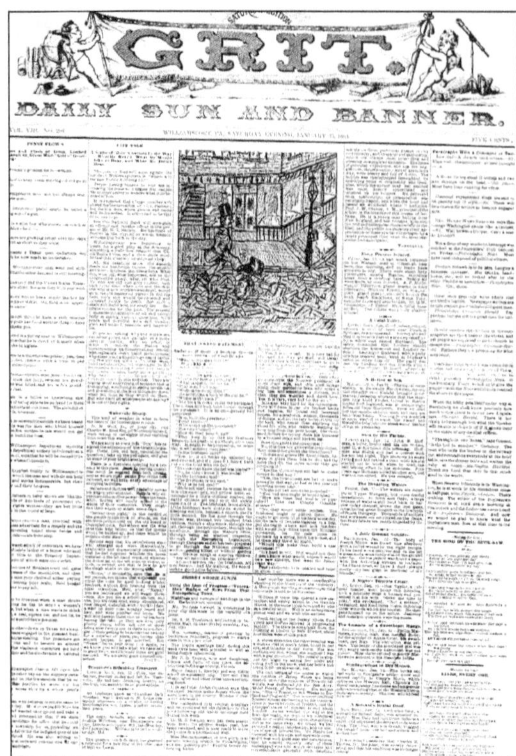

GRIT.

DAILY SUN AND BANNER.

The first issue of *Grit* was published on December 16, 1882. On January 13, 1883, the company printed the first issue with the familiar *Grit* logotype. Originally only 5¢, the *Grit* increased its national price to 7¢ in 1944, 10¢ in 1949, 15¢ in 1959, and 20¢ in 1970. *Grit*'s circulation system was unique; its young salesmen (generally small boys) sold 90 percent of its copies.

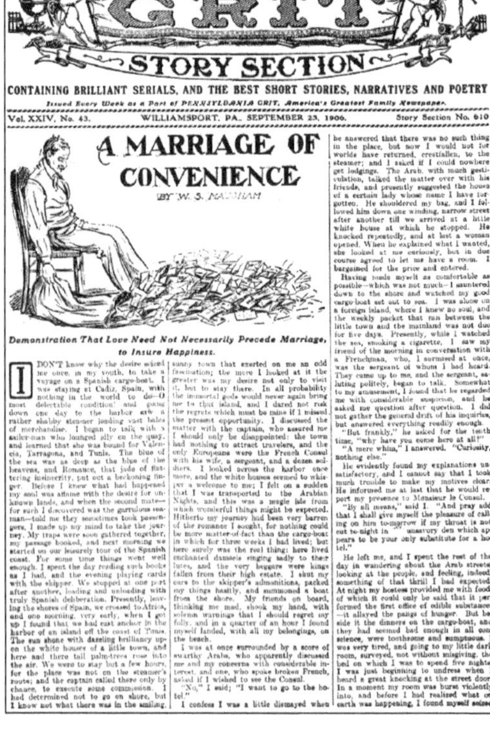

PENNSYLVANIA GRIT

STORY SECTION

CONTAINING BRILLIANT SERIALS, AND THE BEST SHORT STORIES, NARRATIVES AND POETRY

Issued Every Week as a Part of PENNSYLVANIA GRIT, America's Greatest Family Newspaper.

Vol. XXIV, No. 43. WILLIAMSPORT, PA., SEPTEMBER 23, 1906. Story Section No. 610

A MARRIAGE OF CONVENIENCE

BY W. S. MAUGHAM

Demonstration That Love Need Not Necessarily Precede Marriage, to Insure Happiness.

I DON'T know why the desire seized me once, in my youth, to take a voyage on a Spanish cargo-boat. I was staying at Cadiz, Spain, with nothing in the world to do—O most delectable condition!—and going down one day to the harbor saw a rather shabby steamer loading vast bales of merchandise. I began to talk with a sailor-man who lounged idly on the quay, and learned that she was bound for Valencia, Tarragona, and Tunis. The blue of the sea was as deep as the blue of the heavens, and Romance, that jade of flattering insincerity, put out a beckoning finger. Before I knew what had happened my soul was aflame with the desire for unknown lands, and when the second mate—for such I discovered was the garrulous seaman—told me they sometimes took passengers, I made up my mind to take the journey. My traps were soon gathered together, my passage booked, and next morning we started on our leisurely tour of the Spanish coast. For some time things went well enough. I spent the day reading such books as I had, and the evening playing cards with the skipper. We stopped at one port after another, loading and unloading with truly Spanish deliberation. Presently, leaving the shores of Spain, we crossed to Africa, and one morning, very early, when I got up I found that we had cast anchor in the harbor of an island off the coast of Tunis. The sun shone with dazzling brilliancy upon the white houses of a little town, and here and there tall palm-trees rose into the air. We were to stay but a few hours, for the place was not on the steamer's route; and the captain called there only by chance, to execute some commission. I had determined not to go on shore, but I know not what there was in the smiling, sunny town that exerted on me an odd fascination; the more I looked at it the greater was my desire not only to visit it, but to stay there. In all probability the immortal gods would never again bring me to that island, and I dared not risk the regrets which must be mine if I missed the present opportunity. I discussed the matter with the captain, who assured me I should only be disappointed: the town had nothing to attract travelers, and the only Europeans were the French Consul with his wife, a sergeant, and a dozen soldiers. I looked across the harbor once more, and the white houses seemed to whisper a welcome to me; I felt on a sudden that I was transported to the Arabian Nights, and this was a magic isle from which wonderful things might be expected. Hitherto my journey had been very barren of the romance I sought, for nothing could be more matter-of-fact than the cargo-boat in which for three weeks I had lived; but here surely was the real thing: here lived enchanted damsels singing sadly to their lutes, and the very beggars were kings fallen from their high estate. I shut my ears to the skipper's admonitions, packed my things hastily, and summoned a boat from the shore. My friends on board, thinking me mad, shook my hand, with solemn warnings that I should regret my folly, and in a quarter of an hour I found myself landed, with all my belongings, on the beach.

I was at once surrounded by a score of swarthy Arabs, who apparently discussed me and my concerns with considerable interest, and one, who spoke broken French, asked if I wished to see the Consul.

"No," I said; "I want to go to the hotel."

I confess I was a little dismayed when he answered that there was no such thing in the place, but now I would not for worlds have returned, crestfallen, to the steamer; and I asked if I could nowhere get lodgings. The Arab, with much gesticulation, talked the matter over with his friends, and presently suggested the house of a certain lady whose name I have forgotten. He shouldered my bag, and I followed him down one winding, narrow street after another till we arrived at a little white house at which he stopped. He knocked repeatedly, and at last a woman opened. When he explained what I wanted, she looked at me curiously, but in due course agreed to let me have a room. I bargained for the price and entered.

Having made myself as comfortable as possible—which was not much—I sauntered down to the shore and watched my good cargo-boat set out to sea. I was alone on a foreign island, where I knew no soul, and the weekly packet that ran between the little town and the mainland was not due for five days. Presently, while I watched the sea, smoking a cigarette, I saw my friend of the morning in conversation with a Frenchman, who, I surmised at once, was the sergeant of whom I had heard. They came up to me, and the sergeant, saluting politely, began to talk. Somewhat to my amusement, I found that he regarded me with considerable suspicion, and he asked me question after question. I did not gather the general drift of his inquiries, but answered everything readily enough.

"But frankly," he asked for the tenth time, "why have you come here at all?"

"A mere whim," I answered. "Curiosity, nothing else."

He evidently found my explanations unsatisfactory, and I cannot say that I took much trouble to make my motives clear. He informed me at last that he would report my presence to Monsieur le Consul.

"By all means," said I. "And pray add that I shall give myself the pleasure of calling on him to-morrow if my throat is not cut to-night in the unsavory den which appears to be your only substitute for a hotel."

He left me, and I spent the rest of the day in wandering about the Arab streets, looking at the people, and feeling, indeed, something of that thrill I had expected. At night my hostess provided me with food, of which it could only be said that it performed the first office of edible substances—it allayed the pangs of hunger. But beside it the dinners on the cargo-boat, and they had seemed bad enough in all conscience, were toothsome and sumptuous. I was very tired, and going to my little dark room, surveyed, not without misgiving, the bed on which I was to spend five nights. I was just beginning to undress when I heard a great knocking at the street door. In a moment my room was burst violently into, and before I had realized what on earth was happening, I found myself seized

This 1906 issue of the *Grit*'s story section featured a short story by W. Sommerset Maugham, "A Marriage of Convenience." One of the newspaper's most beloved and enduring inserts, the story section promised "brilliant serials, and the best short stories, narratives and poetry."

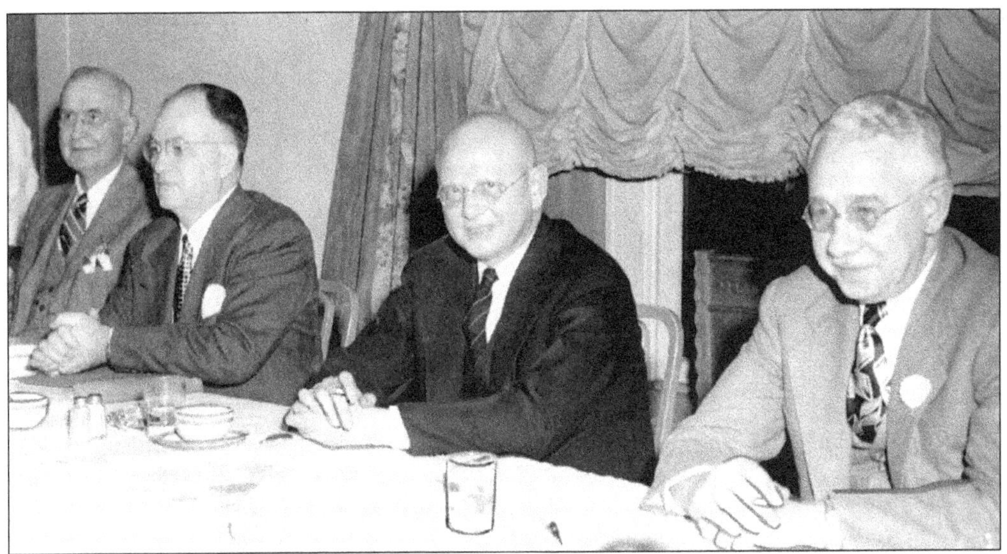

Grit employees attend a banquet in honor of its 66th anniversary in this January 1949 photograph. Seated from left to right are Harry J. W. Kiessling, retired employee and vice president; Russell G. Ross, the guest speaker for the event; George R. Lamade, president and general manager of the company; and Howard J. Lamade, vice president and secretary.

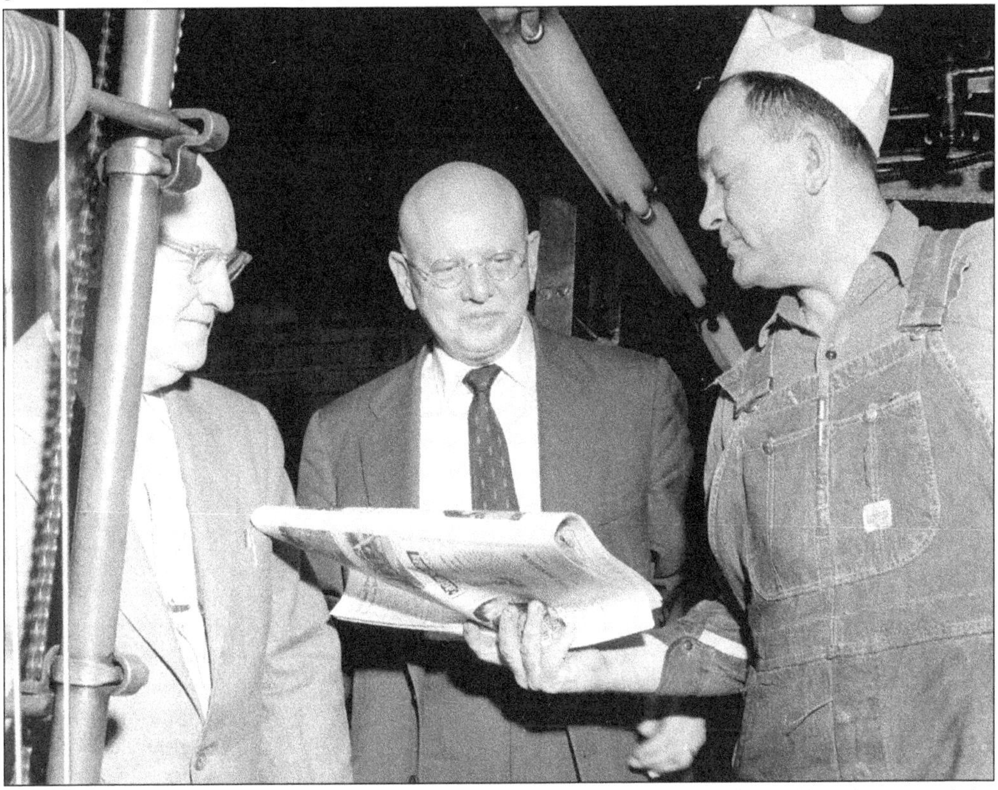

George R. Lamade, president and general manager of *Grit*, receives the millionth copy of the newspaper in January 1958. Fresh off the press, the newspaper is handed to Lamade for approval by Lewis E. Zimmerman Jr. while A. F. Kaufman looks on.

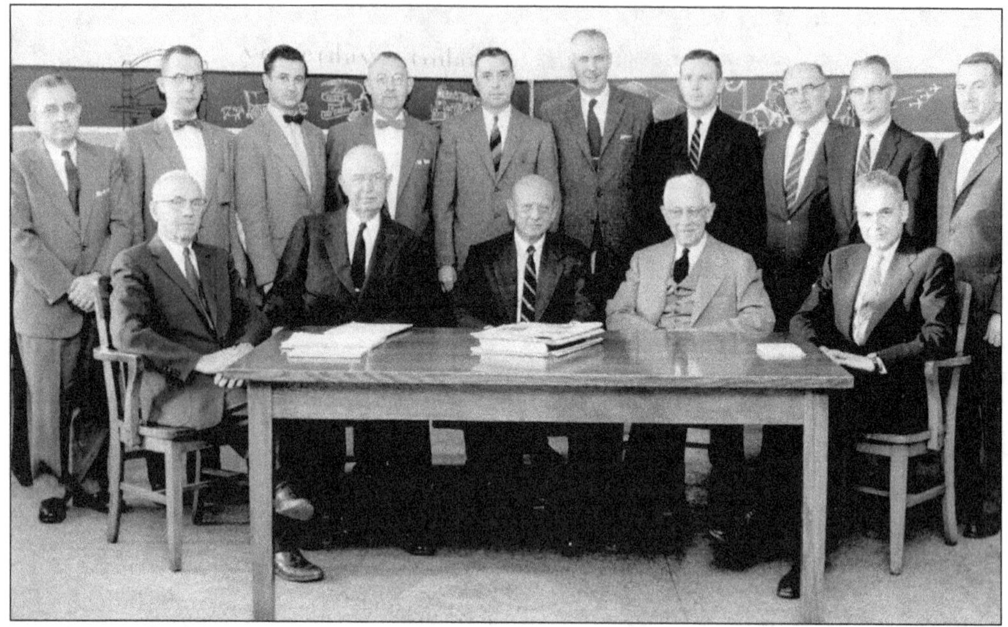

Members of the *Grit* executive board meet in December 1957. Seated from left to right are George W. Stabler, Harry J. W. Kiessling, George R. Lamade, Howard J. Lamade, and Ralph R. Cranmer. Advisory board members are, standing from left to right, Gordon J. Pitman, Howard Lamade Jr., Robert Lamade, Carl N. Stiber, Raul E. Fink, Gilbert E. Whiteley, James H. Lamade, Howard B. Taylor, Kenneth D. Rhone, and Dietrick Lamade II.

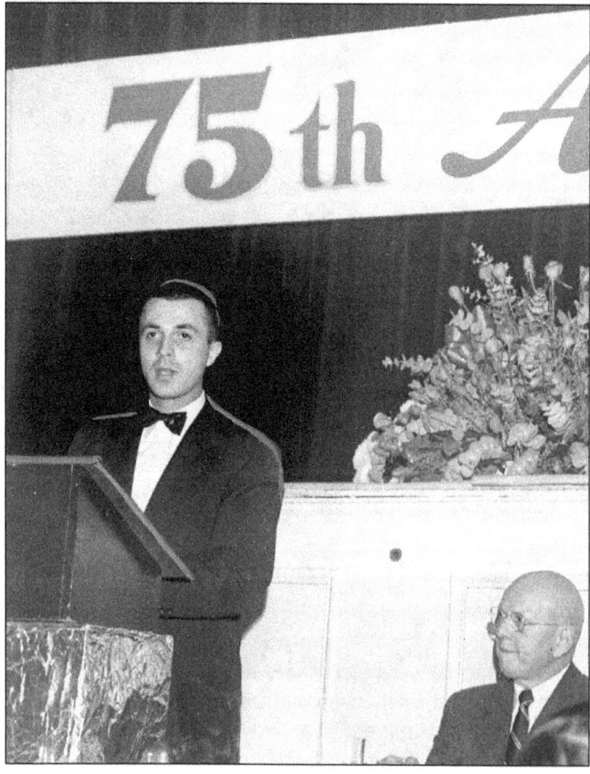

Terry L. Ziegler, city editor of *Grit*, speaks on behalf of the *Grit* family at the 75th anniversary dinner of the company, promising his employees loyalty and dedication in maintaining the publication's high standards. George R. Lamade, president and general manager of *Grit*, looks on at the December 1957 event.

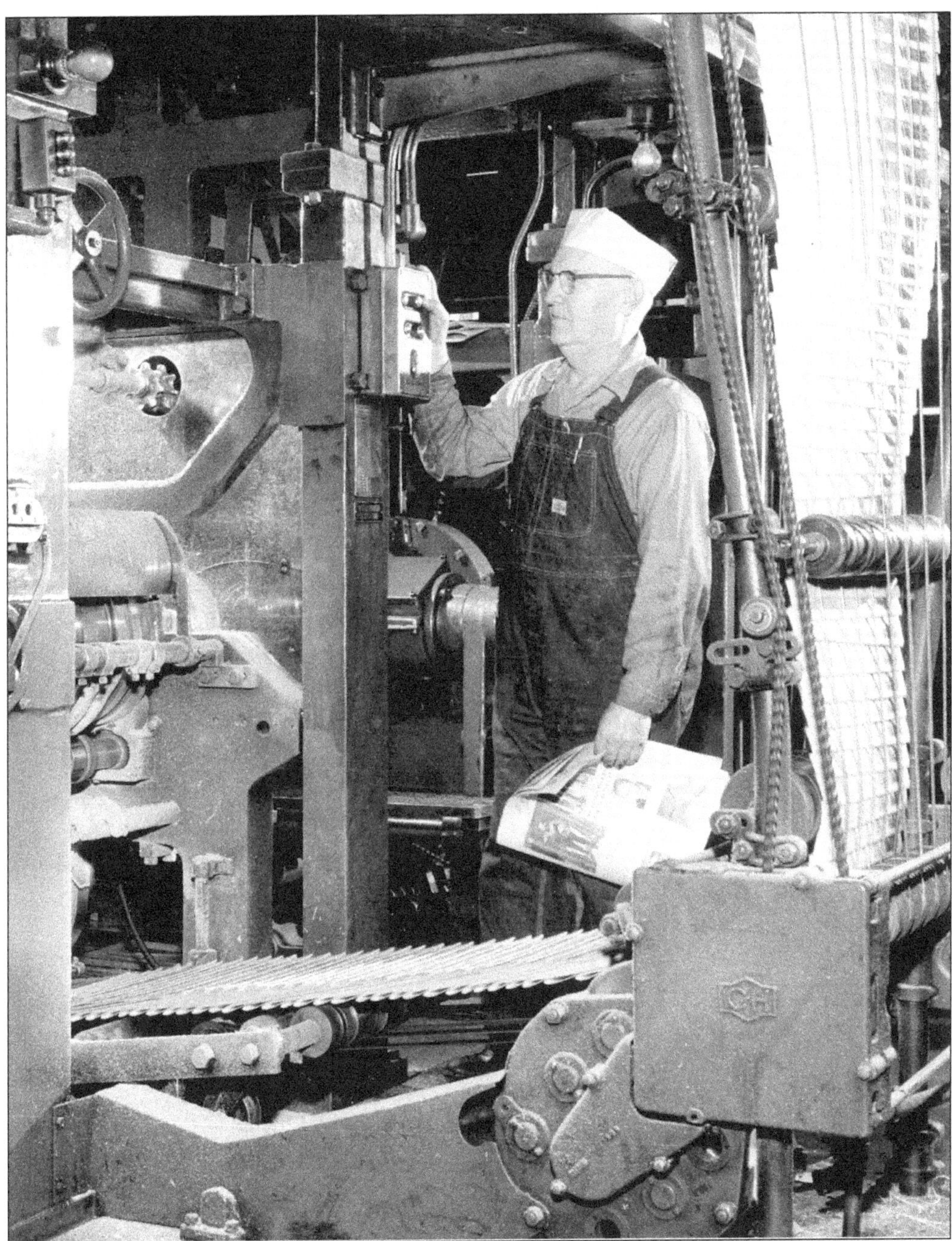

August Frederick Kaufman pushes the master control switch on the huge *Grit* press on his last day as foreman of the news press department on May 3, 1963. Kaufman, then 65, retired after 50 years with the company. He began as the foreman of the department in 1954, exactly 40 years after he began working with *Grit*. He was born April 25, 1898, in North Adams, Massachusetts. With no daily schedule ahead of him, he told reporters that he planned to spend most of his free time fishing and traveling. His successor as foreman was Lewis E. Zimmerman, who joined the company in 1926. The *Grit* had five presses. The original was purchased in 1896, and later ones were purchased in 1925, 1935, and 1963 (a web offset press).

THE WHITE HOUSE

WASHINGTON

June 22, 1972

Dear Mr. Rhone:

Coming home is always the best part of any long journey, but the fine editorial support I received from the GRIT made this occasion particularly meaningful.

In a very real sense, every American played a vital role in the success of the Moscow visit, for what was accomplished there reflected our people's abiding desire for an enduring peace. With the agreements we have an unparalleled opportunity to build such a structure of lasting peace, and I am hopeful that with support such as yours Congress will act promptly in approving the resolution and treaty. Needless to say, I am deeply grateful for your expression of confidence and encouragement.

With my best wishes,

Sincerely,

Richard Nixon

Mr. Kenneth D. Rhone
Editor
GRIT
Williamsport, Pennsylvania 17701

A treasure tucked away in the *Grit* archives, this letter, dated June 22, 1972, is from Pres. Richard Nixon to editor Kenneth D. Rhone following Nixon's visit to Moscow to speak with Leonid Brezhnev, general secretary of the Central Committee of the Communist Party of the Soviet Union. Nixon and Brezhnev were negotiating two treaties at once in that 1972 summit: the Antiballistic Missile Treat (ABM) and the Strategic Arms Limitations Talks I (SALT I) treaty limiting offensive nuclear weapons. The talks, in the midst of the Cold War, were delicate.

www.ingramcontent.com/pod-product-compliance
Lightning Source LLC
LaVergne TN
LVHW081559100826
845153LV00004B/416
9781531620295